BOLLINGEN SERIES XLIV · 2

Victor Zuckerkandl

MAN THE MUSICIAN

Sound and Symbol: Volume Two

TRANSLATED FROM THE GERMAN
BY NORBERT GUTERMAN

BOLLINGEN SERIES XLIV · 2

PRINCETON UNIVERSITY PRESS

THIS IS THE CONCLUDING VOLUME OF
A WORK CONSTITUTING NUMBER XLIV IN BOLLINGEN SERIES,
SPONSORED BY BOLLINGEN FOUNDATION

Library of Congress Catalog Card No. 55-11489
ISBN 0-691-09925-1

Manufactured in the United States of America
BASED ON A DESIGN BY ANDOR BRAUN

To Li Hutchinson

The beneficent spirit of this opus

A PREFATORY NOTE

VICTOR ZUCKERKANDL was born in Vienna on July 2, 1896. He studied music theory and piano in Vienna, conducted operas and concerts there and in other cities, and received the Ph.D. in 1927 at Vienna University. From 1927 to 1933 he was music critic for newspapers in Berlin, and from 1934 to 1938 he taught music theory and appreciation in Vienna. Dr. Zuckerkandl came to the United States in 1940, and for two years was a member of the music department at Wellesley College. In 1942–44 he worked as a machinist in a Boston defense plant. He was on the faculty of the New School, in New York, teaching courses on music theory, during 1946–48. Under a grant-in-aid from the American Philosophical Society, Dr. Zuckerkandl developed a music course especially for the liberal arts student. Instead of being a technical, survey, or appreciation course, it dealt with the nature, structure, and significance of the tonal language which had been used by great composers of the past. After he joined the music department of St. John's College (Annapolis, Maryland) in 1948, the course was adopted as a requisite for liberal arts students at the college. Dr. Zuckerkandl's book *The Sense of Music* (Princeton, 1959) presented this approach to a larger audience.

Dr. Zuckerkandl twice held a three-year Bollingen fellowship. The first award enabled him to write *Sound and Symbol: Music and the External World,* which was translated by Willard R. Trask and published in Bollingen Series in 1956.

Dr. Zuckerkandl had begun to plan the present volume, *Man the Musician,* as early as 1948, after he had finished writing *Music and the External World.* That year, he gave a lecture at St. John's College which became the first chapter of this book. The work proceeded slowly in the ensuing years, while Dr. Zuckerkandl was intensely involved in the music program at St. John's. It was essentially completed in 1960, but he continued to refine and expand the material until 1964.

In the 1960s, Dr. Zuckerkandl gave four lectures at the Eranos Conference, Ascona, Switzerland, which contain ideas advanced in *Man the Musician* and occasionally entire passages. These were published in volumes of the *Eranos Jahrbücher* (Rhein Verlag, Zurich) as follows: "Die Tongestalt," 1960; "Der singende und der sprechende Mensch," 1961; "Vom Wachstum der Kunstwerks," 1962; "Wahrheit des Traumes—Traum der Wahrheit," 1963. A fifth lecture, "Kreis und Pfeil im Werk Beethovens," 1964, was drawn from the work that Victor Zuckerkandl planned to write next and for which he held the second Bollingen fellowship—a study of the creative process in music as exemplified in the Sketchbooks of Beethoven. The 1960–63 lectures, with two other essays, were published in 1964 as a small book, *Vom musikalischen Denken* (Rhein Verlag, Zurich). His other publications included contributions to the *Harvard Dictionary of Music* and articles in British, German, and Swiss journals.

Upon his retirement from St. John's College in 1964, Dr. Zuckerkandl made Ascona his permanent home. He lectured both at the Eranos Conference and at the C. G. Jung Institute, in Zurich. In October, 1964, he returned briefly to the United States to participate in the Thomas Mann Commemoration at Princeton University, when he delivered an address on "Thomas Mann the Musician." Victor Zuckerkandl died on April 25, 1965, at Locarno.

The present publication has had the benefit of close scrutiny by Wolfgang Sauerlander, who had discussed the German text comprehensively with the author before 1964 and was in a position to act in Dr. Zuckerkandl's behalf in consulting on the translation. Dorothy M. Curzon has edited the volume with both musical and editorial expertise. Grateful acknowledgment is made to them; to the Beethoven-Archiv in Bonn for permission to quote a number of examples from the Sketchbooks; to the Alte Pinakothek, Munich, for an illustration of Altdorfer's *The Battle of Alexander;* and to the publishers for a diagram from Heinrich Schenker's *Five Graphic Music Analyses,* copyright 1969 by Dover Publications, Inc., New York.

CONTENTS

THE MUSICAL EAR

MUSICAL THOUGHT

SOUND AND SYMBOL

Man the Musician

FOREWORD

PHAEDO, the great dialogue on the immortality of the soul held on the eve of Socrates' death, opens with a remarkable admission on the philosopher's part concerning music. Socrates' friends are questioning him about a rumor current in Athens that in the last days of his imprisonment he has turned to the practice of music, of all things. In reply, Socrates tells them that repeatedly, throughout his life, he has had a dream in which a voice has told him to "make music and work at it" (Μουσικὴν ποίει). Until recently, he tells them, he had not felt obliged to take the admonition literally. Rather, he had taken it the way a runner takes the urgings of the crowd: isn't he already doing his utmost? After all, had he not devoted his life to philosophy, the true art of the Muses? (To the Greeks, the art of sounds and that of words were intimately related: there was no music without words, and poetry was not spoken, but sung or chanted.) Since his trial, however, Socrates had begun to wonder whether he might not have taken the admonition too lightly, and so had occupied himself in the last days before his execution by composing a hymn to Apollo and by turning into verse some of Aesop's fables.

The story is too ancient and too well known not to be taken seriously. Though it is told self-deprecatingly, its sense is perfectly clear. Like Socrates' last words, "We owe a cock to Aesculapius," it refers to payment of a debt. The philosopher is being scrupulous to the last. His whole life has been devoted to the service of a single power, that of the spoken word. Now, before it is too late, he must make amends for not having served the only power that shapes man's spiritual essence. He will make one last gesture of reverence and gratitude to the power of music: he will raise his voice in song at least once before dying.

Nietzsche was the first to grasp the sense of Socrates as "music maker," no doubt out of some underlying kinship. To him that last gesture in the *Phaedo* is an acknowledgment of the limitations of logical-scientific thinking. Nietzsche views Socrates as the archetypal "abstract thinker," as the "mystagogue of science." "These words heard by Socrates in his dream," he writes in *The Birth of Tragedy*, "are the only indication that he ever experienced any uneasiness about the limits of his logical universe. He may have asked himself, 'Have I been too ready to view what was unintelligible to me as being devoid of meaning? Perhaps there is a realm of wisdom, after all, from which the logician is excluded? Perhaps art must be seen as the necessary complement of rational discourse?' " Yet surely Socrates was already well aware of this. For time and again, in the course of dialogue after dialogue—and at the moment some especially important point is reached—the strict dialectician suddenly starts to tell a story; the logician turns into the purveyor of myth; the Logos is bolstered up and made more vivid with recourse to Mythos. And the voice in the dream is a warning voice: even when Logos and Mythos work hand in hand, words are not enough. To give utterance to the whole of things, to be whole oneself, tones are needed, and song. Nietzsche must have experienced something like it himself when he said of his work, shortly before he went mad, "It ought to have sung, this 'new soul,' not spoken!" No doubt music, song, underwent the most extraordinary developments between Socrates and Nietzsche, but one thing has not changed. Music still is, just as it has always been, the *other* power which, along with language, fully defines man as a spiritual being. No one who has not recognized and honored music as such can be said to have paid his full debt to the world, to himself, to mankind.

The notion to which the *Phaedo* gives expression is that of *homo musicus*, of man as musician, the being that requires music to realize itself fully. This dimension of our humanity has largely been in shadow over the course of Western thought. It is time to bring it into the light.

MUSICALITY

I. The Two Concepts of Musicality

As CURRENTLY USED, the term "musicality" refers to the special gift that brings individuals into close relationship with music. The gift shows itself not only in an active doing but also in passive receiving: we call "musical" not only the composer or interpreter but also the sensitive listener. The gift is always the property of an individual, and as such it is a chance property in the sense that one person has it and another does not. When whole peoples are spoken of as being musical, the observation again refers to the individuality of one people as compared with another. In all cases a comparison is made; and a comparison establishes a dividing line which, like any boundary, creates two fields: musicality makes its appearance by being set off from its negative counterpart, the lack of musicality. In addition, the comparison implies a value judgment: musicality is an asset, its absence a shortcoming. Individuals distinguishable as musical form a minority with the character of an elite that stands in a privileged relationship to music. For the most part, if not exclusively, music is the concern—indeed, the possession—of this minority; the rest can at best participate from the sidelines.

The concept just outlined is fundamentally different from that expressed in the *Phaedo*. There, musicality is not the property of individuals but an essential attribute of the human species. The implication is not that some men are musical while others are not, but that man is a musical animal, that is, a being predisposed to music and in need of music, a being that for its full realization must express itself in tones and owes it to itself and to the world to produce music. In this sense, musicality is not something one may or may not have, but something that—along with other factors—is constitutive of man. So defined, the concept cannot have a negative counterpart; to call a man unmusical would be meaningless, self-contradictory. Nobody is being singled out and set apart. Music is the concern of all, not of a privileged elite, and if musicality represents an asset, it is not the prerogative of a chosen few, but an endowment of man as man.

The two concepts are not mutually exclusive; one cannot say that one is true and the other false. But one of them is originally and unreservedly valid, whereas the other is derived and relative. The concept with which we are familiar is the derived and relative one, and to consider it as universally valid would lead our thinking astray and distort our vision.

To begin with, it is important to realize why the familiar concept must be called relative and derived.

The scholar who has most thoroughly investigated the problem of musicality is Géza Révész. In his *Introduction to the Psychology of Music*, aware of the difficulty of arriving at a definition that fits all cases, he confines himself to describing the essential characteristics of the musical person. (That he conceives of musicality solely in terms of an individual trait is implicit in his psychological approach.) The following excerpts provide a case in point: "That person is to be considered musical who is able to transfer his musical experiences to a sphere in which the art work is the object of purely artistic contemplation. . . . The mental conquest of music as art characterizes the musical person. . . . The musical person possesses a deep understanding of musical forms and the structure or movement plan of the work. He has a finely developed sense of style and of the strict organization of musical processes of thought. . . . He experiences the work of art so inwardly and so profoundly that he feels as though he were creating it." On the other hand, unmusical persons "are unable to grasp the structure of a musical composition and evaluate it in terms of its aesthetic content. . . . They gradually come in contact with music without, however, really attaining the sphere of the specifically musical in which the beautiful-in-music becomes an object of aesthetic perception. . . . No matter how hard they try, they never . . . grasp a composition, are never able to understand its compositional and structural plan."

These statements suffice to indicate the crucial point: musicality as well as its negative counterpart comes into view when a listener is confronted with a musical composition. The musical person measures up to the work; the unmusical person fails to respond. True, this distinction is not one of all or nothing. Révész recognizes degrees of musicality, transitional stages between the two extremes. Yet the ultimate criterion remains the depth to which a person, listening and comprehending, can penetrate the artistic structure of a given composition. Throughout, the confrontation of listener and work is presupposed as the self-evident starting point. Révész explicitly characterizes the musicality he investigates as receptive without, however, thereby implying a contrast to a creative musicality. The latter is viewed—a profound insight—as distinct from the former only in degree, not in kind; it is an extreme special case. For, after all, the composer too is at bottom a listener; he must attain his work by listening to it with the inner ear, and in this sense he too confronts it. Wherever there is a work, there must be a confrontation.

Underlying such reflections, of course, is a specific conception of music (no less specific for not being spelled out) and the assumption that one specific relationship between man and music is universally valid. Music is equated with its most highly developed form, a body of great compositions, and the relationship between man and music is restricted to a listener's encounter with such a composition. Such an equation and restriction, however, can be applied only under special conditions. As we have been born into these special conditions, we tend to forget that they are not characteristic of the whole of music but merely of one phase in the course of its history. It is a pre-eminent phase, certainly, but still only one: the culminating phase.

In a twofold sense we are witnesses of the culminating phase: as members of Western civilization and as contemporaries of this century. With the epochal discovery of polyphony—that is, the possibility of producing a musical whole by combining different, simultaneous strands of tones—Western music has made a clear break with every other kind of music and embarked on a path that within a thousand years of breathtaking development has led to the ultimate distillate of pure instrumental music. The process has no parallel in the history of any other art; it can be compared only with the more or less simultaneous development of mathematical science. The building of these two worlds, the world of tones and the world of numbers, will surely remain Western man's most signal achievement during this period. Be that as it may, a development like this necessarily generates its own special forms, and it is no surprise that our musical life manifests itself in forms that are very different from those of other ages. They may be summed up under four heads: work, composer, performer, audience.

Work, above all: we live in an age of individually composed works. To us music is scarcely conceivable save in terms of symphonies and sonatas, operas and oratorios, cantatas, lieder, concertos, string quartets, and so on, each of them a work of art, a little world unto itself, as unique and uninterchangeable as an individual person, a microcosm, a creation. A creation implies a creator, a man of the highest mental powers, capable of achieving again and again the ultimate and pushing the ever advancing boundaries of the art still farther. Works are preserved in musical notation which must be transformed into living sound, and this calls for interpreters and performers who can do justice to the ever increasing demands of the compositions. All this leads to a division of functions. Composing and interpreting are the business of a few experts; all other people are confined to participating in music as mere listeners, as an audience. Music is largely something produced by a small minority for a larger public. This division of functions determines the attitude in which we experience music today: we sit in front of something—a stage, a podium, a record player, a radio set—and wait for the music to come to us. Music always comes to us from the other side, from beyond a boundary; it is given to us and we receive it.

Another boundary runs through the audience itself. As a superior creation of the human spirit a composition is a challenge for the listener; the extraordinary gift requires an extraordinary recipient. In the presence of the work the listeners are being sorted out according to the varying degrees of intensity, sensitivity, and comprehension with which they respond. A few listeners split away from the rest and gather closely around the work, as if under a spell; obviously they hear things to which others are deaf. The sense of hearing, it seems, is not uniformly the same. Some people have a special listening faculty: their ears are specially attuned to understanding music. In short, hearing can be musical or unmusical: there are musical and unmusical people. This observation is not intended as a slur or a criticism; it states facts which cannot be otherwise. Our familiar concept of musicality is the direct result of the conditions under which the encounter of man and music presently takes place, the conditions of the culminating phase.

For us, music is simply the music of the culminating phase. Overwhelmed by its magnificence, we have turned our backs on anything outside it. And yet great art music, as we know it, is an exceptional event, something unique and quintessential, whereas music pure and simple is part of the general human endowment. It is not confined to the masterworks of art music, but inherent in people everywhere. There is no people or tribe without music, however primitive. Wherever there is speech, there is also song. The harps from the graves of Ur and the sounding stone disks from the Malayan jungle bear witness to the fact that music is older than recorded history. Nor is there any real argument against the assumption that music is coeval with language and that the appearance of the human race in time announced itself both in word and sound. From this music of the beginning we who witnessed the culminating phase are the farthest removed, so far indeed that we have lost sight of it. How, then, can we hope to understand the innermost essence of music, including that of the culminating phase, unless we consider its entire trajectory and take into account both the beginning and the culmination? The beginning of music is not a historical event—man had music long before he had a history—nor is it a prehistoric event, something that occurred at an indefinitely remote time of the human past. If we cannot separate man, time, and music in our thinking, then it is impossible to think of a beginning of music; in other words, the beginning of music lies in the realm of myth. As legend has it, music was the gift of a god to mankind. What this means is quite clear. It could not have been that a god intoned a song for people to sing after him. Gods do not give in this way, from the outside. A god's gift comes from the inside; he opens men's hearts and unseals their lips. Another legend is even clearer on this point: men first raised their voices in song when they witnessed the death of a divinely beautiful young hero. At the beginning, music comes from men, not to them—or, rather, also to them but on the rebound. The singer or player cannot help hearing what he sings or plays: the circle must be closed. Here the notion of a confrontation between listener and work makes no sense. Music is both the gift and the giving, the musician both giver and recipient.

Among the periods about whose music we are adequately informed, the centuries of Gregorian chant offer the best instance of forms prevalent in the situation of the beginning. At the time, Western music was still in its precompositional stage. As we look back from the culminating phase the Gregorian melodies may strike us as works of art, but to those who created, sang, and heard them, they were nothing of the kind, and though Gregorian melodies may be recorded in notation they were never considered as compositions to be performed for or listened to by an audience. Gregorian chant is something else entirely: it is prayer—in praise, supplication, thanksgiving—an offering rather than something received. Giving and receiving have changed places; if there is a recipient it is the man in whose mind the melody first takes shape. Far from thinking of himself as a composer, or even a humble craftsman, he sees himself as having been graced with the gift of being able to hear the angels singing; all he does is set down the sounds vouchsafed him by heaven. And when the melody rings out during divine service, chanted by the priest or the choir, nothing is farther from anybody's mind than the idea of performing music for an audience. The melody will be sung whether anybody is listening or not, and if there are listeners they are not an audience but a congregation. They have assembled not to listen but to worship. The chant is not sung to them but for them, on their behalf. The division into singers and listeners remains on the surface, beneath which all of them, singers and listeners alike, are one. Only in the most obvious physical sense do the sounds come to the listeners from outside themselves; the true source is inside the listeners. The melodies are their prayers, and the singers only serve to voice them transmuted into sound.

We come closest to the beginnings of music when we consider what today, in the culminating phase, is called folk music. In no sense can the tune of a folk song be regarded as a musical composition. Never (until our own day) set down in notation, it exists only in sounds transmitted from generation to generation. As it lives on, it undergoes change and takes on new forms. It is never finished, as a composition is, and indeed resists fixation. Collecting and transcribing folk songs is the concern of a higher stage anxious to preserve neglected treasures. The same is true about performance. In their own habitat folk songs are not performed. People get together to sing songs, not to listen to them. They sing to themselves, and if there is any listening, it is to learn a tune so as to sing it oneself. (The ballad in which a story is told in poetic musical form marks the transition to a higher stage.) New melodies may well occur to some individual, but that does not make him a composer, a person permanently singled out from the group and charged with a special function. He stands outside the group only as long as he launches the new tune; when he is done he merges again with his fellow singers, who may adopt his contribution or reject it. When certain lines are intended for a solo voice, the solo singer is not a performer in front of an audience; his voice remains the voice of the group, which may join in at any time, as it indeed does in the refrain. The situation is that of an all-together, not of a confrontation. The three functions—composing, performing, listening—so sharply differentiated at the culminating phase are still interchangeable facets of one overall function residing with the group. This is true even when music seemingly is being made by some for others, as happens with dance music. Here again, the others are not listeners, they are participants, and the music and music making are part of their own activity. The music, as it were, is behind them rather than in front of them. Even in the extreme case of the magical rite where the magician uses certain musical formulas which in fact are his own jealously guarded possession, the formulas are not addressed to those present as if they were an audience, but jointly with them to the god or demon so invoked. Again, the music comes from human beings, not to them.

There is a trace of snobbery about the term "folk music" (*Volksmusik*), as when a noble condescends to his inferiors. The term is not simply one of classification; it also expresses a value judgment. Beyond the boundary it establishes lies something lesser, no more than a primitive model, a humble seed, showing no trace of the splendor of the organism when fully developed. Occasional expeditions to this lowly region may turn up valuable finds, and in times of crisis it may lure us into an ephemeral return to nature. But the "real" music, the embodiment of truth and value, lies on this side of the boundary. Here, and only here, in composed masterworks, does music reveal its true essence and full range.

Nobody will deny that the tune of a chorale and a chorale prelude by Bach belong to different stages; but the stages differ in degree, not in kind. The tune is not some plebeian product that is being ennobled when touched by Bach's genius; it contains in a nutshell everything a great musical mind may bring to fruition. Folk music is like childhood, not like an embryo; the fetus is not yet a human being, but an infant is. Folk music is music in the full and proper sense because it contains all elements that make up the nature of music. The decisive act that brought music into being precedes it, or rather is one with it: the discovery of tones and the system of tones.

Occasionally one still encounters the opinion that man found the tones ready-made in nature (in birdcalls, for instance) and out of these created music. Nothing could be more mistaken. No more than numbers do words or tones exist in nature. And from birdsong to melody it is just as far as from a jackal's bark to a sentence. Tones exist as little before music as numbers before mathematics: one was born with the other. In a sense one might even say that tones were created by music: "It is music that gave birth to the tones," according to the *Li Chi* (*Book of Rites*). It was the impulse to create music that created the tones. They were not random tones, however, subsequently put in order and arranged in a system; tones *are* in order and have no existence except within a system. The tone system represents the completion of the act of musical creation, and with folk music this act has been fully achieved because the system is wholly present in it. What followed later, including the greatest masterworks, is but the realization of everything inherent in the tones. Here again music resembles mathematics: it is not that somehow there first are numbers, which then are brought into systematic order. Numbers are in order. All this will be discussed in greater detail later. To detect the slightly false shade in the term "folk music" we need only imagine that elementary addition and subtraction be called "folk mathematics."

Those who make so-called folk music are not "folk" or "people" but "man." Not some people or all peoples and certainly not specific individuals, but man as such, one of whose uniquely human attributes is to be musical. Now, it makes sense to speak of "musicality" not as the distinguishing characteristic of this or that individual but as an overall human endowment: man as man is musical. Not that first there was man, who in the course of time acquired music to make his life more attractive by easing the strain of work or filling his leisure time; rather, man and music are so fundamentally interlaced from the beginning that one cannot exist without the other.

We see that the concept of musicality that we have called original in contrast to our familiar concept, which is derived and relative, is no figment of the imagination. It corresponds to the reality of music at the beginning, of the primordial musical condition. The conception which considers musicality as a gift of privileged individuals and music as the prerogative of musicians and music lovers turns out to be too narrow because it leaves out the essential. What it leaves out may be seen when we draw the rather startling logical conclusion: in the framework of our current thinking about music we can imagine a world without music. But seen from the vantage point of the beginning and the original concept of musicality, a world without music is unthinkable.

It is astonishing that we who have witnessed the culminating phase of music should be able to envisage a world without music. Yet such is the case: in our thinking we isolate phenomena and approach music with analytic concepts. When we think of music as art we isolate it from the everyday world of reality; when we consider it as the art of sounds we isolate it from other arts; composer and performer are singled-out, privileged individuals; knowledge of music is a specialized field for experts; and the many, the public at large, view music as a special gift. If we expunge music the world will be poorer by one art form, a few specialists will lose their means of livelihood, and the public will be deprived of a source of great pleasure; it would be an impoverished, a darker world, but it would still be the same world as we know and understand it: we can imagine a world without music.

Not so when we look at music from the phase of its origin. If man and music existentially belong together, and music is an essential element of the human endowment, then man without music is not man and a world without music is not our world: both man without music and world without music are unthinkable self-contradictions. In other words, to our current thinking music is a matter of chance, whereas when viewed from the origin it is a matter of necessity. Which of the two views comes closer to a real understanding of music? That which relegates it to the realm of the contingent or that which considers it as necessary?

Other ages, other civilizations have endeavored to understand music as necessary in this sense. We recall Plato's vision of the Demiurge (in the *Timaeus*) who places the order of the diatonic scale firmly into the foundation of the universe. The wisdom of the ancient Far East may be less familiar to us. The following two passages are quoted from the *Li Chi* again (from Richard Wilhelm's German version):

"Spring creates, summer makes grow: this is love. Autumn gathers, winter shelters in the barns: this is justice. Love corresponds to music, justice corresponds to rites."

"Music effects union, the rites effect separation. In union men love one another, in separation men respect one another. If music predominates, there arises the danger of dissolution; if the rites predominate, there arises the danger of stagnation."

These statements suffice to indicate how the style of this thinking about music and the attitude it reflects differ from ours. The words associated with music are not "art," "artist," or "work of art," but summer and winter, separation and union, love and justice, dissolution and stagnation. Where our thinking tends to analyze and isolate, the Chinese sage contemplates an ordered whole. He does not compare one thing with another or search for traits they may have in common or progress from a particular to the general. Rather, he strives to understand how music, as what it is, must necessarily fit into the whole.

(The whole is not the same as the general: separate particulars making up the general are accidental, whereas the part of a whole is necessary. The general remains the same when a particular is removed, but when a part is missing the whole is no longer the whole.) Here music is something in itself but not for itself. It is one-half of a pair, one of two poles, the other pole being the rites. Again, music and rites are not taken as existing for themselves, but as mediators, earthly mediators between the two superterrestrial powers whose polar tension keeps the universe in permanent balance. Only if the mediators are balanced and in a sound state is the soundness of the whole guaranteed. The opposition of the poles is in reality a mutual dependence. Danger is not threatened by the existence or power of the other pole but from its nonexistence and weakness. Each pole must will the existence and the power of the other and dread its nonexistence and weakness. If one pole were to vanish, dissolution and stagnation of the whole would immediately set in. It is obvious that within the framework of such thinking the idea of a world without music finds no room.

The foregoing may, of course, be rejected as metaphysical speculation and mythological fantasy, inadmissible without a substantiation of their claim to validity. Our thinking about music and musicality may be less ambitious, but it has the incontestable advantage of sticking to the facts as we experience them and explaining them adequately. And there is no reason why an explanation of music as necessary should by itself be superior to one that considers it as contingent. Why should music not have been a sublime accident? The touchstone, surely, must be which conception fits the actual facts better. And it cannot be gainsaid that the evidence of our experience does not support any high-flown claims to universal validity. It is a matter of fact that in its highest development music separates people rather than uniting them. There may be many listeners, but many more never listen, and among those who do listen only a few will really be able to hear what goes on in a Bach cantata, a Mozart string quartet, or a Beethoven sonata.

Are we not, then, bound to conclude that in its highest and strictest sense music is the special possession of a very small minority? Ought not our conceptions of music and musicality take this fact into account?

What is wrong with this argument is that it uses the term "experience" in too gross and narrow a sense. To be sure, the confrontation with a musical masterpiece seemingly divides people rather than uniting them; only a small band is being united, clustering around the work, separated from those who may give occasional attention and go away unaffected and from all the rest who are too distant to be aware of music at all. But only a very superficial view could conclude that music does not concern all these others too, that it does not exist for them at all. Beethoven wrote the words "From the heart—may it reach other hearts" before the opening chords of his *Missa Solemnis*. Was he thinking only of the musically gifted? He of all people could not have been unaware that only a very few would ever be capable of following the highly complex and utterly abstract musical thought processes of this Mass. And yet the work is not addressed to these few or to any larger groups; it is addressed to all, to the whole of mankind, to the human heart. If there were only one person ever able to understand the work, he would be the representative of all mankind; on its behalf he would widen the understanding of the human heart; in him consciousness would have extended its reach and through him a new reality would have entered its ken. For what has occurred is shared by all men, just as many may share in a new illumination without seeing the source of the light. In this sense the greatest works of art—and indeed particularly the greatest—are, if not addressed to all, created for all. The evidence furnished by the confrontation in the concert hall is superficial. Behind the surface evidence we sense, though we cannot pin it down, the reality of an all-together in which everybody—composer, performer, listener—stands together and gazes, as it were, with the eyes of the work in the same direction, the very situation we found at the phase of the beginning. Nor are the walls of the concert hall an enclosing limit: the all-together reaches beyond them. The fact that the work exists and is understood by a few simply means that henceforth many others will be different in their poetry, their emotions, their thinking, perhaps even in their movements and their breathing.

Although the full range and impact of the fundamental problems raised by music could be revealed only to those of us who witnessed the culminating phase, it seems that at the same time we have lost the ability to focus on these problems, let alone think them through to the end. Is it that the proximity of the culmination has overwhelmed us, made us speechless, and stifled our thinking to such a degree that we can only take tiny steps in a small circle? Seen from the phase of the beginning, music appears as one of the main faculties of human consciousness in its advance toward ever wider horizons. What we must do is take the problem of musicality out of the context of the culminating phase and place it back into the context of the beginning. The search for answers can no longer proceed along the lines of metaphysical speculation; it would be a fruitless endeavor. The task simply is to have a close look at the facts, describe them faithfully, and interpret them correctly.

II. The Meaning of Song

WHY DO people sing?

Notoriously, "why" questions lend themselves to ambiguity. They may refer to the cause of a given phenomenon, to its antecedent, or to its meaning, its implications. In the former case, the answer will refer to observable facts of which the given phenomenon is the effect; in the latter, to the idea of which the phenomenon can be the logical consequence. The answers are not mutually exclusive, but they are of different types. The distinction between the two is analogous to that made by Dilthey between a demand for explanation and a demand for comprehension. For instance, to the question "Why do people die?" replies of differing types are possible. If the question refers to the cause, we will go into the physical and chemical processes of the organism involved, and the interplay of those processes with other processes going on in that organism's environment; if it refers to the meaning, we might look for the answer in the Book of Genesis, in the Fall of Man.

Which type of reply is the more appropriate will depend on the subject of the question. What the question refers to is often obvious at once. For instance, listening to a piece of music, I may well ask, Why just that chord just there? Clearly, I do not expect to be told it is because certain instruments produce particular sound waves, thus accounting for my perception of that chord just there. Rather, what really interests me is comprehending the meaning of this chord with reference to the work as a whole. In other contexts, however—such as "Why is the moon so much bigger and redder when it comes up over the horizon than when it is high in the sky?"—obviously I want a scientific accounting for the phenomenon, an answer in terms of its cause. Indeed, to ask what the rising of the moon really means seems meaningless in the first place. This is not to say, of course, that every question calls for an answer which falls neatly into one of two mutually exclusive classes: causes and meanings. Even when dealing with phenomena of nature it is possible to seek and find meaning over and beyond any mere accounting for them. Thus, it is generally believed that the only question about rainbow colors is "How are they produced?" But Goethe thought it possible to inquire into their meaning and found the answer in the conception of the *Urphänomen*, the "primal phenomenon." Goethe also wrote that all things ephemeral are but a reflection—in other words, that supreme wisdom consists in the search for meaning, not for causes. This is an attitude directly opposed to that of latter-day science, which eliminates any search for meaning and looks only for causes—more accurately, for specific laws governing the successive occurrence of observable facts. In this latter perspective, the question "Why do people sing?" will automatically be interpreted as a question about causes, and will accordingly be answered in the sense of psychophysiology. We shall refer to this interpretation of our question at a later point; here we are concerned not with causes but with meaning.

The first question with which we must deal, however, concerns neither the causes nor the meaning but the immediate purpose of music, especially of the earliest music available to us in any quantity—folk music. The farther back we go, the more it seems as though music, far from being an end in itself (as it has eventually become in Western "art music"), was always subordinated to ends outside itself—religious, social, practical. Nor has music today ceased to lend its aid to such extramusical endeavors. Children are still being sung to sleep, soldiers still sing to give themselves courage, and laborers lighten their work with song. Western religious rites do not dispense with music, and civil rites seem drab without it. And though no one pays much attention to it, a certain amount of music is an indispensable ingredient of every film.

When one and the same means serves many different ends, and serves them all equally well, it is natural to look for what these ends have in common. In our case, this common element is easily identified. However different the behavior of people praying, marching, dancing, watching a spectacle, working, or celebrating, and however the ways in which they express themselves may differ—action or contemplation, motion or rest, physical or psychic alertness or the lack of it, tension or relaxation—in all these situations, the people involved abandon themselves wholly to whatever they are doing. They do not abandon themselves in this way for the sake of self-abandon, in order to forget themselves or—the extreme case—to find release in Dionysiac frenzy. Yet there is an element common to all these diverse expressions of a need for self-abandon, and this is not a turning away from the self, not a negation, but an enlargement, an enhancement of the self, a breaking down of the barriers separating self from things, subject from object, agent from action, contemplator from what is contemplated: it is a transcending of this separation, its transformation into a togetherness.

Imagine a hillside in a warm country; it is morning and the sun is shining brightly. A young man is up in a pear tree, picking the fruit, and as he picks he sings. Why is he singing? I suppose most of us would say, Because it is a beautiful day, and it is good to be young on a beautiful day in a beautiful countryside, picking luscious pears. All this may be so, but there is another, deeper, more essential reason for song in this situation. Our young man might not sing as he picked if the day were not so fine or if troubles weighed on him, but if he sang at all as he picked pears, he would sing the same song—and a different song if it were grapes. The song he sings is the immemorial pear-picking song in his part of the world, a tune that musically makes fruit and picker one, that "brings" the pears to the picker's hands and consecrates his harvesting of them. It is as though the picker's hands did not reach out for the fruit but surrendered to it, as though the fruit, instead of resisting the hands, were meeting them halfway, dropping into them of its own accord. Instead of opposition, distinction, we have togetherness, unity.

It might be objected that not every type of activity is furthered or enhanced by music. Thus, scientists and scholars need yield to no one in capacity for self-abandon, and it is a fact that they do not sing as they work. Faust alone in his study, singing, as Gounod portrayed him, strikes us as ludicrous. A game like chess, similarly, does not lend itself to a musical setting: imagine a chorus of kibitzers! Hunters, too, sing only in operas, and then only before or after they shoot (if the composer knows his business). In real life, hunters keep still, not just so as not to alert the quarry—they would keep still even if the birds or animals they seek had no sense of hearing. In the kitchen you hear singing only from persons doing routine tasks, like peeling potatoes, never from the chef nervously preparing a delicate sauce. What the objection overlooks is that the kind of person-object relationship characteristic of thinking, study, or any other activity requiring concentration is not correctly designated by the term "self-abandon." For here the opposite is true: self and object are sharply distinguished. When engaged in such activities we are wholly with ourselves and wholly with the object at the same time. True, we do not focus on ourselves, yet we are entirely absorbed in observing the object, concentrating on it, and in doing this we keep the object away from ourselves, distinct from ourselves. This is an attitude incompatible with any sounds. The man singing in the pear tree does not focus on the fruit. Nor does Orpheus act like a hunter when he encounters wild beasts.

Thus music is appropriate, is helpful, where self-abandon is intended or required—where the self goes beyond itself, where subject and object come together. Tones seem to provide the bridge that makes it possible, or at least makes it easier, to cross the boundary separating the two.

There exists a type of music making at this level which does not—or, at any rate, not as obviously as other types—serve as a means to an end. Wherever folk music is still alive, people come together to sing. To be sure, many songs, such as dance tunes, lullabies, martial airs, religious chants and hymns, have a specific, immediate purpose; but there are also others which are sung for their own sakes, just for the sake of singing. What is the meaning of this practice?

A folk song is primarily a poem, that is, a verbal structure. It tells a story, evokes a situation, expresses feelings. There can be no doubt that the words of the song are all-important; the tune takes second place. The title of the song refers to what the words say, not to the melody; indeed, different songs are often sung to the same tune. In many collections of folk songs the main part of the book is given over to the verbal texts, followed by the indication "To be sung to the tune of . . ." What each text is sung to is usually given in an appendix; the number of tunes is invariably inferior to that of the texts.

It would seem, then, that even in those folk songs where the tune is not just a means to an end, its function is clearly secondary. It might even be maintained that in folk songs the contribution of the tune is less essential than in other forms of early music making. Dancing and celebrations without musical accompaniment lack something essential, whereas a poem is a self-contained whole, lacking nothing.

This is no doubt true of the unvocalized poem, the poem I think about or read silently, perhaps to recite it to myself or to someone to whom it is unfamiliar; it is not true of the poem that is actually meant to be vocalized, to represent the voice of a community. Can one imagine that people come together to *speak* songs? One can, but only as a logical possibility; in real life this would be absurd. It would turn something natural into something utterly unnatural. Looked at in this way, what the musical tones contribute to the folk song is essential:

only in so far as it is sung does the folk song really exist. Take the tune away, and what remains is something entirely different.

A trivial explanation suggests itself: the naturalness of singing and the artificiality of speaking in chorus are supposed to be accounted for by the fact that meter regulates the temporal succession of tones but not that of words. It is argued that the meter alone makes possible orderly group performance, but that to keep time when speaking is unnatural. This explanation overlooks the fact that only with the advance to genuine polyphony—in other words, the advance to art music—did meter become an indispensable element of musical language. Music in its original state is free to comply or not to comply with a meter. Gregorian melodies which know no meter are nevertheless sung by choirs. In folk music outside the boundaries of the West, group singing and group playing without meter are nothing less than alien. We may marvel at the accomplishment, but it is taken for granted. On the other hand, there is no reason why a poem, an utterance in rhythmic language, could not be merely spoken metrically under certain circumstances. At any rate, the reason why it is unnatural to recite folk songs rather than sing them must be sought elsewhere, not just in the fact that tones have become inseparable from meter.

It seems that the spoken word is unsuitable in the situation naturally presupposed by the existence of folk songs. The spoken word presupposes a speaker and someone spoken to, is directed by one person to another, implies a communication. "All speech," we read in Bruno Snell's *Der Aufbau der Sprache*, "consists in this: that a sound reaches an ear, another being. . . . Speaking is always the speaking of someone to someone about something." The words of the folk song, however, are not directed by one person to another or by many persons to many others; the voice is that of the group, which includes all those present; here, there is no "other being," no mere listeners. More accurately, the speakers are also the listeners, not in the sense that every individual speaks to all the others, but in the sense that all of them together speak to themselves taken together. Nor can there be any question of communication: what is there to be communicated where everyone knows exactly—indeed, must know—what is to be said in order to take part in the collective speaking? If one member of the group happens to lead the chorus, his words are certainly not addressed to the others; each of the latter could say them as well. He does not tell them anything they don't know; he does not speak to the others but *for* them; he is still the mouthpiece of the group. Nor does a comparison with the special situation of the monologue get us anywhere: to soliloquize is merely to think aloud, to voice thoughts that could just as well remain unvoiced, whereas a song does not really exist until it has been voiced. People do not come together to think of songs silently, to imagine them in common. And so the question arises, What is the element of the tune whose addition to the words of the folk song turns something meaningless into something meaningful?

The answer must be sought in the difference between the human interrelationships created by the word, or speaking, and those created by the tones, or singing. The spoken word presupposes "the other," the person or persons to whom it is addressed; the one speaking and the one spoken to are turned toward each other; the word goes out from one to the other, creating a situation in which the two are facing each other as distinct, separate individuals. Wherever there is talk, there is a "he-not-I" on the one hand and his counterpart, an "I-not-he," on the other. This is why the word is not the natural expression of the group. In the group, person and person are brought together, not separated; the barriers between individuals are not emphasized, they are minimized. An individual may certainly step in front of the group and speak to it; but when he speaks within the group from out of the group, as a member, and when the group includes all individuals present, when there is no "other," no "facing each other," then one of the conditions under which speaking is meaningful is canceled out by the realities of the situation. Now, if adding tones to the words results in transforming the meaningless into the self-evident, it is reasonable to assume that singing is the natural and appropriate expression of the group, of the togetherness of individuals within the group. If this is the case, we may assume that tones—singing—essentially express not the individual but the group, more accurately, the individual in so far as he is a member of the group, still more accurately, the individual in so far as his relation to the others is not one of "facing them" but one of togetherness.

A closer look at the situation involved in each case confirms this: the nature of tones expresses the situation of togetherness as closely as the nature of the word expresses the situation of "facing each other." Tones are not directed to others (Géza Révész's hypothesis that they originate in the call—that is, the caller's intention to give greater range to his voice—is just as well- or ill-founded as any other attempt to rationalize the primordial and to penetrate even behind the beginnings). Tones do not refer to things; they say nothing about anything. And yet they are not mere "expressions," either, are not merely emitted: they are also intended to be heard, namely, by the singer himself. Invariably, they are both outgoing and incoming. Whereas the word goes out from me, the speaker, and remains outside with the person spoken to, who replies with another word, I, as a singer, go out of myself with the tone and at the same time, as a listener, return to myself from outside with the tone. In the tone, and only in the tone, the singer encounters himself coming from the outside, and not just himself if the singer is the group. In the one tone that comes from all, I encounter the group as well as myself. The dividing line between myself and the others loses its sharpness. Here the situation is not one where two distinct parties face each other; here the others do not address their singing to me. Whereas words turn people toward each other, as it were, make them look at each other, tones turn them all in the same direction: everyone follows the tones on their way out and on their way back. The moment tones resound, the situation where one party faces another is transmuted into a situation of togetherness, the many distinct individuals into the one group.

If this is the case, why do not people simply sing songs without words? Why do the words in songs give way to the tones only for short moments, at the most? Why is there no folk song that is not a sung poem?

Mere melodies would be sufficient if the meaning of song were exhausted by the transmutation of the face-to-face encounter between persons into a togetherness, if the singer were concerned only with feeling at one with the community. Something else must be involved in a form of expression where words are necessarily linked to tones. The singer who uses words wants more than just to be with the group: he also wants to be with things, those things to which the words of the poem refer. A person using words only is never with things in this sense: he remains at a distance from them; they remain for him "the other," that which he is not, "outside" him. By contrast, if his words are not merely spoken but sung, they build a living bridge that links him with the things referred to by the words, that transmutes distinction and separation into togetherness. By means of the tones, the speaker goes out to the things, brings the things from outside within himself, so that they are no longer "the other," something alien that he is not, but the other and his own in one. Thus a form of speaking that is addressed to no one and communicates nothing becomes intelligible. So long as the words of the poem remain silent within myself, what they are intended to say is not yet "something other," a thing "outside" myself; I must utter them, project them out of myself, in order to transform what they say into a "thing" other than myself, encountered from the outside. Only then can the tones fulfill their purpose: remove the barrier between person and thing, and clear the way for what might be called the singer's inner participation in that of which he sings—for an active sharing, an experience of a special kind, a spiritual experience. This experience is not a dreaming-oneself-out-of-oneself, not a dreaming-oneself-into-something-other, as though one were different from what one is. The singer remains what he is, but his self is enlarged, his vital range is extended: being what he is he can now, without losing his identity, be with what he is not; and the other, being what it is, can, without losing its identity, be with him. This kind of experience is not to be confused with sympathy. Sympathy is directed at immediate action, like compassion meant to shorten or to allay another's suffering, whereas the active sharing of suffering—for instance, expressed in a song that tells a story of suffering—consists precisely in this, that the suffering is fully re-experienced in the singer's mind. Here the emotion is secondary, is the effect not the cause of the sharing, and together with the latter is spiritualized, "put into brackets." (This is why the evil to which the poet refers is just as good, just as lovable, as the good.)

Thus our question on the meaning of song has been given a preliminary answer: it lies in the transmutation of the twofold confrontation between person and person and between person and thing into a twofold togetherness: the I-not-he and I-not-it become the I-and-he and the I-and-it. The tones are the medium in which the transmutation takes place.

III. Words and Tones in Song

SINCE the interpretation of the word-tone relationship given here differs substantially from the interpretations generally current, it will be well to discuss these others for purposes of orientation and further elucidation. Thinking about music today is almost entirely dominated by one or the other of two mutually exclusive theories. According to certain writers, music is essentially a language of feeling, an expression of emotion; according to others, music is made up of "dynamic sound patterns" which constitute a purely formal game (in the most serious sense of the term), one that conveys no meaning whatever, whose sole and entire content is itself. The word-tone relationship is accordingly interpreted in two very different ways. In terms of the second of the two theories, this relationship is external, no more than a close metrical correspondence (e.g., the words "rauschender Strom, brausender Wald" fit ♩ ♪. ♪|♩ ⅄ |♩ ♪♪|♩, do not fit ♫|♩ ♩ ♫|♩ ♩). According to this theory, then, the problems with which we are dealing never arise. According to the other theory, the tones expressively enhance the feelings the words arouse. (Whether the feelings are those of the singer or of the personages referred to in the poem is a question we leave in abeyance here.) Inasmuch as the term "song" today denotes primarily the art song, and inasmuch as many art songs exhibit strikingly the power to enhance feeling, it is understandable that the "emotional" interpretation is rarely contested. However, the earliest stages of song— true folk songs—do not provide nearly as good evidence in support.

The example given below is a well-known German song, "Death the Reaper." I did not choose it to refute the one theory or to bolster the other, but out of considerations that will become apparent in the next chapter. As far as the word-tone relationship is concerned, any number of examples would serve as well.

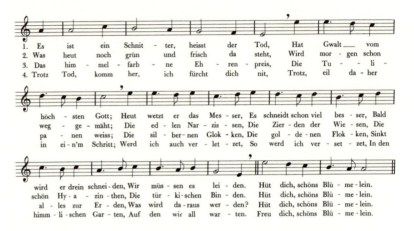

1. Es   ist   ein   Schnit - ter, heisst   der   Tod,   Hat   Gwalt ___ vom
2. Was   heut   noch grün   und   frisch   da   steht,   Wird   mor - gen schon
3. Das   him - mel - farb - ne   Eh - ren - preis,   Die   Tu - - li -
4. Trotz Tod,   komm her,   ich   fürcht   dich   nit,   Trotz,   eil   da - her

höch - sten Gott; Heut   wetzt   er   das   Mes - ser, Es schneidt schon viel   bes - ser, Bald
weg - ge - mäht; Die   ed - len   Nar - zis - sen, Die   Zier - den der   Wie - sen, Die
pa - nen weiss; Die   sil - ber- nen Glok - ken, Die   gol - de - nen   Flok - ken, Sinkt
in   ei - n'm Schritt; Werd   ich auch ver - let - zet, So   werd ich ver - set - zet, In den

wird   er drein schnei - den, Wir   müs - sen es   lei - den.   Hüt   dich, schöns Blü - me - lein.
schön Hy - a - zin - then, Die   tür - ki - schen Bin - den.   Hüt   dich, schöns Blü - me - lein.
al - les zur   Er - den, Was   wird   da - raus   wer - den?   Hüt   dich, schöns Blü - me - lein.
himm - li - schen Gar - ten, Auf   den   wir all   war - ten.   Freu   dich, schöns Blü - me - lein.

1. There is a Reaper men call Death, And God has given him Pow'r. The blade is whetting, Sharp, sharper it's growing, Soon will he be mowing, We all must suffer this. Beware, O lovely flower.

2. What is still green and fresh today, Will be mowed down tomorrow: The noble narcissi, The gems of the meadows, The fair hyacinths, The bright scarlet poppies. Beware, O lovely flower.

3. The sky-blue-hued forget-me-nots, The tulips brilliant white, The silver bellflowers, The golden sweet sultans, They all fall to the ground. What will become of them? Beware, O lovely flower.

4. Dare, Death, come here, I fear thee not, Dare, come in a single bound. Should I too be struck down, I would be transported To the heavenly garden, Which will receive us all. Rejoice, O lovely flower.

Can the tune of this song be interpreted as an expression of the feelings its words release in the singer?

First of all, the sense in which the term "expression" is used here must be clearly defined. Words are said to "express" what they denote; gestures and cries, to "express" the emotions that give rise to them; handwriting, to "express" the writer's personality. Tones are said to "express" emotions in a sense intermediate between the first and second of these three senses, somewhat closer to the second. Those who view music as a language of feeling say that tones express emotions in a way similar (but no more than similar) to that in which words express the things they denote, that is, that tones serve as a means of communicating emotions. It must be kept in mind, however, that the correlation of words and things is superficial, accidental. There is no intrinsic necessity for a given vocable to denote any one thing rather than another; identical vocables may denote different things, and different vocables one and the same thing. By contrast, every emotion gives forth its own characteristic expression, as a flower its scent; the correlation between the two is direct, inherent, leaves no room for ambiguity. Every emotion expresses itself—if at all—down to the subtlest nuances in its own distinctive way. Thus, whereas we must be told what the words of a language mean in order to understand them, not only people but even animals directly grasp the meaning of an angry or conciliatory gesture, never mistake a cry of fear for a cry of joy.

Let us now go back to our example, and see whether the word-tone relationship in this song is actually of this type.

We realize at once that the gravity of the melody matches that of the words. This observation is necessarily trivial. Obviously our poem, if taken seriously, not parodied, cannot be sung to a gay dance tune. Seriousness, however, is not an emotion but a mood, is not something that stirs us but a certain receptive state in which we happen to be. We would have to say, then, that the melody expresses the emotions which are released in me by my serious mood.

Clearly, this statement does not get us very far, does not contribute significantly to our understanding of the song and the particular way in which it affects us. There are countless serious moods, countless serious melodies. The answer to our question must be more specific. We might say, for instance, that the melody expresses the singer's emotions when the transience of earthly things—not just the vain things, but precisely the natural, innocent things of this world—is brought home to us as forcefully as it is by the words of our poet.

Even this formulation is still too vague, too general: it still does not come to grips with the substance of this particular song. Of course, no one will be unaffected by its forceful evocation of the transitoriness of all things earthly; of course, the color of the emotion it arouses is consonant with the tenor of our melody. But this emotion, taken in this general sense, is no more than the monochrome background for the manifold images suggested by the words, whereas the melody is much more than mere musical background for the words. What we hear is not merely some soft music accompanying the recital of the poem, but rather an intimate, indissoluble union of tones and words; the melody, so to speak, merges with the words, moving in complete accord with them, from syllable to syllable, from nuance to nuance. It is this accord that determines the high quality of the song, and it is this accord that is in question here and that we are trying to understand. Here the theory of music as a language of emotions fails to pass the test of experience. Instead of clarifying experience, this theory renders it unintelligible.

We must proceed, if not word by word, at least line by line.

(There is a Reaper men call Death)

The barely differentiated motion of the opening tones of the song is in keeping with the opening words, whose meaning does not become explicit until we hear the word "death." Accordingly, with this word the tonal motion comes to a brief halt at the lowest tone.

Hat   Gwalt____ vom   höch - sten   Gott;

(And God has given him Pow'r)

In this line a definite melodic contour, a definite rhythmic pattern emerges. Severity and restraint characterize the tonal motion—comparable to a series of carefully measured steps along a narrow path—in keeping with the reference in the words to the highest court, from which there is no appeal.

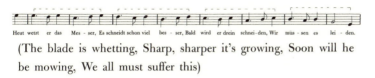

Heut wetzt er das   Mes - ser, Es schneidt schon viel   bes - ser, Bald wird er drein schnei-den, Wir   müs - sen es   lei - den.

(The blade is whetting, Sharp, sharper it's growing, Soon will he be mowing, We all must suffer this)

The harsh, indeed cruel, words, the inexorable events referred to, are matched by the rigid rhythmic pattern, the inexorable repetition of the same melodic phrase, the step-by-step descent (indicated in the musical example) from phrase to phrase. Unexpectedly, the phrase is not repeated at the end; instead we have a descending sequence. The tones drop suddenly, as though yielding of their own accord to the abrupt switch from activity to passive suffering. Finally, nothing could convey more forcefully the emphasis, the whole weight of the warning expressed in the last words than the upswing of the melody to the "Beware" directly followed by its descent to the concluding tone:

Hüt   dich, schöns   Blü - me - lein.

(Beware, O lovely flower)

Severity, restraint, harshness, cruelty, inexorability, activity and passive suffering, forcefulness, gravity, warning: all these terms denote not emotions but attitudes or states of being. What we have observed is only that the tones correspond closely to attitudes or states. To bring emotions into the picture, we would have to assume that they are released by the attitudes and only indirectly expressed by the tones.

But this would be an *ad hoc* hypothesis: the tune as perceived by an attentive listener can be adequately described without reference to emotions. That emotions are present will certainly not be contested, but they seem to be produced by the tones, not the other way round. (This is why it would be utterly wrong to sing this song "with feeling"—for instance, the first stanza "cruelly," the second and third "mournfully," and the fourth "defiantly.")

The second stanza shows that the matter can be settled without going into all those subtleties.

Was heut noch grün und frisch da steht, Wird mor - gen schon weg - ge - mäht;

(What is still green and fresh today, Will be mowed down tomorrow)

The opening words are closely related to those of the first stanza, which merely enunciates the law whose meaning is spelled out in the second. You can, if you will, assume that these words are said by the Reaper: the fact that the same tones are sung to different words would thus be accounted for by the similarity of the emotions expressed in either case. But beginning with the next line, all such explanations break down. The words now turn away from the executioner, toward his victims:

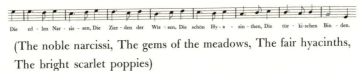

Die ed - len Nar - zis - sen, Die Zier - den der Wie - sen, Die schön Hy - a - zin - then, Die tür - ki-schen Bin - den.

(The noble narcissi, The gems of the meadows, The fair hyacinths, The bright scarlet poppies)

It is unthinkable that these words arouse the same, or even similar, emotions as the corresponding words in the first stanza, "The blade is whetting," and so on. And yet the tones are the same, and they fit the new words just as well. The rhythmic and melodic parallelism of the phrases, the gradual descent are now perceived as the correct tonal antitype of the images suggested by the words: flowers and flowers and flowers threatened by the knife. Thus we see that one and the same expressive gesture fits different emotions equally well.

The third stanza confirms this. The words now refer only to the Reaper's victims. The congruence of words and tones—

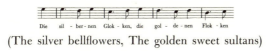

Die sil - ber-nen Glok - ken, die gol - de - nen Flok - ken

(The silver bellflowers, The golden sweet sultans)

—produces the most intimate accord.

Sinkt al - les zur Er - den,

(They all fall to the ground)

This is now as true of the tones as of the flowers.

Was wird da - raus wer - den?

(What will become of them?)

The hopelessness, the collapse expressed in this question could not be conveyed more forcefully than by the steep descent of the tonal line at this place. It is inconceivable that the melody was not invented to fit these very words.

And now the last stanza. After proclamation of the law and submission to the law, rebellion against the law: "Dare, Death!" The emotions corresponding to these words are undeniably the direct opposite of those aroused by the preceding stanzas. And yet the firmness, the resolve now revealed by the beginning of the melodic movement fit perfectly the attitude expressed in the words. And how exactly the sharp, trenchant tonal motion (but its emotional significance is very different) corresponds to the words.

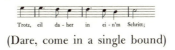

Trotz, eil da - her in ei - n'm Schritt;

(Dare, come in a single bound)

The song reaches its culmination when the melodic upswing—the tonal gesture which, by having been repeated three times, has become associated in our minds with the "Beware"—conveys the "Rejoice" with the most deeply moving effect.

Consider only the last-mentioned effect: in terms of the emotive theory, it would make no sense. One and the same gesture cannot be an equally forceful, equally convincing expression of the feeling of being threatened and the feeling of joy, indeed, of triumph. According to the theory, the use of the same tones to express both feelings can be attributed only to a weakness or a miracle. That we are not dealing here with a weakness—as though the inventor of the melody could not think of a more adequate, more suitable expression than the one he had used before—is shown by direct experience. It is enough to change the melody of the last line so as to make it conform to the emotive theory—replace it, say, with

Auf   den   wir all   war - ten.   Freu   dich, schöns   Blü - me · lein.

(Which will receive us all. Rejoice, O lovely flower)

—to realize at once that the special effect of the ending rests precisely upon the repetition of the phrase, precisely on the fact that the melody of "Beware" unexpectedly discloses the aspect of a "Rejoice."[1] To speak of a miracle, on the other hand, would only too obviously suggest an attempt to cover up the failure of the theory. The miraculous is not the incomprehensible. A true theory proves its worth not by ignoring the miraculous but by making it understandable. A theory that dismisses

---

1. Changing of tones to adapt them to the emotional values of individual words is (as a secondary factor) characteristic of the art song. When Hugo Wolf, in the song "In der Frühe," lifts the [music] "Fear no longer, torment thyself no more, my soul" to the [music] "Rejoice" of the next line, the change is exactly right.

observable facts as incomprehensible proves only its own inadequacy.

Reduced to the shortest formula, the facts with which this song confronts us, and which concern us here, can be stated as follows: (1) the tones fit the words, and (2) one and the same tone can fit equally well words that say different, even diametrically opposite, things. It follows that this "fitness" cannot rest upon an accord such as between emotion and expression. We come closer to the facts, understand them better, if we assume not that tones are messages sent from within us to the external world (which they would be if they were expressions of emotions), but that in tones our inwardness itself goes outside and encounters itself outside—that tones serve not to communicate our feelings but to help us share actively in what is said.

An incidental remark: The reader of these pages encounters the words and tones of the song "Death the Reaper" as printed characters in a book, that is, from without. In no way do they come from him: they are said to him, sung to him soundlessly; he confronts them from outside. By contrast, the singer—and he is in question here—has the words and tones within himself; they are "behind" his singing (he must know the song to be able to sing it); he lets them go out and come back to himself. Since what follows refers solely to the attitude of the singer, the reader is expected, without ceasing to be a reader, to imagine that he is a singer, more accurately, a member of a group of singers.

"There is a Reaper men call Death. . . . What is still green and fresh today. . . The sky-blue-hued forget-me-nots . . . Dare, Death, come here"—what does "active sharing" refer to in this context? What is does *not* refer to is clear. The words do not evoke something outside the singer, say, mental images of the Reaper whetting his tool, a green meadow, a blue flower, and a knight fighting Death and the Devil. There can be no question of anything like that, no question of the singer's identifying through empathy with what such images evoke, with Death and his doings, with the flowers and their suffering, with the challenger and his triumph. The imagination as the faculty to conjure up mental images is therefore not involved; nor is illusion, the putting oneself in place of the imagined, the substitution of another being for one's own. But it is equally clear that the singer does not just let the words and tones go out of himself, staying behind as a mere observer. He shares actively in what he says; he "lives" it. How? In what sense?

Words that do not serve to evoke vivid representations of things, events, feelings are nothing but empty signs—signs I understand without thoroughly exploring their meanings. "Death," "flower," "challenge"—I can understand these words without visualizing the things they denote. I can understand them as "mere words," "empty words," which provide superficial communication, nothing else. Words that are sung, however, are not empty, even though they do not aim at concrete visualization. For the singer, the words acquire a very special plenitude and depth of meaning. Something that remains silent in words merely spoken begins to flow, to vibrate; the words open and the singer opens to them. It is as though the tones infused the words with a force that reveals a new layer of meaning in them, that breathes life into them in a special way: not by making the word a tangible thing, as it appears when seen from outside, and certainly not in the sense of submerging it in a universal life in which all particularity, all distinctions are abolished, but exactly in its determined content when seen from inside, from a point where the word is, so to speak, an "I."

Die sil - ber-nen Glok - ken, Die gol - de - nen Flok - ken, Sinkt al - les zur Er - den

(The silver bellflowers, The golden sweet sultans, All fall to the ground)

To the singer, these words do not suggest anything like an endless falling of bright, fragile shapes. In fact, he sees nothing at all, imagines nothing; nor does he "empathize" with all those things, including himself, that must fall to the ground. He simply *is* this falling and the falling is he. He does not observe the falling; he "lives" it and the falling "lives" him. In the layer of meaning opened up by the tones, things that are separated meet; speaker and spoken word, "person" and "thing" come into direct contact. It is as though a door had opened through which the speaker's living self goes out to what has been said, and what has been said enters him as something that has a life of its own, as an "I." Although neither of the two swallows up the other, the antithesis "I" and "it" is transcended: the singer can say "I" to that of which he sings, and say "it" to himself. The full reality of the person and the full reality of things are now fused into a fuller reality.

To express all this in words may be somewhat complicated, but what actually takes place is simple. The process is almost automatic, comparable to the switching on of a light. What we have here is not—far from it—the result of a particular emotional effort: it takes place below the layer of affectivity (this is why singing "with feeling" inhibits rather than furthers the process). But if exactly the same tones which fit so uniquely specific words that they bring to light their innermost meanings can just as uniquely fit different words, producing the same effect—if the same musical phrase can hit different marks with the same accuracy—it is clear that words, which emphasize what distinguishes one thing from another, cannot play the decisive part in this process. ("Thing" stands here for everything that is not an "I," whether it is material or spiritual, an object or a state of mind, a feeling or an event.) The whetting of the blade, the falling of the flowers, the transience of all things earthly, the ecstatic ascent to the heavenly garden—each of these is sung in the same tones, each is made equally alive by the same melody. We must conclude that in the layer of reality whence the tones come and toward which they lead, not only the antithesis of "I" and "it" but also the distinctions between things are transcended. There must be a layer in which all things have their roots; then tones must, so to speak, activate this layer and thereby bring us closer to the roots of things. Mystics speak of a place where "all things are together," implying not an undifferentiated mixture of all things, but the common source that feeds each particular thing. This source is also the domain of tones. The characteristic experience of the sung word, which connotes both the concrete individuality of the things referred to and their submersion in a larger whole, thus becomes intelligible. One and the same melody could not express "Beware" and "Rejoice" with equal truth if such a domain did not exist, if it were not at the source where fear and joy, doom and salvation, though certainly different, are linked in a single meaning. The very existence of tones is evidence of a stratum of reality, in which unity shines through diversity.

Accordingly, a second answer to our question about the meaning of song might be: people sing in order to make sure, through direct experience, of their existence in a layer of reality different from the one in which they encounter each other and things as speakers, as facing one another and separate from one another—in order to be aware of their existence on a plane where distinction and separation of man and man, man and thing, thing and thing give way to unity, to authentic togetherness.

It may seem that this interpretation of the word-tone relationship is not incompatible with the second of the above-mentioned theories, the formal theory. If a melody is to be invented for a poem, and if its tones are not correlated with the words on the basis of objective meanings or released emotions, it can be based only on the metric scheme of the poem. Actually, it is the inflection of words as words—as metric and phonetic units, not as vehicles of meaning—that sparks off the invention of a suitable melody: only in this way can we explain why poems entirely different in content but of the same or similar metric structure can be sung to one and the same melody. This is true not just of folk music: even the greatest composers did not hesitate to use the same score twice, for entirely different texts. Thus, the formal theory justifiably denies any link between words and tones as far as meaning is concerned, and interprets melody purely in terms of tonal relationships. But this theory breaks down because it does not go beyond the superficial aspects of the word-tone correlation, and overlooks the deeper aspect—the opening of new layers of reality and meaning. The definition of music as a "game" (in whatever sense of the term) and of *homo musicus* as a variety of *homo ludens* misses the essential. Another question, however, is left open here. What we have said so far might give the impression that any tones associated with the words in a suitable metric order, that any melody whatever, whether clumsy or masterly, noble or trivial, can serve equally well. This question, the question of the melody's quality and of the part it plays in determining how words are linked with tones, will be discussed in a later section.

IV. The New Dimension

WHAT HAS BEEN said about "the other layer of existence," "the other layer of reality," must now be brought into sharper focus.

The term "layer" is not precise enough. "Another layer" might be understood: (1) as "background" to the tones, in a perspective sense—for the tones take us "behind" the words and what the words say; (2) as the "polar" complement of the words—for the reality expressed in the song is complete only in the union of words and tones; and (3) as a dialectical synthesis—for the tones resolve the antinomies present in the earlier layer. Strictly speaking, none of these interpretations hits the mark. (1) "Background" implies "foreground" and "viewer": from the viewer's standpoint it is the farthest layer, whereas tones, although they do indeed take us "behind" the words, reveal a layer closer to the viewer, not farther away. (2) The tones do indeed complement the words, but the two are not opposed as pole and antipole, as the inner and the outer, or as the spiritual and the physical. Whereas pole and antipole are always on the same plane, the union of words and tones resolves the antinomies of one plane by recourse to another. (3) This resolution cannot properly be called a dialectical synthesis. Such a synthesis transcends both thesis and antithesis by showing that neither is valid and thus abolishing both, whereas the tones abolish verbal opposites without negating the validity of a single word. On the contrary, they enhance and deepen the meaning of every word in its very particularity, and by the same token produce the union.

The unity expressed by the tones consists in the very fact that the particularity of each word is preserved as such. Think of numbers, of how every number exists precisely as a plurality of distinct units: $1 + 1$ becomes one as 2; the one 2 is $1 + 1$. We are reminded of the old saying that music making is ultimately an unconscious counting: should we grant its truth in this sense?

"Another layer" denotes neither background nor antipole nor synthesis; it denotes a new dimension, in the geometrical sense of the term. What is distinct, what is multiple in the first dimensional layer becomes one in passing to the second. Two points become the one line, three lines the one triangle, four triangles the one pyramid. In each case, a new meaning is revealed by the passage to the higher dimension, where elements previously distinct and separate form a unified whole without losing their identities as elements of the lower order. Indeed, their very distinctness is reasserted. The one straight line does not merely join the two points; it also keeps them apart forever. The one triangle cannot exist unless the number of straight lines is three. Only in a higher dimension so understood can elements of a lower dimension be unified; their unification presupposes the reality or possibility of the higher dimension. Once the unification has been effected, the higher dimension is created, the potential has become the actual.

Thus singing actualizes a new dimension of the word and of its meaning. The background to the word disclosed by the tone is not comparable to a second plane behind the plane of the foreground: it is three-dimensional space—space that extends both in back and in front of the plane. What is miraculous in this event is well illustrated by the geometrical analogy. The emergence of a new dimension is always the greatest of miracles. What is more inconceivable than the possibility that two points, which know nothing of straight lines, should become unified while remaining two? Imagine a being that communicates with the world only through the sense of touch, is aware of surfaces only;

now suddenly it opens its eyes and sees light, spatial depth. Imagine a being that has no auditory sensations (most animals have no auditory organs; only vertebrates and some crabs and insects are equipped with ears), a being that can only see and touch, that is aware of the world only as the sum of visible and tangible things in space, and suddenly this being can hear, can perceive sounds, a depth behind the spatial depth, an existential depth.

(To avoid possible misunderstandings, we may note that here and elsewhere in this book, the "spoken word" denotes words as elements of speech used in their most important social function, that is, to communicate facts, ideas, feelings, orders. This includes the written word but not poetry, not words used for magical or ritual purposes. The latter were probably always sung, and as such open to the depth dimension. After poetry separated itself from music and became a purely verbal art, it retained the additional dimension; more accurately, in this art spoken words perform the function of tones. Poets have learned to use words in such a way that these "surface" forms evoke depth, just as painters learn to suggest spatial depth by the proper use of two-dimensional forms. Accordingly, poetry stands in the same relation to song as, say, perspective painting to architecture.)

In one of his "Muzot" letters, Rilke refers to *"the depth dimension of our inwardness."* He writes: "I have come to think more and more that our ordinary consciousness is situated at the very tip of a pyramid, the base of which lies within ourselves (even, in a sense, beneath ourselves), and that this base is progressively wider and wider; as we descend into ourselves, we find ourselves more and more included among the data of our earthly existence (the *world* in the broadest sense) that are independent of space and time. Since my earliest youth I have had the feeling (and have lived in accordance with it as far as able) that if we could just get far enough down into this pyramid of consciousness, we could experience pure *being*, the inviolable presence and simultaneity of all things which at the upper 'normal' level of consciousness we are vouchsafed to experience only as a succession in time."[1] Here, and also in later passages, Rilke stresses the temporal components, the simultaneity of elements that are successive in time. It is clear, however, that what he has in mind is the world of things in general, the place where "all things are together." Only seemingly does he dispense with the passage to another dimension (pyramids are three-dimensional both at the top and at the bottom): the passage to a new dimension is implied in Rilke's reference to the base of the pyramid as being "within" us—in a dimension where the psyche and the world are at one, where the many exist simultaneously at the same place without ceasing to be many.

An image that perhaps more vividly than any other conveys the becoming one of the many as many is that of the sphere, particularly if it is taken in both the dynamic and the geometric senses. The center of the sphere is the source of energy: from the center, lines of force radiate outward in all directions, filling the space without leaving any gaps. On the surface of the sphere figures are visible in any desired number and shape. From every point of every figure, a radius, a ray of energy, runs back into the sphere, to its center. The figures stand for the many: as two-dimensional forms they are a mere plurality, nothing but the many. But as they step out of the surface—carried by their radii, so to speak—they converge toward the center, where all of them become one. Here all are perfectly, purely together; they are one, yet have not been swallowed up, have not become indistinguishable from one another, for in the one central point each figure is present as what it is, each defined by a particular sheaf of radii. Each individual figure on the surface finds an inner path leading to the other figures via the center common to all. The energy-suffused sphere makes this possible. (In an early work Kepler says that the sphere symbolizes the trinitarian Christian godhead: " 'The image of the triune God is in the

---

1. Rilke, *Briefe,* p. 871 (Rilke's italics).

spherical surface, that is to say, the Father's in the center, the Son's in the outer surface, and the Holy Ghost's in the equality of relation between point and circumference.' The movement or emanation passing from the center to the outer surface is for him the symbol of creation.")[2]

Such images, needless to say, paraphrase rather than define the specific nature of the word-tone relationship. However, they make us see more clearly how this relationship must *not* be interpreted. The unity expressed by the sung word as against the plurality expressed by the spoken word is not that of a *Gestalt;* nor is it something transcendent.

When we are dealing with a plurality of phenomena constituting a unified structure or pattern, the idea that first springs to mind is that of a *Gestalt.* The tonal *Gestalt:* the one melody that does not do away with the plurality of tones but is built of them, that is one precisely as a plurality; the verbal *Gestalt:* the one sentence consisting of many words; the rhythmic *Gestalt:* the one wave made up of many phases; the visible *Gestalt:* the one figure made up of many lines—in each of these, the many become one in the same way. The unification that takes place when the spoken word is sung has another sense. More generally, are we justified in speaking of a *"becoming* one" in the case of the *Gestalt?* After all, the crucial point of Gestalt theory is the demonstration that in the *Gestalt* the whole is not only more than the sum of its parts but also that the whole exists prior to the parts. The experience of the *Gestalt* is not that of parts coming together to form a whole but of parts being singled out in a whole: the parts do not *become* a whole; they have always formed the whole, their places in it being predetermined. For example, this figure △ is not perceived as an open figure with four sides, but as a triangle one side of which is incomplete. (Gestalt psychology shows conclusively that

---

2. Cf. W. Pauli, "The Influence of Archetypal Ideas on the Scientific Theories of Kepler," pp. 159 ff.

this is not primarily due to habit, in this case, the habit of seeing triangles.) Not only do the parts as such fit into the whole of the *Gestalt*—lines as lines into the figure, words as words into the sentence, tones as tones into the melody—but they are, so to speak, eager to do so of their own accord: it is well known how hard it is *not* to hear successive tones as a melody, *not* to see connected lines as a figure. Consequently, this kind of unification of distinct elements does not presuppose the existence of a new dimension. Not so the unification of words: nothing in the spoken word suggests the possibility of unification, which is only revealed when words are being combined with tones; the spoken word alone could never discover and actualize it. "Beware, little flower" is one verbal *Gestalt,* "Rejoice, little flower" is another, and each is a component of the greater verbal *Gestalt,* the poem in which the opposed meanings of "Beware" and "Rejoice" are fully retained. This opposition cannot be bridged by other words, but it can be bridged by the tones. Earlier we have referred to the three lines and the one triangle; now it turns out that our statement contained an ambiguity. The triangle can be conceived of as a single structure, as a linear figure consisting of straight lines, even apart from the surface; but the fact that the lines as such belong together is different in kind from the fact that they are unified by grace of the surface. The unity of the *Gestalt* rests on the former fact; the latter characterizes a unification that cannot be brought about with a passage to a higher dimension. The unity created by the sung word is of this latter type.

Furthermore—and this is crucial—the passage to another dimension is not a passage to a "beyond." The "new dimension" is not another world, is not something mysterious as opposed to the self-evident, is not something supernatural. To be sure, a two-dimensional being cannot conceive of spatial depth; to such a being, the third dimension is an impenetrable mystery, its emergence a miracle beyond understanding. However, spatial depth is still space, a form of extension just as the surface is—a new, richer form of extension, not something beyond extension, another reality of the world, not the reality of another world.

Music is not (as Robert Musil put it) "a little terrestrial back door leading to the supraterrestrial." Singing man does not step out of anything, does not leave anything behind him, says no farewell to speaking man. Quite on the contrary, it is speaking man who gets to the bottom of himself, and he does this not by turning his back on the world, not by looking into himself in search of a "better," "inner" world; he does not go "into himself," he goes out of himself; he does not shut himself in, he opens himself. The change from the spoken to the sung word is not a turn of 180 degrees, does not involve a change of direction. Singing man reaches back deeper into himself, reaches out farther, and thus also gets farther out, penetrates deeper into things, than speaking man. The spoken word and the sung word do not refer to different things; the things are the same and yet not the same, just as the things I see with my eyes are the same and yet not the same as those I blindly touch with my hands: I see them in a new light, my relation to them is different, and things illumined by tones are in a new relation to me. The tone the singer adds to the word does not cancel out the word, but rather gives it the sharpest edge, makes it vibrate with the highest frequency, so that it penetrates things to a greater depth, down to a layer where their separatedness tilts over into togetherness. Singing man reaches a new depth of the world, and by the same token a deeper level of himself.

In all of the foregoing, "singing man" stands for "music-making man" in the broadest sense: after all, it does not really matter whether one makes music with the natural instrument of the vocal cords or with a man-made instrument. Directly or indirectly, tones are always man-made: music-making man is singing man. The conception of musicality as an essential characteristic of man, as man's innate predisposition to music—not a characteristic one may or may not have but a constitutive element of man's nature—thus postulates the reality of the additional dimension, of a depth behind spatial depth, an existential depth in the precise sense of the word borrowed from geometry, and a conception of man as a being that lives in this dimension, a being that would be incomplete without it. This means, however, that musicality, in addition to being an attribute of man, is also an attribute of the world. The one without the other makes no sense: the existence of the new dimension is revealed precisely in communication between man and things, in the fact that the singer shares actively in what he sings about. Singing man verifies his own reality in the new dimension, but at the same time, thanks to the tones, he steps outside himself and recognizes the reality of the new dimension in things. Of course, music is not the only means of attaining the broader, deeper levels of existence, nor is it the only testimony to them. There are many means, many testimonies. Music, however, surely provides the shortest, the least arduous, perhaps even the most natural solvent of artificial boundaries between the self and others, just as language is most apt and useful for expressing every sort of distinction and difference between them. Because man can accede to the "new dimension," he may properly be called "musical."

v. Music and Inwardness

THE INTERPRETATION of music presented here is in sharp contradiction to a theory which has been well and ably urged by a number of profound and logical thinkers. In their view, music's essential character is its turning away from the world; it has no relation to material things, is absolutely nonobjective—in a word, is turned "inward." The language of tones, it is claimed, is just as unsuitable for giving expression to phenomena of the external world as it is ideally suited to express the inner world or soul. To quote one illustrious witness: "In the tone, music forsakes the element of external form. For musical expression . . . only the inner life of the soul that is wholly devoid of an object . . . is appropriate. This is our entirely empty ego, the self without further content. . . . The fundamental task of music will therefore consist in giving a resonant reflection, not to objectivity in its ordinary material sense, but to the mode and modifications under which the most intimate self of the soul, from the point of view of its subjective life and ideality, is essentially moved. . . . The tones merely resound in the depths of the soul, which are thereby seized upon in their ideal substance, and suffused with emotion. . . . It is precisely this sphere, the intimacy of soul-life, the abstract appropriation of its own reality, which is grasped by music."[1] It would be impossible to find a more lucid and forceful statement of this point of view than these words of Hegel's.

1. Hegel, *The Philosophy of Fine Art*, Vol. III, pp. 341, 342, 344, 361.

The phrases just quoted refer to music at its most advanced stage. They were written at a time when music had moved very far from its origins and was within sight of its supreme achievement in Beethoven. What had been unthinkable before—vast structures consisting of nothing but tones, overwhelming manifestations of energy divorced from matter, capable of arousing the highest admiration and the deepest emotions— had become facts of musical life. How are we to account for this phenomenon? Such a musician stirs us deeply, but what is he saying, what is he talking *about?* Not about this, not about that, not about anything that can be named, not about any object—he is speaking about *nothing;* yet this "nothing" is an "all." And there is no contradiction here. For what do we find within ourselves when we resolutely turn away from the world of things to our interior selves? Why, just such a "nothing" that is at the same time "all." This is pure subjectivity: "nothing" so far as things, objects, are concerned, nothing that can be pointed to, called by name (if it could, it would be object, no longer subject). And yet it is "all" at the same time, because the objective existence of all objects presupposes it. Pure inwardness: an "all" that is the source and ground of all expression, all utterance, and a "nothing" so far as precise utterance is concerned—strictly speaking, something unsayable. Could it be said, it would lie outside the being of the utterer; it would be external to him rather than pure inwardness. The "nothing" of which the tones speak to us is the "nothing" of pure subjectivity, pure inwardness.

("Subjectivity," "inwardness," in the sense used here must not be confused with feeling or mood. One "has" a feeling or one does not have it; one "is" in a mood or one is not. Subjectivity, on the other hand, is what one is, and that cannot be otherwise. Feelings and moods are "objects"; they can be pointed to, given a name—fear, joy, devotion, defiance—and their consequent "objectivity" makes them external to pure inwardness, just like everything else in the external world. There- fore tones have as little to say of feelings and moods as of anything else. Yet if they do *not* have anything to say about feelings and moods, they either are about something else entirely, or they are, strictly speaking, meaningless. Thus the two opposed theories of music, as a language of feelings and moods on the one hand and as a mere formal game on the other, are complementary in that both are based on the same faulty premise.)

If Hegel's words are taken as rigorously as intended, they would seem to represent the thinker's last word on the meaning of Beethoven's symphonies. What does this extreme view imply? In emancipating the tones from the spoken word, music seems to have taken the momentous step that cleared the way for its highest development. What the tones liberated themselves *from* makes it possible to infer what they liberated themselves *for*. Words refer to things, to "objects"; anything named by a word becomes an object, that is, becomes severed from the subject, external to it. Even the word "subject" turns the subject into an object; even the word "inner" turns the inner into the outer. What else can the divorce of the tones from the spoken word mean but the most radical shift from the "outer" to the "inner"? Only tones freed from their bondage to words can faithfully express the meaning of "subjectivity" or "inwardness," can express it without perverting it. In thus fulfilling itself, music reveals that its true purpose has always been to grasp "the intimacy of soul-life." So long as linked with words, tones retain an embarrassing residue of earthiness. This is the reason why, in the last analysis, adherents to Hegel's view of music cannot regard music set to words as music of the highest rank, as "absolute music." Down to this day, the more severe among them bear Beethoven a grudge for having permitted tones to make their way spontaneously back to words in the last movement of his last completed symphony. Others regard this as the exception that confirms the rule: after all, Beethoven's thirty-six other symphony movements, his sonatas, and his chamber music speak about nothing and to nothing but "the inner life of the soul that is wholly devoid of an object." "From the heart—may it reach other hearts": the heart knows no objects.

And yet Beethoven wrote these words as a motto for his Solemn Mass, not a symphony or a sonata. Moreover, the interpretation of the word-tone relationship necessarily implied or presupposed by Hegel is not quite consistent with the phenomena of music's culminant stage; in view of what we know about the early stages of music, this interpretation is downright absurd. As musical evidence, that from the beginnings is no less weighty than that from the culmination, and it is absurd to suppose that music has somehow become involved in self-contradiction in the course of its history. Words naming things, referring to objects, turned outward; tones expressing the life of soul wholly devoid of objects, referring to the purely subjective, turned inward: we would have to conclude that words and tones pull in opposite directions. If this were the case, tone meanings would be at odds with word meanings; each would conflict with and weaken the other. That this cannot be the case is attested by every folk song. The tone the singer adds to the word is not at odds with the word, does not pull in the opposite direction, away from what the word says; rather, it accompanies the word on its way to the thing, to the object. Only, unlike the mere word, it does not stop at the object: it breaks through the dimension of objective existence, thus making it impossible for what the word denotes to be nothing but object, to remain frozen in its existence as object. The tone does not blur the word's meaning but rather deepens it. Incontestably, the sung "Beware" conveys more of a warning, and the sung "Rejoice" more of a rejoicing, than the same words merely spoken. It would be utterly mistaken to imagine that the tones take the singer away from the words; rather, thanks to the tones, the words are no longer confined merely to denoting objects. Sometimes, usually at the end of a line or a stanza, the tones detach themselves from the words and the melodic movement continues freely on its own, but the wordless tones never turn their backs on the words preceding them; on the contrary, they serve to explore and savor their meanings more deeply. The last word of the stanza clings to the melody, which, so to speak, retains its color. To be sure, tones are "nonobjective":

in itself says neither "Beware" nor "Rejoice," says nothing of the kind: if it did, it could not say the one as well as the other when combined with words. But the nonobjectivity of tones is not that of the "other side," of inwardness devoid of an object, of pure subjectivity; it is a nonobjectivity *behind* the objects. "The intimacy of soul-life is grasped by music": when the song resounds, when we hear the words "Beware" and "Rejoice," and words speaking of resignation and defiance, of reaping and falling, *whose* inner life is grasped here? Is it the singer or the composer who is warning, rejoicing, resigning himself to his fate, rebelling, reaping, falling? No, it is the inner life of warning and rejoicing, of resignation and defiance, the inner life of the flowers and of the blade. The dimension disclosed by the tones can certainly be called "inner life," but this is not the inner life of the subject as opposed to the object, to something external; it is not the inner life of the self but of the world, the inner life of things. This is precisely why the singer experiences inner life as something he shares with the world, not as something that sets him apart from it. As he sings (and hears himself sing) he discovers that the things of the world speak the language of his own inwardness and that he himself speaks the inner language of things. The tones express this accord. The antithesis of "inside" and "outside" is not thereby abolished, but it is, so to speak, turned on its side: the vertical becomes the horizontal. The wall separating the self from the world now runs straight across everything, becomes a bridge joining the two.

Hegel's statements—and all statements of the same or related kind—are untrue or, more accurately, a travesty of the truth, precisely because, taken in the strict sense, they imply a radical antithesis of the inner world and the world of things. "The fundamental task of music will therefore consist in giving a resonant reflection, not to objectivity in its ordinary material sense, but to the mode and modifications under which the most intimate self of the soul, from the point of view of its subjective life and ideality, is essentially moved": this statement is riddled with false antitheses. It might be rearranged to read: "The fundamental task of music will consist in bringing to light, not the aspect of things that distinguishes them from me and opposes them to me, but the aspect of them already turned toward me, what they have in common with me, by giving a resonant reflection to the mode and modifications under which the things themselves are moved from the point of view of their inner life." This formulation is certainly more consistent with the facts. For the truth is that Hegel does not view music as it really is: he sees it through a web of concepts, categories— subject, inwardness, soul, self, on the one hand, and object, outward- ness, world, on the other. He thinks in these antitheses; he thinks as a logician, in terms of the logos, the word, spoken language. This is why, in the last analysis, he must arrive at a false conception of the tone, of music. As long as subjectivity (the self) and objectivity (the world of things) are conceived as mutually exclusive, music can only refer to subjectivity, the self. Were the inner world wholly devoid of objectivity, the outer world nothing but object, the music's theme could only be an inner life devoid of objectivity. But this is the crux of the matter: the existence of music puts these categories and antitheses in question. It is impossible to understand music in such terms; the categories themselves have to be revised in the light of what music actually is. And the first step toward understanding music is to grasp that singing man has no place in the world view of speaking man. However encompassing a conception of himself and of his world speaking man may formulate, the conception must remain parochial if it excludes music, as it were, by definition.

vi. "The Limits of My Language Are the Limits of My World"

The foregoing remarks do not in any way imply a value judgment: that music is superior to spoken language, tones more essential to human existence than words. No single essential characteristic of a given entity can be said to be more essential than another. The three angles of a triangle are not more essential than the three sides. It is true, however, that when we consider not the essence of a thing but the way it comes into being, one essential characteristic may indeed take precedence over another. The triangle starts with one side, not with one angle. I cannot draw a triangle starting with an angle. From the evolutionary point of view, speech unquestionably ranks higher than music.

I do not claim that speech existed before music. It is impossible to ascertain the exact sequence of facts buried so far back in time. What I do say is that man begins with the word. The word marks the crucial advance which sets man apart from all other living beings. With the power of speech he breaks through the closed circle of action and reaction that keeps other living organisms bound to their immediate environment. Unlike the animal, once man acquires the power of speech he exists no longer only *in* nature and begins to conceive of "nature" as something distinct from himself. The word does not completely divorce man from nature, to which he remains bound, but it loosens his ties, sets him apart, creates things. Nature becomes world. The word is the sign by means of which man's being-in-the-world is distinguished from the animal's being-in-nature. The endlessly debated question of whether the power of speech is actually man's distinctive attribute, whether some highly developed animal species are capable of speech, essentially centers around the definition of the term "language."[1] If language is defined by its social function, if the word is primarily seen as the instrument used by individuals of a given community to communicate with one another, then there is no doubt that bees, for instance, possess a highly developed language. If language is viewed primarily as an expression of the "soul," of inner life, feelings, states of mind, or as a game composed of sounds and gestures, whether imitative or merely playful, then it is clear that human as compared with animal language differs from the latter only in degree of efficiency, not in kind. But human language is actually something else, something more: it also has a purely denotative function; it designates things, names them. No animal names things. An animal can give the sign "water" when water is supposed to be found or avoided, it can express pleasure or aversion when encountering water, it may even perform a "water dance," but it would make no sense for an animal to say "water" in circumstances in which water had no relevance to the animal's life functions. If language is defined by its specifically human characteristics, as something never found outside the human world—for no human language, however primitive, functions purely as sign, as emotive expression, as a game, or fails to be first and foremost a language of words—then the term refers to a power of speech different in kind from any and every animal language, a power that could not have just grown gradually out of animal language. None of us has ever been an animal, so none of us can take the measure of this decisive step. We can get an inkling of how momentous this step was from the autobiography of Helen Keller, in which she describes how she first realized that "water" was not just a sign or expressive sound but a name, and that it made sense

---

1. Cf. Ernst Cassirer, *An Essay on Man*, part I, ch. 3.

to say "water" even when she was not wet or thirsty. The step from functional designation to meaning, the emergence of meaning, is the crucial one: with it, the human spirit rises above nature. The word marks the moment when man comes into the world and becomes aware of the world. Thus he can call the word "God": the word created man.

Since man has sought to understand himself at all, he has understood himself primarily as a being that possesses the power of speech. This could not be otherwise. The idea man forms of his own essence may center on practical activities, on tools and technology, or on theoretical activities, art, thinking, science: what essentially characterizes all of them is man's language-born attitude toward the world as something distinct from himself. Animals, too, work, fashion, think in their own way, but only man does all this as an "I" confronting a world. Only man has a world, and he has it only because he has the word. I have said that tones open up a new dimension: the same can be said more justly of words. For the singer's sense of being at one with his world has a sort of precedent at a prehuman stage, in the animal's relationship with its natural environment, whereas the word marks the emergence of something utterly new, something that had never existed before. The passage to a new dimension here involves a radical break, a stepping out of nature: speaking man faces the world, sees it from "outside," speaks *to* it; in speaking to it, he views it as distinct from himself, and himself as distinct from it; what the word names becomes thing, object. Philologists and psychologists agree that in the evolution of the race as well as of the individual, objects make their appearance concurrently with the advance from expressive sounds or signs to words. The dimension opened up by the word is called "objective reality." This is not something that existed prior to speech, that speech merely discovers; it is first and foremost a creation of speech. Comparative linguistics is gradually destroying our naïve notion of objective reality as an absolute, that is, absolutely autonomous, entirely self-determined reality to which our words or our thoughts slowly find their way, guided by language. "It must be remembered, disconcerting though the fact may be, that so far from a grammar—the structure of a symbol system—being a reflection of the structure of the world, any supposed structure of the world is more probably a reflection of the grammar used."[2] For this reason the term "object" and terms designating the object-subject relationship have different connotations in differently structured languages: each language "discovers" its own objective reality. There is no reality "behind" all these different objective realities; the very notion of an objective reality "behind" language is meaningless. All this is not to belittle the importance of the idea of objectivity; it only helps us understand in what sense the word can be said to have created man *and* his world. Now it also becomes clear that Ludwig Wittgenstein's proposition in his *Tractatus Logico-Philosophicus*, "the limits of my language are the limits of my world," must not be taken in a restrictive sense, but is valid without reservations.

At this point it might seem that our reflections have become self-contradictory, incompatible with our earlier assertion resulting from a longer chain of reasoning, that speaking man's image of himself and his world needs to be broadened and supplemented. Actually, the incompatibility is only apparent. For although the limits of my language are the limits of my world, music lies *within* these limits: after all, we do name it, say "music"; the word places it before us, makes it a human thing in the human world. Music is not alien to us. We can appropriate it because we have the word, because we name it, because we can ask questions about it—questions concerning music not only as a "thing" or "object" but also as a reality not encompassed by the terms "thing" and "object," questions concerning the intrinsic nature of music, its essence. True, many writers deny that such questions concerning the essence of music have any rational meaning. According to them, it is possible to speak rationally only about the "object" music,

---

2. Ogden and Richards, *The Meaning of Meaning*, p. 96.

a specific human activity viewed historically, psychologically, socio-
logically—the periphery, the shell of music, not the kernel; the latter,
we are told, eludes verbal expression. To take this view, to conclude
that music is by nature inaccessible to the word, to language, is to
exclude it from the world of language, that is, the human world. But
to regard any discourse on the essence of music as fruitless on the
ground that the essential core of music eludes verbal expression is to
misconstrue the significance of both tones and words. If rational discourse were possible only where the essence of a thing did not elude
verbal expression, what would be left? Who besides a mathematician
could say anything rational about color, for example? (Goethe's mon-
strous folly!) No one could speak about himself, let alone about God.
Man as a rational being would be forbidden to ask the very questions
that more than anything else reveal him as a rational being, the questions
concerning himself and the meaning of his existence.

All this, however, makes us more sharply aware of the paradox
involved in our position. How can something—music—that extends
beyond word language nonetheless lie within the boundaries of word
language? How is it possible to capture in words that which eludes
verbal expression? We are reminded of an old philosophical paradox:
What is "nothing"? If every thought is a thought about something,
how is it possible to think "nothing"? How are we to interpret the
fact that when someone says "nothing," he does not say nothing?
Should not a man who wants to say "nothing" remain silent? Those
who try to say something about music are confronted with similar
questions. Our discussion of the tone-word relationship in folk song
brought the paradox fully into the open. It has been shown that the
word "tone" names a thing, that is, makes it an object whose essence
manifests itself in negating every kind of objectivity and in reaching
beyond anything that can be said in words. Our analysis could proceed
only in the medium of language; it was an attempt to say in words
not only *that* tones say what words cannot say but also *what* it is they

say: *to say in words what words cannot say.* Is this absurd? Only those who read the proposition falsely may allege so, as though we had written: "to say in words a thing which words cannot say." But surely no one could mean to say anything so absurd, for this would amount to asserting and denying simultaneously the difference between tones and words. What is actually meant can only be: "to say in words *what it is* that words cannot say." Anyone who denies that it is possible to do this is like a man who says that it is futile to try to see the *inside* of things because the eye sees only their surface, and so sees only the *outside.* Such a man misunderstands what the phrase "to say in words" means. It does not mean that words can take the place of things, as though words were things all over again, in another form. Words do not duplicate things, nor do they represent the "spirit" of things, nor do they merely point to things already given. Words are boundaries: they create things by setting them apart, by tracing their boundaries. But a boundary is not the same thing as that which is bounded. That which is in this sense created by the word always extends beyond the word, extends "inward." Sometimes this inner part is "empty"—when a thing is entirely defined by its boundaries, when word and thing coincide, when the thing is identical with its definition, as is the case with many scientific and abstract concepts, especially the symbols of logical calculus. Normally, however, the "inside" of things is not "empty"; the thing is not identical with its definition, is more than its boundary. But this does not mean that words must now lag behind: what extends beyond the word is not for this reason inaccessible to it. The naming word will be followed by other words, directed inward, away from the boundary—words that reach into that which was circumscribed, words that trace ever closer boundary lines around the things, as though to rope them in. The things respond in various ways: depending upon their nature or structure, they submit readily or resist. To put it differently, about some things it is easier to speak; more can be said about them than about others. A visible thing, for instance,

being itself delimited, accommodates itself more readily to the requirements of speech than a mood or a feeling, the static more readily than
the dynamic, "words" more readily than "tones." In a general way
words, by their very nature, tend to emphasize boundaries, to draw
attention to them; to counteract that tendency always requires a special
effort. When words are given too much scope, when our thinking relies
exclusively on words, on language, it may happen that the things, giving
way to the words, seemingly shrink more and more within their boundaries, become identical with their definitions: the world becomes unreal.
In this sense, we have said above that the mere word "subject" turns
the subject into an object. If the same is allowed to happen to the
word "tone," our discourse about tones will very soon be confined
to frequencies and sinus curves, to figures and numbers, that is, to
physics; if this happens to the word "music," we will soon confine
our discourse to cultural history or the rules of musical theory. But
language is never powerless. Words can say "no," can time and again
undo what words have done, can upset the thing's fixation in its
existence as object, pry open what they have enclosed within their
boundaries, trace new boundaries and pry them open again—words
acting against words, language against language, yet never ceasing to
be words, language.

Once again the metaphor of the sphere comes to mind. The prelinguistic stage could be represented by the undifferentiated sphere.
With the emergence of speech a differentiation sets in, the sphere
articulating into a center and a spherical surface seen from within—as
we see the horizon, for instance, or the starry sky. The center stands
for speaking man, the surface for his world. The words trace boundaries
on the surface; the figures they delimit are things named by words,
"objects." This does not, however, reduce the sphere to a central point
plus a surface. Not only speech exists; there is also music, tones, and
the tones do not trace figures on the surface, do not extend in two
dimensions on the surface but cut through it; they move outward and

inward without creating something confronting them; they are pure beings of the third dimension, depth; they are, so to speak, perpendicular to the surface that represents the words. Consequently, we must assume the reality of such a "perpendicular": before and behind the surface there is not nothing. The sphere is not merely a central point plus a surface; it also has depth. The tones put the two-dimensionality of the verbal world in question. In the perspective of the tone, the surface is a cross section of the spherical space and the figures on the surface are projections of three-dimensioned structures. This division, however, is not as simple as might appear, does not imply that the surface is the domain of the word, and depth the domain of the tone. The depth opened by tones is not inaccessible to words. Although the word remains surface, this surface is not fixed at a definite place, a definite distance from the center: it can shift its position, can move closer to the center and move away from it. The tones do not run away from the words; the words catch up with them. To whatever depth the tones reach, words can reach too, but they never cease to be two-dimensional. Direct expression of depth is denied to words, is reserved to tones. Tones, for their part, are denied the sharp outlines, the definiteness of figures, which require the two dimensions of the surface to be represented. In itself, the dimension of depth can produce no figure. Thus both, words and tones, have each their own limits and their own limitless possibilities.

"The limits of my language are the limits of my world": only now does the meaning of Wittgenstein's proposition become entirely clear. "The limits of language" does not imply the existence of a domain inaccessible to language. No such domain exists. Nothing actually or potentially relevant to human existence is beyond the grasp of language; the domain of the word is limitless. The limit beyond which words cannot go is their own delimiting activity. The limit of language is its being-a-limit. However broad or narrow the limits it may trace, there is one thing it never reaches: that which is delimited. This is the unutterable—Wittgenstein calls it the "mystical." It is not mystical in the sense of being infinitely remote, utterly hidden; it is what is closest to us, most manifestly present in everything that is not an intellectual or linguistic fiction. This is what Aristotle means when he says that the individual is the ineffable. This is what Rilke has in mind when he says, "Wagt zu sagen, was ihr Apfel nennt!"—"Dare to spell out what you're calling apple!" He himself dares just that, in one of his poems of the "Orpheus" sequence. Wittgenstein was wrong to write, "What we cannot speak of we must consign to silence." Not at all: what we cannot speak of we can sing about.

Just what we mean here should be clear. Singing man does not raise himself above speaking man; musical man does not supersede rational man. The otherness of tones is not of another world. It does not derive from some transcendental beyond or from some "purely interior" self or thought or feeling. It is singing man's different attitude toward his world. That from which speaking man sets himself apart and which he holds in front of himself, singing man brings as close as he can to himself, becomes one with. The two acts are like breathing in and breathing out, in one process, or the Chinese sage's complementarity of love and respect.

VII. Music and Magic

WE HAVE still to consider a not infrequently expressed opinion, briefly referred to above, that singing man, far from marking any sort of advance over speaking man, actually marks a reversion to earlier, prelinguistic, prerational stages of development. If it is true that speech creates objects, objective reality, sharp boundaries, and a radical opposition between subject and object, then—it is argued—music, which tends to abolish this opposition and to blur these boundaries (as we have shown), can aim at nothing other than annulling the achievements of speech and reviving the superseded prerational stage. This leads to two contradictory evaluations of music. Briefly stated: where "spirit" is looked upon as the "adversary of life," music is praised as the healing power that keeps open our lines of communication to the wellsprings of life; by contrast, where salvation is sought in a spiritual order, it is felt that music tempts us to relapse into animal darkness, and therefore that we should shun it. Common to both evaluations is the mistaken opinion that music originated at some prelinguistic stage of evolution, and that the radical opposition between subjectivity and objectivity can only be transcended "from below," by going back to some prerational stage. That the same result can also be achieved by going forward to a broadened rationalism is overlooked.

This mistaken opinion finds its strongest support in the widespread belief that song is first and foremost an expression of emotion. The assertion that music is to speech as feeling is to thought is rarely contradicted. Furthermore, because the child's development is generally viewed as an abridged version of the development of the human race, and because the child passes through a period of predominantly emotive utterance before learning to speak, we conclude without further ado that singing man existed prior to speaking man. "Man sang out his feelings long before he was capable of uttering his thoughts."

This sentence and the passages quoted below are taken from Otto Jespersen's *Language, Its Nature, Development, and Origin*. It is astonishing that even in a discipline as exact as modern linguistics the popular correlation between musicality and emotionality should be uncritically accepted and serve as foundation of a theory according to which speech marks an advance over an earlier "musical" stage, just as rationality marks an advance over a primitive "feeling" stage. "It is a consequence of advancing civilization that passion, or at least the expression of passion, is moderated; and we must therefore conclude that the speech of uncivilized and primitive men was more passionately agitated than ours, more like music or song. . . . There was once a time when all speech was song, or rather when these two actions were not yet differentiated. . . . Our comparatively monotonous spoken language and our highly developed vocal music are differentiations of primitive utterances, which had more in them of the latter than of the former. These utterances were at first, like the singing of birds and the roaring of many animals and the crying and crooning of babies, exclamative, not communicative. . . . Our remote ancestors had not the slightest notion that such a thing as communicating ideas and feelings to someone else was possible. . . . How did the association of sound and sense come about? How did that which originally was a jingle of meaningless sounds come to be an instrument of thought? . . . We may perhaps form an idea of the most primitive process of associating sound and sense. . . . In the songs of a particular individual there would be a constant recurrence of a particular series of sounds with a particular cadence. . . . Suppose . . . a lover was in the habit of addressing his lass 'with a hey, and a ho, and a hey nonino.' His comrades and rivals would not fail to remark this, and . . . banter him by imitating and repeating his 'hey-and-a-ho-and-a-hey-nonino.' But when once this had been recognized as what Wagner would term a 'person's leitmotiv,' it would be no far cry from mimicking it to using [it] . . . as a sort of nickname. . . . It might be employed, for instance, to signal his arrival. And when once proper names had been bestowed, common names (or nouns) would not be slow in following." Thus, according to Jespersen, speech developed from song.

We may leave aside the question of whether it is legitimate to call a living being still incapable of speech "human": actually we know no human community, however primitive, whose language consists only of calls, does not include names, words. That prelinguistic utterance, however, should unhesitatingly be designated as a kind of song will certainly not pass unchallenged. Utterances such as meaningless noises, animal growls, and infant gurgles have just as much and just as little in common with speaking as with singing. The "hey-and-a-ho" is certainly just as far (perhaps even farther) removed from the primitive musical phrase as it is from the primitive sentence. However primitive, a musical phrase is a structure no less meaningful than a verbal phrase. Nonsense plus feeling does not make music. Such notions are based on a totally mistaken conception of what music and song really are. A sound of more or less defined pitch, no matter how expressive, is not a musical tone; a sequence of sounds of varying pitch, by which feeling is expressed, is not yet song, nor can it become song merely by repetition. Song begins precisely where successive sounds rise above their ties to feeling and form new ties—ties with one another. A tone is a sound of definite pitch, referring primarily not to a feeling expressed by it—or, more generally, to a thing—but to other sounds of definite pitch, to other tones. A sequence of tones is a musical structure, a melody, when its unity results primarily from the audible relations of sounds to one another, not from their relations to something else—for example, feelings. Tones can be audibly interrelated only because they form a system, an order. The step from the prelinguistic call to the primitive melody is in no way less fundamental than the step to the primitive sentence. In either case, the step leads to order, signifies the discovery of structure; it is a spiritual act that creates meaning. The meaning of the sound is constitutive of the tone just as it is constitutive of the word; and even though tones are not meaningful in the same sense as words, the problem of how sounds became associated with meaning is a musical as well as a linguistic one. The same gulf separates prelinguistic utterance from the first melody *and* from the first sentence. As measured by this gulf, the most primitive song is not a bit closer to prelinguistic stages of culture than a Bach fugue is. Similarly, the most primitive sentence and the most fully developed speech are, as word language, just as different in kind from prelinguistic utterance. There is no evidence against the hypothesis that the step which led to the word was the same which led to the tone, that man began to sing and to speak at the same moment, and that later differentiations of musical and verbal modes of utterance hark back to a stage when speech and song had not yet been clearly separated. But such a stage would in any case lie on this side of the gulf: in respect of origin, singing man and speaking man stand together. Singing man did not precede speaking man; he misunderstands himself when he sees himself as the representative of an evolutionary stage closer to the animal stage. It would be more just to ascribe a higher spiritual rank to song than speech, for speaking man finds a kind of material support in the fact that words refer to tangible things, but where can the musician find such tangible support? This may be the reason why Greek and Chinese myths associate mankind's emergence from the state of barbarism with the appearance of a *musician*, half man, half god.

To view musicality as falling within the domain of the rational, however, is merely to shift the problem to another plane. Human rationality did not come into the world at one stroke, ready-made.

Beginning at a primitive stage, it ran through a long evolution before fully unfolding in the advanced civilizations. And it is precisely at the early stages of this evolution that music, as a cultural phenomenon, played a dominant part. The domain in which its importance is most strikingly manifested is defined by the notion of magic.

We believe that early man's relation to the world is most comprehensively characterized by what has been termed his "magic mentality." As can be inferred from anthropological studies of today's primitive tribes, the basic traits of this mentality are as follows: The distinctions between animate and inanimate nature, between persons and things, also between one person and another, lack the sharpness and exclusiveness that today are taken for granted; the world is not yet split into subject and object, matter and mind. Thinking remains at a concrete level, does not yet tend to generalization and abstraction; life manifests itself most intensely in the group, is not yet concentrated in the emancipated individual, remains in an intermediary state before falling asunder into extremes. The negative features of the magic mentality include inability to make clear distinctions and decisions; the vagueness is an obstacle that must be overcome before rationality can develop. The positive features—which are largely lost on the way to the next stage—are the original closeness of man to man, man to thing, and thing to thing; the oneness of man's being with nature was once actually experienced, not merely conceived. This is not the same thing as the "unconscious" oneness with nature of prehuman living beings. Man at the magical stage might well see nature, but he sees it from the inside, so to speak. (It was to express this that Edgar Dacqué coined the term *Natursichtigkeit*.) He was probably able to influence nature "from within" in ways incomprehensible to us. At this stage man already faced nature, conceived of it as something distinct from him, but his sense of being at one with it was still much stronger.

That music is closely related to magic is obvious at first glance. No primitive magic ritual can do without music, and even in modern civilized societies scattered islets of ritual have survived. The church no less than the circus, the ceremonial of public as well as of private life, cannot do without music. Conversely, certain principles of magic ritual—repetition, structures based on the numbers three, four, and seven, to name only the most important—play a crucial role, not just in primitive music but in the culminating stages of art music. To how surprising an extent even today musicians practice magic in the literal (not the metaphorical) sense, Jules Combarieu's voluminous work *La musique et la magie* demonstrates with a great many documented examples. The affinity between music and magic does not just come down to superficial similarities; it is rooted in their very nature. The same terms serve to characterize the essence of musicality and of the magical mentality; in both, man's sense of being at one with the world outweighs his sense of being distinct from it: what links man to man, man to thing, and thing to thing outweighs what separates them. If it is true that tones build a bridge over the boundaries which words spell out between subjectivity and objectivity, the correspondence between music and magic seems complete. Thus it is natural to recognize in music the form in which magic survives down to our day.

In his book *Ursprung und Gegenwart*, Jean Gebser does not content himself with noting a close correspondence, as well as affinities, between music and magic: according to him, music actually determines the very structure of magic. "If the links between music and magic disclose that they are closely related," he writes, "and thereby that music is eminently magical, it will not be surprising if we believe we are justified in singling out the ear as the inner organ that plays the predominant role at the magical stage. The magical world, and with it an essential part of what constitutes our own world, originated in magical sound, operating through the ear, giving rise to an audible world." In this book's broad perspective, expounding the overall development of mankind in terms of a few decisive evolutionary steps, the mythical stage supersedes the magical stage at the same time as the word supersedes the tone in the latter's fateful function. Music and speech would stand for two stages of development. The magical stage: the world experienced as one; existence as egoless, timeless, spaceless; the opposition between man and world not yet present to waking consciousness but as though in a dream, buried under the awareness that man and nature are originally at one; the individual dissolved in the group, not yet opposed to it. The mythical stage: awakening of the individual spirit, opposition between man and the world felt as a polarity; awareness of self as existing in time; the individual in process of emerging from the group. At the magical stage the crucial organ was the ear, the crucial sense the sense of hearing. At the mythical stage it was the mouth, the organ of speech. There is no mouth in the earliest representations of human figures; only later is the mouth fully delineated.

In this view of mankind's development, words and musical sounds are sharply contrasted and assigned radically different origins. Their relationship is reduced to one of temporal succession, a crucial evolutionary leap in the history of the human race. The two are diametrically opposed, musical sounds treated as something due to be superseded by words, and it is claimed that the supersession has actually occurred. Even though Gebser lays special emphasis on the fact that in every living development the earlier stages remain operative in the later ones, his interpretation helps us understand why fanatics of the word look upon the presence of music among us as a dangerous atavism, while those who have lost hope in the word believe they hear in music the glad tidings of ultimate return to a lost paradise. Such overstatements dictated by partisan passion are frequent enough; relegating music to the status of magic makes it all possible.

I am listening to people singing: they are rehearsing one of the miracles of art music, a double canon by Purcell. Two melodies closely intertwined are being sung by different voices at different times. To what stage does such a microcosm of the highest quality belong? Is this the mode of utterance of a still slumbering soul, without awareness of self or time, a spirit still imprisoned within nature? What is so splendidly unfolded here is nothing other than an order of tonal space and tonal time, the same order already contained in germ in the musical tone as such. If with the creation of the word man emerges as a principle of order, if the word marks the rise of a spiritual order above nature, then tones and words must have a common origin. Where could a spiritual order, where could man conceiving of himself as a spiritual power distinct from nature be more purely revealed than in tone structures? Where could the soul be more awake than where it represents itself in tonal movement? Where could it be more deeply aware of time as one of the roots of its existence than in music? Verily, the mouth that opens to sing, no less than the mouth that opens to speak, is the human organ par excellence. As long as the mouth opens only to cry, to call, to utter merely expressive sounds, it is not yet human, and can be omitted in representations of the human figure confined to the essential. Only when pictorial representations disclose that the mouth has been discovered as the organ of human expression in the pregnant sense—i.e., at the mythical stage, not earlier—must we look for the origin of the tone as well as of the word.

It is easy to see how this conclusion can be reconciled with the undeniable fact that music is closely related to magic. We must only keep clearly in mind that the same word, "tone," denotes something different at each of the two stages in question. The tone of the still dream-imprisoned soul, unaware of self and time, is a biological phenomenon, an expressive sound or sign (warning, calling, direction-showing) or both: an element in a chain of actual events. The tone of awakened consciousness, the musical tone proper, is a semantic phenomenon: part of a system of audible relationships, a structural element, a member of a symbolic whole. The special significance of the musical tone rests upon this, that here the crucial achievement of the mythical stage, the discovery of the symbol, becomes fruitful in the audible world itself, i. e., in the element that was the essential one at the superseded magical stage, the element that embodies that interpenetration of man and world. Music's content is magical, its form mythical. Music takes over and resettles the old in the new; it does not conjure up the past, does not glance backward, is not a reconstruction but, first and foremost, a construction: the past becomes symbol and in this form continues to be a living force in the present and in what is to come. Music achieves the appropriation of the magical by the spiritual: the essential core of magical existence is integrated into a spiritual order. To infer from the affinity between music and magic that music originated in the world of magic is fallacious. Music did not originate in magic; it originated precisely because of the loss of the world of magic, following the law of all living development that each successive stage must incorporate the modes of existence of the preceding one. Speech and music are not antagonists representing two developmental stages, one of which superseded the other. Our discussion of the word-tone relationship in song has shown that the two work together, not one against the other; that they are not at cross-purposes, but enhance each other. Words divide, tones unite. The unity of existence that the word constantly breaks up, dividing thing from thing, subject from object, is constantly restored in the tone. Music prevents the world from being entirely transformed into language, from becoming nothing but object, and prevents man from becoming nothing but subject. Nor can the word aim at this; the objectifying word *needs* the tone, *demands* it: the stronger the tones, the freer the words are to perform their task of objectification. It is certainly no accident that the highest unfolding of the power of tones in modern instrumental music and the highest unfolding of the power of objectifying words in modern science coincide historically with the sharpest divisions ever drawn between subjectivity and objectivity. Not because the tone expresses the subject as adequately as the word expresses the object, not because the tone feeds the irrational element as the word feeds the rational element. Such either/ors are false and superficial. What the tone expresses is not the subject but the interpenetration of subject and object. Music does not thrive at the expense of rationality. Music originates, grows, and reaches its culmination within human rationality, together with it, not outside it or against it.

VIII. Problem and Solution—Question and Answer

MODERN SCIENCE views all living processes, physical and psychical, as resulting primarily from interchange among living centers and between organisms and their environment—as processes in a field of energy that encompasses the organisms and their world, the entire domain of their possible interactions. The central concept is that of behavior: the behavior of living beings continually discloses in what ways they interact with their environment. The basic assumption is that every change in behavior is caused by a disturbance of balance in the field of energy, and aims at restoring the balance. The cause of the disturbance may be located within the organism or outside it, in its inner or outer environment; the tension produced is discharged in an action which, if it is successful, restores, at least temporarily, the balance between organism and environment. The old rigid interpretation of animal behavior as one-sided adaptation to a ready-made environment, as mere response to a stimulus, has been broadened and refined, so that the concept of behavior now can encompass all living processes, from the mechanisms of conditioned reflexes and the purely vegetative processes of growth and metabolism to the highest achievements of the mind in symbolic operations with words and numbers. Also art and its products can be included here; formative activity, whether in the medium of words, tones, or visible shapes, is viewed as a kind of behavior, springing from a specific need—a tension, a disturbance of balance—and gratifying this need, restoring the balance. "Art is born of the search for adjustments that are felt to be right."

Our attempt in this work to understand music in terms of an encounter between man and world, and musicality as an essential attribute of man corresponding to an essential attribute of his world, seems at first glance to proceed along behaviorist lines. The fact that speech fails to express an important aspect of man's encounter with both his outer and inner world can be interpreted as the result of a defective adaptation, of a tension between different levels that seeks to be resolved. But at this point we must part company with behaviorism. According to the latter, music is the means of resolving the tension; according to our view, the tension is the means of discovering music. Every form of behavior aims by definition at the zero point of resolved tension; it is judged successful or unsuccessful according to whether this goal is or is not attained. What matters, from the point of view of music, is not the transition from disturbed to restored balance but the by-product of the transition—what is left behind after the transition has been effected. Interpreted in behavioristic terms, that is, as a way leading from disturbed to restored balance, music making does not differ essentially from the inarticulate utterance in which an emotional tension is discharged, and listening to music does not differ essentially from quenching one's thirst. But the musicality of music does not begin in the first place until it is something other than emotional discharge, something other than quenching thirst; bad music, bad listening to music is precisely characterized by the predominance of the nonmusical, behaviorist element—the emotional discharge, the quenching of a thirst for tones. If music is understood as a type of behavior, it must be true of music as of any other type of behavior that its main purpose is to eliminate something from the world: as a result of successful behavior, the living being finds itself, in relation to its environment, exactly where it was before the disturbance of balance. From our point of view, however, the most important thing about music is not that it eliminates something from the world but adds something to it—indeed, that it creates a world; not that it brings man back to where he was in the world, but that it takes him to a place where he has never been before. In short, what we are trying to understand is in what ways the world and man are changed by music.

The pupil of the eye reacting to a ray of light, the warning call when a danger is perceived, the seeking and finding of food, the solving of a crossword puzzle, the solution to a scientific problem: to the behaviorist, all these are gradations of *one* basic phenomenon, successive terms of a series which, to use Jean Piaget's terminology, extends between physico-chemical causation and logical-mathematical implication. The reaction of the eye represents a maximum of physico-chemical causation and a minimum of intellectual implication; the solution to a scientific problem represents the reverse. In between there is a more or a less of each ingredient, the seeking and finding of food being located approximately at the center. If we were to trace a boundary from the viewpoint of behaviorism, it would run between the seeking of food and the solving of the crossword puzzle: this boundary would separate animal behavior from specifically human behavior. The mouse that solves the riddle of the maze does so to reach a bit of bacon; man solves puzzles for the sake of solving them. But the crucial boundary, which behaviorism cannot trace because it marks its own limits, runs elsewhere—namely, between the puzzle and the scientific problem. The solution of the former can still be interpreted adequately as a type of behavior; not so the solving of a scientific problem. Both puzzle and problem are experienced as disturbances of the intellectual balance; but the puzzle is solved in order to do away with the disturbance, whereas the scientific problem is solved in order to discover a truth. The solved puzzle ends up in the wastepaper basket; the solution to the scientific problem rises as a new star in our intellectual firmament. Puzzle and problem belong to different worlds. The puzzle is a task to be performed; the problem, for its part, is a question and, properly speaking, requires not a solution but an answer. Problem and solution, question and answer: therein lies the difference. Even an animal can see a situation as a problem to be solved and solve it. But only a living being with a mind can see a situation as a question. The question-and-answer situation cannot be interpreted in purely behavioristic terms.

Music, as we said at the beginning of these reflections, must be understood as *necessary*, i.e., in such a way that a world without music or a mankind without music would be unthinkable. What makes music necessary as a whole and in its individual manifestations, at its early stages or at the peak of its development, is that it answers a question. Being musical is having the ability to question. Even after everything nameable, including God, has been given a name, there is still a void to be filled, a darkness to be lit up; even after it has given its all-inclusive answers, language still leaves some questions unanswered. In music man finds answers to those very questions. Our task is to understand the nature of the questioner on the basis of music's answers to his questions.

THE MUSICAL EAR

IX. The Audible World

THE BASIS of any encounter with music is the act of hearing. Music exists in and for the ear: apart from being heard, it does not exist. Like all other encounters, there are two sides to this one: we experience music by listening to it, and at the same time we experience ourselves as listeners to music. What does the phrase "I hear music" actually say, especially the words "I hear"?

We sometimes run across statements that seem to discredit the ear as our only means of access to music. A famous poet once extolled the "sweetness" of "unheard" melodies above those actually heard, but he could not have written these words had the meaning of "melody" not already been made clear to him in the exercise of his sense of hearing. Musicians maintain, and they are doubtless right, that no performance can attain the perfection of sound present in the imagination when they go over a score silently; many subtle details can be appreciated only in this way, details which go under in the acoustical welter of actual performance. But does this imply, as is so often asserted, that musical masterpieces contain many things never intended to be heard, only to be seen? Hearing in the imagination, in the mind's ear, is certainly a kind of hearing, not of seeing. This is the exercise of a sense of hearing so practiced, so sensitive through long and intimate intercourse with tones, that actual sound waves are not required to set it off; the eye serves merely as a subordinate organ for the reception of musical notation. Master composers who set down such passages did so for their appeal to the mind's ear, not for their appeal to the eye. No road leads from the world of the visible to that of music without passing through the auditive sense, whether actually or in the mind. There is no visual approach to music, although the experiment was once made, in an American institution, to understand Bach's *Goldberg Variations* in purely visual terms, working chiefly from the graphic image without any reference to sound. Not surprisingly, the experiment was one of a kind.

Another objection might be suggested by our considerations on musicality and on music at the original stage. If the functional division into producers, reproducers, and recipients had not yet become fixed at that stage—in other words, if the overwhelming majority of people did not yet confront music as recipients, as mere listeners—then one may doubt whether originally music existed to be heard. Where music comes from people instead of merely going to them, it must surely be something they produce actively rather than receive passively. But this activity is essentially the production of sound, a making oneself heard: to make music is to be actively producing sounds and working with sounds, whether listeners are or are not present. This activity is, so to speak, circular. The circle closes only when the sound produced returns to its producer as something audible. This is true of the player as well as of the singer; even a recluse does not make music on a silent piano. The composer, in turn, hears in his mind what he creates; even while creating he is always a listener as well. No matter how you look at it, there is no way out of the circle of the audible. The world of music is part of the audible world, the world of the ear.

The audible world, the world of the ear—how many among us, men of this century, still know what kind of world this is and that it *is* a world? Surrounded by the noises of the technological age, deafened by its never ceasing din, we are alienated from the audible world to an extent of which we are not even aware. In so far as seeing goes, we are better off: the eye still finds a bit of sky even above the ugliest, dreariest corner of a metropolis. The wall of machine-generated pseudosounds that surrounds us has no such gaps; natural sounds hardly ever penetrate it. The street noises muffle even the roar of thunder. Occasional stillness strikes us as unnatural; it makes us ill at ease and we hasten to switch on an artificial noise to get rid of it. Our image of the audible world has become distorted, a caricature. There is nothing in it save the racket of machines, and then, God knows where and whence, unconnected with the rest, an alien body—music.

The true image looks different. What infinite riches, what authenticity, what inexhaustible multiplicity and diversity of sensations! The murmur of breaking waves, the roar of the storm, the sound of ringing bells, the echo of a gunshot in the mountains, the report of the shot itself, the thud made by an apple falling on grass, the humming of bees, the laughter of a child, the sound of a violin, the cry of the gull, the belling of the stag, the rumble of an avalanche, the crackling of a fire, the clinking of glasses, the sigh of falling snow, the patter of raindrops, the scraping of steps in the sand, the rustle of dead leaves—how could one ever enumerate them all? Moreover, the nuances of sounds of the same kind: the rustling of the wind in pines, deciduous trees—oak, olive, palm—in a solitary tree, in woods dense or sparse, at high altitudes, in an enclosed valley: language has long since fallen behind, unable even to name sensations that our ear distinguishes and identifies most accurately. References to the physical causes of these differences, to slight variations in the form of air waves, far from accounting for the efficiency of our organ of hearing, make it appear all the more miraculous.

In the above enumeration the reader will have noticed that language invariably makes use of two words to designate auditory perceptions. The first—murmur, echo, roar, crackle, clink, creak, and so on—is always imitative of the sound referred to. Since language is at home in the audible, which, unlike the visible, is its natural medium of communication, it must be natural for it to name what can be heard by imitative sounds. The sign and what it signifies belong to one and the same world. Yet language is not very accurate in its imitations. It contents itself with the approximate and the polyvalent: what rustles can be water, but also the wind or the silk of a garment with many folds; a crunching sound is made by stones, but also by steps in dry snow. The second of the two associated words serves to make the designation more specific; however, it names not the quality of the sensation but of the visible, tangible, material object that is the source of the sensation of sound: the murmur of the *sea*, the ringing of *bells*. Therein, too, language is faithful to its most important task—to make possible communication concerning visible-tangible things in an audible content. Its method of naming sound perceptions is to associate sounds with their physical sources. In the mirror of language, that which is heard appears as an attribute of that which is seen or touched.

This is not the place to settle the question of whether, in such cases, language reflects the natural history of perception or imposes its own new order upon the latter. What is certain is that language and sensation run parallel to each other: when we hear a sound, we usually perceive, in addition to the sound, the thing or event that produces the sound. We hear the sea or the storm, not merely a roar; bells, not a ringing; an apple, not a falling. Our hearing does not, so to speak, stop at the sensation but reaches out through it toward its objective source. Sometimes it reaches out into the void. When we hear a sound whose source remains undetermined—a rustle, for example, but not something that rustles—then the sensation is unsatisfying, disquieting; it impels us to listen, to try to discover the material source of the sound, and we will not rest until we have succeeded in associating what we hear with something visible-tangible. In this way we perceive the entire audible world, as an adjunct to the world of visible and tangible things, as though wrapped around it. Visible-tangible things that treat themselves to the luxury of being audible—for a change, for the sake of colorfulness, of enriching the picture, to please us, disquiet us, warn us—eye and hand acting as lawgivers, the ear as an auxiliary organ: this is how one might describe the world opening to our senses.

This description would be correct if our enumeration of audible sensations did not include the item "sound of a violin." At this point the audible breaks away from that order, from its correlation with visible-tangible things. As tone follows tone, as the tones become melody, in the midst of the audible world a door opens; we enter, as though in a dream or a fairy tale, not so much into another world as another mode of existence within our familiar world. The audible has broken its ties with material objects. On hearing other kinds of sound, if I ask, "What is it?" I expect an answer such as "An airplane" or "The wind." If I asked the same question when hearing a violin, and someone answered, "A violin," I would laugh at him. This is not what I asked about. A correct answer, such as "Bach's Partita in E major," will refer not to the connection of the sounds with a material source (this would be trivial; all tones of the Bach partita are violin sounds) but to the way the tones are connected among themselves. In this case, hearing does not go beyond what is heard, does not reach out toward the visible-tangible source of the sensation; what we hear is self-contained, is whole and complete in itself. A world of the purely audible opens, a domain in which the ear is lawgiver. Needless to say, the existence of such a domain confers an entirely new dignity upon the audible world as such. In the presence of music we should not be inclined to say that the audible is a colorful garment in which the visible world wrapped itself; we should speak rather of the gift the Creator bestowed upon the visible world—the gift of sharing in the audible, in the dignity of being audible.

The phenomenon is unique. That within a sensory domain a sensation otherwise tied to things as one of their "qualities" should emancipate itself and build an autonomous world of its own, free of any objective reference, does not occur elsewhere. The analogous phenomenon in the visible world, the art of pure colors and forms, offers nothing comparable, for the colors and forms are either the same as are found in objects or derived from objects, whereas man finds no tones in the audible world; he must supply them himself. It is man who creates the *purely* audible, in which the audible world reveals itself in a form that is entirely its own. Without music, hearing would be like seeing with one's ears. Only in music does hearing come into its own.

Thus we discover that there is something special about the sense of hearing. "To hear" does not always denote the same act. I hear the marching of troops, and I hear the march they are playing: here language obscures the true state of affairs, for it has only one word to signify two very different functions. In the first case, to hear is to perceive a physical event; the function involved is essentially comparable to the functions of other senses. In the second case, hearing is something entirely different, completely *sui generis*. If one tries to understand hearing on the basis of any given sound sensations, as most psychologists do, one can never get beyond what hearing has in common with seeing and touching. What hearing really is, what we really are as listeners, can be understood only on the basis of hearing music.

By way of anticipation we may sum up the reflections that follow. Hearing music is a many-layered process. We may distinguish four layers: hearing tones, hearing dynamic qualities, hearing motion, and hearing organic structure. And all of this lies wholly within the purview of the sense of hearing: the other senses and functions do not enter in.

Our "layers" are not to be mistaken for successive stages, as though we heard first one, then the next, and so on. When we hear music all this goes on at once. Necessarily, to analyze a unitary experience is to break it up into parts.

x. Hearing Tones

To KEEP technical detail to a minimum we shall base our study on the simplest musical structures: tunes or melodies. There is a difference only in degree, not in kind, between hearing a tune and hearing some complex, lengthy musical composition.

The old hymn of Resurrection—the Hallelujah Chorale—resounds, sung in unison. What exactly do we hear when hearing this melody?

Surely we hear primarily tones, a succession of different tones. Melody, every melody, is primarily heard as that.

What a tone is, what constitutes the difference between one tone and another, cannot, strictly speaking, be defined. The only adequate answer to the question "What is a tone?" is to sing or play a tone. No matter how many words we use, no matter how correct and apt they may be, they will not give a deaf person even the vaguest idea of a tone. Such a person may know and understand all the words that have ever been said about tones: the essential core of the reality referred to by the words will remain a blank.

The same is true of the differences between tones. Different tones are first and foremost tones of different pitch, and what pitch is can similarly only be heard. It may be said that pitch is a characteristic comparable to warmth or brightness, in which we can distinguish between a "more" and a "less"; that consequently tones can be arranged in a series according to pitch, so that of two different tones one is always higher and the other lower, and of three tones one is the highest, one the lowest, and one intermediate. But according to *what* the tones are so distinguished and arranged remains forever inaccessible to those who cannot hear them.

It is still possible to encounter persons who imagine that they have the true answer to the question of what is a tone or what is pitch. This answer is: A tone is the vibration of air or another propagating medium; pitch is the rate of vibration, frequency. The word "is" here stands for "is actually" or "is truly." It is scarcely possible to put oneself into the frame of mind of someone who could accept such an answer uncritically. Vibrations or the frequency of vibration can be seen or felt; tones must be heard; they are not seen or felt—only the deaf "feel" tones. How can something audible be something visible or touchable? The two may correspond to each other most exactly; the visible or touchable may be the material cause or the material vehicle of the audible. But this does not justify the assertion that one *is* the other, and certainly not "actually" or "truly." Why should the senses of sight and touch have access to that which is actually, truly, and the sense of hearing be denied such access? Why should the ear be less trustworthy than the eye or the hand?

Apart from pitch, tones are characterized by timbre and loudness. Both play no essential part in so far as hearing melody is concerned. Clearly, I hear the same thing—that is, the same melody—whether it is sung softly or loudly, blown on a trumpet or plucked on a guitar.

But after pitch the most essential characteristic is duration. Different tones are also of different lengths, and a change of tone duration, like a change of pitch, has the result that I no longer hear the same thing, that I hear a different melody. Were the beginning of our example ♩♩♩♫♩ instead of ♩♩♩♩♩, I would hear not the hymn of Resurrection but "Brother Martin."

Here a qualification is necessary. Everyone knows that one and the same melody can be sung by a soprano or basso, played on a violin or cello. Despite the completely different pitches the melody remains identical. What remains unchanged is the relation of the pitch of each tone to its neighboring tones. What makes a melody is not, properly speaking, the tones but the relations between tones. A melody taken as a whole can be shifted back and forth in tonal space, can be transposed to another key without being changed, just as a geometric figure remains unchanged if we imagine it moved from one plane to another in space (more accurately, Euclidean space). This trivial statement conceals musical and geometric problems of equal weight. The same is true of tone duration: shortening or lengthening of all duration values in the same ratio will not affect the melody. In other words, a melody remains the same when played at a faster or slower pace (within reasonable limits). What cannot be changed without changing the melody itself is the relationship of tone durations, the ratio of each tone's duration to the duration of the neighboring tones.

To hear a melody is thus first of all to hear a sequence of tones which stand in specific relation to one another in respect to pitch and duration. When I hear a melody, I do not hear first one tone, then another, then a third, and so on; at the same time as each tone, I hear the relation in which it stands to other tones, preceding and following. Previously we have observed that hearing music differs from all other kinds of hearing in that what is heard here is self-contained, whereas elsewhere hearing reaches out beyond the sound itself toward its material source. Now we discover that also in the case of a melody, hearing does not stop at the immediate sensation of the tone just sounded, but reaches out beyond it, this time not toward a material object but toward other tones—tones which either have already faded away or are still to resound, tones not heard at this moment. Hearing beyond what has been heard to other audible elements, hearing the relation of something heard to something no longer or not yet heard: how is this to be understood?

How, more generally, are we to understand the fact that hearing reaches out beyond the immediate sense datum? Heidegger writes: "We hear the motorcycle racing through the street. We hear the grouse gliding through the forest. But actually we hear only the whirring of the motor, the sound the grouse makes. As a matter of fact, it is difficult to describe the pure sound, and we do not ordinarily do so, because it is *not* what we commonly hear. From the standpoint of sheer sound we always hear *more*. We hear the flying bird, even though strictly speaking we should say: a grouse is nothing audible . . ." But, taken just as strictly, is that "more" really something heard? A blind man who has never encountered a motorcycle or a grouse will hear neither: he will hear two different sounds, not something "more." Hearing in itself cannot go beyond the sensation of sound. No one *hears* a bell: we hear a sound and we know what makes the sound because we see or remember or have been told that it is the sound of a bell; in other words, we know from experience. The function of the sense organ ends with having and conveying the sensation; other functions, mostly intellectual, do the rest.

This raises the fundamental question whether the same is not true of hearing melodies and music in general. Strictly speaking, is not, here too, the going beyond the immediately given sense datum something other than hearing? Can I *hear* how one tone is related to other tones, preceding and following, which I do not hear? If melody is actually defined by these relations, how can I say that I *hear* melodies? Would it not be more correct to say that here, too, the function of the sense organ is confined to having and conveying sensations, whereas tone relations, and by the same token melodies and all music, are apprehended by other, nonsensory functions? Must we not conclude that music is primarily intended not to be heard but to be apprehended by those other functions, whatever they may be?

Surprisingly, many philosophers, psychologists, theoreticians, historians, and even composers (in so far as they theorize on music) largely agree in answering these questions in the affirmative. According to these witnesses, sound, the musically audible element, is of secondary importance, no more than an outer coating, a pleasing garment; the real core of music is not heard, is not perceived by the senses, but apprehended by other, nonsensory functions. Sound, they maintain, is merely a mediator, a messenger; there is no essential difference between hearing music and hearing a lecture: the sound of words reaches the ear, but what matters is obviously the meaning of the words, not the sound, and to grasp meaning is not a sensory but an intellectual function. Similarly, they conclude, when we apprehend musical meaning, the function involved cannot be hearing; strictly speaking, musical experience is not an auditory experience. Paul Hindemith—to cite a prominent witness—distinguishes "sound, the external quality" from "the immaterial, the spiritual aspects" of music. We must, he says, "outgrow the mere recording of sensations, the superficial sentimental dependence on sounds"—not in order to develop a more adequate attitude toward sound, but to emancipate ourselves from sound as such, to achieve a pure comprehension of music's spiritual aspects, purged of all sensory elements.

Certainly no one will deny that musical experience involves functions other than sensory, that there is something more to music, speaking colloquially, than meets the ear. But the question remains, at what point does music cease to be tone and begin to be something else, something that is not heard? If it is taken for granted that "to hear" is merely "to record auditory sensations," we must ask whether the tone itself is not more than the tone that is heard. For all his outstanding merits as a composer, Hindemith the thinker has fallen into the trap of a false alternative. The fact that external sound qualities can be distinguished from the spiritual aspects of musical experience does not yet prove that everything that is not external sound quality is automatically "spiritual" and must be apprehended by nonsensory functions. Apart from their external qualities, musical sounds, tones, may very well possess "inner" qualities; sound itself may very well have an immaterial aspect. Similarly, the fact that we must outgrow superficial sentimental dependence on sound in order to gain a better understanding of music does not by any means prove that we can outgrow such dependence only by going beyond sound. Why should it not be possible to outgrow it in the very act of hearing, in another dimension of hearing itself? These are legitimate questions which can be settled not by speculation and debate but only by carefully observing musical phenomena. The results of such observation will provide conclusive evidence that musical hearing performs tasks very different from the apprehension of external sound qualities.

How can we account for the fact that a prominent contemporary composer, than whom no one could be closer to the flesh and blood of music, should ignore this evidence? There is only one explanation. Those who question today the part the sense of hearing plays in musical experience simply take it for granted that they know what the sense of hearing is. They approach musical experience with settled convictions about sense organs in general, not least about the ear. Their convictions are popular-science convictions, involving such outmoded notions as the "fact" that all a sensory organ does is to react to an external stimulus and, via the nerves, carry its message to some center in the brain, which then produces some corresponding sensation in the mind. In this view, the function of the sense organ is to inform the organism about events external to it. Every sensation corresponds exactly to the event that produces it: there is nothing in the sensation that does not have its counterpart in the external event. However, sensations do not give such information—at least, not fully or explicitly; they merely serve as signals. And as such they still have to be interpreted by other, intellectual functions in order to be recognized as pointing to specific objects or events. What has been said about noises—I hear a sound, and I know that it comes from a bell—is true of all sense perception. Sensation in itself is never more than a bit of raw material—a sound, a spot of color, a tactile quality—as meaningless as an individual letter in the compositor's typecase; it acquires meaning only after being incorporated into relevant contexts, the most important of which associates the sensation with the thing or event in the outer world that produces it.

However convinced we may be that musical hearing does not primarily consist of relating sensations of sound to things or events in the external world, as long as we conceive of the sense organ as the mere supplier of data, we exclude all views other than that in music, too, hearing serves merely to record individual tone sensations. If there is nothing in these sensations that does not have its counterpart in the events producing them, and if, on the other hand, music only begins with tonal relations—that is, with something that is *not* in the event which produces tone sensations—then, strictly speaking, music cannot be *heard*. Whatever the thing may be that relates tones to one another, it cannot be audible; it must be apprehended by other, nonsensory functions; it falls under the "spiritual" aspects of music. Accordingly, it must be concluded that in hearing music the ear performs essentially the same function as in hearing noises. In both cases, its function ends with conveying the sensation to consciousness; the task of interpreting, understanding it and giving it meaning, has nothing to do with the function of hearing. To enjoy the mere sensation, the sound, is like enjoying the harmonious sounds of a language without understanding what the words mean. The assertion that what is heard in this way is music can hardly be justified.

Clearly, in the light of the traditional notion of hearing as a purely sensory function, music is no more than a meaningless sequence of pleasing sounds, the function of hearing can play only a subordinate part in musical experience, and the crucial problem of whether and how musical hearing differs from merely acoustical hearing does not even arise. It is impossible to deal with this problem, and so to learn what music is, if we adhere rigidly to this obsolete conception of hearing.

XI. Hearing Dynamic Tone Qualities

TONE, as discussed in the preceding section, that is, as a specific aural sensation characterized by pitch, timbre, loudness, and duration, produced by vibrations in a physical medium and corresponding to these vibrations in every respect—in short, tone as an acoustical phenomenon—does not exist in the world at large. It is at home only in laboratories where, in accordance with the rules of science, physicists and psychologists study its constituents and the conditions under which it is produced. The tone we know from musical experience is of a different kind—a musical phenomenon. Someone familiar only with the acoustics of the laboratory would never suspect that tones could also be something different, *audibly* different. And yet if our ears were capable of taking in acoustical sounds only, there would be no music.

The individual tone removed from its musical context, the laboratory product, is fully characterized by its acoustical qualities. But if the same tone is restored to its natural environment, that is, a musical context, something happens to it: it comes alive. Its being alive manifests itself in an additional quality, a quality nothing in the acoustical phenomenon has led us to expect. This is the tone's dynamic quality. Because music is through and through a manifestation of tonal life, and because the very possibility of music rests ultimately upon this quality, we must recognize it as the specifically musical, as distinct from acoustical, quality of tones.

A detailed discussion of dynamic quality may be found elsewhere.[1] The gist of it is given below.

As musical events, tones are characterized by specific dynamic states of balance or disturbed balance, states of tension. Each of the seven tones of the tonal system on which Western music is based (and was based exclusively for two and a half millennia) has a dynamic quality of its own; each differs from the others in the character and direction of its tension. The tone qualities are not rigidly defined one for all; rather, they fully define themselves as they succeed, and for all their definiteness admit of a certain range of individual variations. Only one among the seven tones is characterized by a state of perfect balance. This balance does not mark a zero point; it is active, but its activity is, so to speak, directed toward itself. The other six tones are audibly directed toward this one tone, which functions as the center of attraction; they gravitate toward it, point to it, each from its position and in its own way. They tend to move away from themselves to it; they lack balance and strive for it. Their lack of balance is quite obvious in four tones—the second, fourth, sixth, and seventh of the system: these tones are clearly unstable. The two remaining tones, the third and fifth, exhibit an intermediate state: though more stable than the others, they are clearly directed toward the perfectly balanced tone; in other words, they are in a state of internal tension.

The idea of a dynamic field suggests itself. Musical tones can be interpreted as events in a dynamic field. The balanced tone stands for the field's center of action; from the latter radiate the forces that act upon the other tones in various ways. The dynamic quality of each tone is determined by the dominant constellation of forces at the place where it is sounded. Since all octaves of a tone have the same dynamic quality, there are as many dynamic fields of identical structure as there are octaves.

---

1. *Sound and Symbol: Music and the External World*, pp. 11 ff.

The dynamic tone qualities are qualities in the literal sense of the term: they are perceived by the ear; they are *audible*. We can clearly *hear* the pressing ahead, the striving of the unstable tones, the peculiar inner tension of the relatively stable tones, the perfect balance of the central tone; we can *hear* the particular character and direction of each of these dynamic states with the same distinctness, immediacy, and definiteness as we hear pitches. They are as audible as any acoustical quality. In a sense, differences between dynamic qualities are even more tangible, so to speak, than differences in pitch: the dynamic qualities are the basis of elementary ear training in the tonic sol-fa method, although its implications are rarely recognized. The property by which the method distinguishes and identifies tones is not, as is often mistakenly assumed, pitch distance from other tones, but the peculiar character and direction of tonal tension.

Thus we discover that our first answer to the question "What do we hear in melodies?"—namely, a sequence of tones that exhibit specific ratios of pitch and duration—was quite inadequate. In the first partial phrase of our Hallelujah Chorale, for instance, we hear, if we listen attentively, that events other than ascending and descending motions take place. The end of the short sequence ♩♩♩♩ seems to mark a resting point: consequently, the preceding tones must have introduced an element of unrest. At the end of a later partial phrase ♩♩♩ the phenomenon becomes unmistakable. In the terminal tone ♩ I not only hear that it is "lower" and "longer"; I also recognize a certain restlessness, an urgency, a pointing beyond, a will to go beyond. Not until the final tone of the line, ♩ , will this striving and urging achieve its goal. To my ear, what primarily characterizes this tone is, once more, not its pitch or duration, but the balance it achieves. Therefore, it is not ratios of pitch and duration that we hear in this instance, but relations of tonal direction and tension.

Even granting that when the acoustical phenomenon is in question, we may be justified in doubting whether we can *hear* tonal relations (indeed, it is impossible to *hear* that one acoustical event relates to another not yet or no longer present, i.e., audible)—even granting this, it was rash to conclude that tonal relations can never be apprehended by the ear but only by nonsensory functions. When the tone qualities manifest themselves in music, tonal relations do become audible. To hear dynamic tone quality is, after all, nothing other than to hear the tone relating itself to other tones, ultimately to the central tone: the dynamic situations prevailing at various places in the dynamic field make themselves heard in the tones. We become aware of these relations solely by means of hearing them; no other, nonsensory functions are involved. What takes place is not that the tone heard is related to a tone remembered or expected. When I hear the tension tone 𝄞 in our chorale melody, I do not have a mental picture—recollection or anticipation— of the perfectly balanced tone 𝄞; the tension, the direction, the pointing beyond are all within the tone itself, are all fully audible; they fill my awareness to the brim, leave no room for anything else. Hearing melody is essentially an act of hearing—that is to say, an immediate perception of tonal relations.

What is peculiar to the dynamic quality of tone is that nothing in the physical event which produces the sensation corresponds to it. The tone quality that makes music possible has no counterpart in the material world. When a tone resounds, a luminous curve appears on the screen of the oscilloscope; an experienced observer can read from this curve all the acoustical characteristics of the tone; the only thing he cannot read from it is the dynamic quality of the tone. The slightest change in the tone's acoustical properties will immediately be registered by a corresponding change in the curve; but no change, however radical, in dynamic quality will ever show on the screen. Musical and physical events belong to different orders of existence.

Thus, what takes place here is a real breakthrough in the realm of perception. All aural sensations (including sensations of tone as an acoustical event) are either the ear's reactions to external stimuli or hallucinations. Hearing dynamic qualities is neither. It is direct perception of nonmaterial events. The dynamic tone qualities give the ear direct access to such events. The tone's unique position—as compared with noises or other sounds—its audible self-sufficiency, has so far been characterized only negatively, by the fact that tones do not refer to visible and tangible things. We can now characterize it positively: the tone transcends the auditory sensation within the audible, an inner transcendence. Unlike nonmusical sounds, which, going beyond the audible, reach out toward objects, the tone goes to an audible beyond. It enters the latter at the point where the acoustical phenomenon turns into the musical. At this point the scope of hearing itself broadens; hearing is no longer confined to reactions to external stimuli. "More than tone" is still tone; "more than hearing" is still hearing. Thus, the usual division of musical experience into external sound qualities and spiritual aspects, reactions to sound stimuli and nonsensory functions—feeling, imagination, thinking, or whatever we call them—leaves out of account the phenomenon's very essence. What lies beyond the domain of external (i.e., acoustical) sound qualities is not the domain of music's spiritual aspects—they are not reached until much later—but first of all, and for long stretches, the tone's musical qualities proper. Where nonmusical hearing (perceiving acoustical qualities only) ends, what begins is not feeling, thinking, imagining, but true musical hearing. The world of music in its full breadth and richness extends *between* the domains of acoustical hearing and nonsensory functions. Its reality, that of a nonmaterial process, is audibility: it is entirely perceived by the ear.

The purpose of the following lengthy discussion of Gestalt psychology and modern physiology (which have discarded or profoundly modified the traditional view of sense perception) is to cast light on the ear's performance in perceiving dynamic tone qualities. To this end we shall carefully define what this performance seems to be but is not. It will become apparent that the new theories of sense perception in general, and of hearing in particular, developed by Gestalt psychology and physiology still cannot adequately explain how music is heard.

GESTALT AND DYNAMIC TONE QUALITY

The Gestalt school rejects the traditional view that the primary sense datum is an individual sensory element—a sensation of color or tone—a bit of raw material, meaningless in itself, which is conveyed via the nerves to the brain and once there is combined, by a higher nonsensory function, with other relevant elements into the meaningful whole of a perception. According to this school, the immediate, original sense datum is itself a whole, a *Gestalt*, i.e., a meaningful structure consisting of directly interrelated parts. The eye does not see individual spots of color, nor does the ear perceive individual tones, which some higher function transforms into the image of a visible thing or the line of a melody. Rather, the eye itself directly perceives the visible object; the ear itself perceives the melody. Moreover, this is not to be interpreted in the sense that the unifying factor is a subjective contribution of the mind, and that the individual datum alone is objective; on the contrary, it is precisely the notion of the elementary sense datum that is devoid of any real content, being an abstract notion derived from the originally perceived whole.

This seems sufficient to dispose of the difficulties arising from the traditional conception of hearing and so to bring theory into agreement with the facts of musical experience. If what I hear is not individual tones, not tone–tone–tone, but always portions of a tonal whole, so that I do not have to relate one tone to another at some later point; if I actually hear tones within a context, a melody, in the first place, not "elements" but audibly interrelated parts of a whole, each needing to be complemented and each pointing beyond itself, then direct perception of tone relations is certainly not as inexplicable and impossible as it must appear to be from the traditional point of view. Then hearing music can be regarded as one among other forms of *Gestalt* perception. The reason music is assigned a privileged position is that the crucial characteristics of *Gestalt* and *Gestalt* perception are more clearly and purely exhibited in music than anywhere else. I hear a transposed melody and recognize it as the same I heard before in another key, although not a single tone was left unchanged. This fact demonstrates clearly that I hear the whole before the parts, that the *Gestalt* is prior to its constituents. Significantly, the study of *Gestalten* began with music: the term *"Gestalt* quality" was first used to designate the unknown something that remains unchanged when melodies are transposed. The maxim that the whole is more and different from the sum of its parts is nowhere more strikingly confirmed.

This being the case, it would hardly be correct to maintain that musical hearing, as distinct from all other kinds of hearing, marks a "breakthrough." If perception is always *Gestalt* perception, different kinds of hearing can differ only in degree. Indeed, we must ask whether our earlier assertion involving the essential problem of music's reality—that nothing in the physical context of the external world corresponds to dynamic tone qualities—can be upheld in the face of the discoveries of Gestalt psychology. Once we abandon the notion that the individual tone is a primary sense datum, we are no longer justified in regarding the physical event, the individual sound wave that produces the sensation of tone, as the counterpart of the musical tone. If the musical tone is never heard as an individual tone, as though at the moment we heard it no other tones existed, but always as part of a whole, related to other tones and to the whole of the tonal *Gestalt* in process of actualization; if, being a part, it is determined by the whole and is heard as, or even *is*, the same or another, depending on the context to which it belongs; if, in other words, we always perceive a whole when hearing an individual tone, the physical counterpart of the musical event must be looked for in the totality of the processes that run parallel to the hearing of the whole. True, a sound wave will not show changes in a tone's dynamic quality, or, indeed, that the tone has any dynamic quality at all. The frequency range of the isolated tone 𝄞♩ does not differ in the slightest from that of the same tone in the phrase 𝄞♩♩♩♩♩♩♩♩♩; nothing in the picture of the last ♩ will show that 5̂ has become 1̂;[2] nor would the picture change in the slightest if the tone ♩ in the melody were replaced with ♩ so that ♩ would still be 5̂. But after all, the tone ♩ is 5̂, becomes 1̂, or remains 5̂ not in itself, as an individual tone, but only in context with other tones, as part of the given whole. Consequently we should look for the counterpart of the dynamic tone quality not in the representation of an individual sound wave but in the spectrum of all the waves corresponding to the given tonal whole. And from this latter picture it will certainly be possible to read the difference between ♩♩♩ and ♩♩♩ .

It would seem, then, to follow from the Gestalt theory that (1) the dynamic tone qualities are determined by the whole of the tonal *Gestalt*, remain the same or change when the *Gestalt* remains the same or changes, and (2) each *Gestalt* is characterized by a spectrum of wave dynamics which remains the same or changes concurrently with the *Gestalt*. Dynamic tone qualities and physical events are thus correlated via the *Gestalt*. The possibility of transposing melodies, in particular, shows that identity and difference of *Gestalt* depend not on individual pitches but on pitch ratios; what is relevant in the correlated physical event is not frequencies but frequency ratios. It is, then, in these ratios

---

2. The symbols 1̂, 2̂, etc., stand for the dynamic qualities of the tones of the diatonic system. Cf. *Sound and Symbol: Music and the External World*, pp. 11 ff., especially 34 ff.

that we would have to recognize the physical counterpart of the psychological event of musical hearing in general, and of hearing dynamic qualities in particular.

The following reflections are in no way directed against the Gestalt theory. Our concern is simply to point out that although it solved a number of problems, there are still many more to be solved. The theory could not attack all the problems confronting it at one stroke. Methodologically speaking, the Gestaltists were right in soon turning from audible to visible, spatial *Gestalten*. After all, their purpose was to clear the way for a radically new conception: that primary sense data are not parts which are subsequently combined into wholes, but wholes which are subsequently analyzed into constituents. For this reason they had first to consider *Gestalten* actually perceived as wholes, that is, those in visual space. Audible *Gestalten* such as melodies, purely temporal *Gestalten*, because they are never directly apprehended as wholes and only individual parts of them are directly perceived by the ear, inevitably confront the investigator with different and far greater difficulties. The Gestaltists certainly did not overlook music, with its purely temporal *Gestalten*—in fact, they have repeatedly mentioned music as a specially promising field of study—but until now they have taken it no further than that. (Characteristic of this state of affairs is the fact that in his survey entitled *Probleme der ganzheitspsychologischen Wahrnehmungslehre*, Walter Ehrenstein devotes more than two hundred pages to visual perception and only eight pages to all kinds of aural perception, not just musical.)

The main concepts and ideas of Gestalt psychology have been developed on the sole basis of visual, spatial *Gestalten*; whether they can be applied to audible, temporal *Gestalten* remains doubtful, and these may not take us very far. (It is enough to mention the concepts "figure" and "background" so essential in descriptions of spatial patterns: what corresponds to them in the tonal pattern?) To treat the problems of the audible *Gestalt* as materially related to those of the visible *Gestalt* (as has so far been the case) is inevitably to treat hearing as a subspecies of seeing. Now you can, if you insist, interpret hearing in general as a kind of auditory seeing; but musical hearing above all cannot be so interpreted. Nevertheless, Gestalt theoreticians study the tonal *Gestalt* as though it were not essentially different from other auditory *Gestalten*, that is, study it predominantly in its acoustical, nonmusical aspects: here, as elsewhere, the fundamental problem of musical hearing is not even raised. Similarly, when the tonal *Gestalt* is studied on the basis of our knowledge of the spatial *Gestalt*, the temporality of the former necessarily takes on a tinge of spatiality, as though time were a succession of spaces; sequences in time are viewed in terms of a simultaneity in space transformed into a succession. What is peculiar, however, to the temporal *Gestalt* is not that it transforms juxtaposition in space into succession in time but the exact opposite; it gathers successive elements into a simultaneous presence.

Gestalt psychology has so far failed (1) to distinguish sharply enough between seeing and hearing (and between hearing tonal patterns as acoustical and musical), and (2) to recognize that the temporality of tonal patterns is radically different from the spatiality of visual patterns. These two sins of omission—if they may be so called—have a long history. A decade before publication of Christian von Ehrenfels' pioneering work "Über Gestaltqualitäten," Ernst Mach wrote in his *Analyse der Empfindungen*: "According to earlier views"—this refers to the traditional theory of hearing developed on the basis of Helmholtz's theory—"an important fact, to be discussed below, remains incomprehensible, and yet no theory can be complete without accounting for it. If two tonal sequences begin with two different tones, and the ratios between frequencies do not vary as one tone is followed by another, we hear the same melody in both as directly as we see that two similar and similarly positioned geometric figures are of the same shape. Identical melodies in different positions can be called . . . tonal structures of the same tonal pattern." The problem, program, and method of Gestalt psychology are here formulated in advance. Its problem is the *Gestalt* phenomenon, the immediacy of *Gestalt* perception; its program calls for broadening the earlier view or replacing it by another which must be able to account for the *Gestalt* phenomenon; and its method is anticipated in that the problem is formulated in geometric, not musical terms: the audible, temporal *Gestalt* is to be studied on the basis of the visible, spatial *Gestalt*. That the two rest upon a common foundation is tacitly assumed; otherwise it would be pointless to compare them. To be sure, this assumption is not arbitrary: the fact that the pattern remains the same is determined by the persistence of quantitative ratios —frequency ratios in the musical *Gestalt* and ratios between side lengths in the geometric *Gestalt*. Why are [musical notation] and [musical notation] the same melody, the same tonal *Gestalt?* The tones are not the same, nor are the frequencies, but the same ratios are preserved as tone succeeds tone. The initial tone [musical notation] in our first example has the frequency number 468, and the initial tone [musical notation] in the second example 390; the second tone in the first example [musical notation] has the frequency 312, that is, exactly two-thirds of 468; the frequency of the second tone [musical notation] in the second example, 260, is exactly two-thirds of 390. In either example, the next step leads to a tone whose frequency is nine-eighths of that of the preceding tone, and so on. If the frequency ratio between the two initial tones [musical notation] and [musical notation] were 468:390, that is, 6:5, all following pairs of tones would disclose the same 6 : 5 ratio. We obtain analogous results when we compare geometric figures. Why are the two triangles [triangle] and [triangle] similar, that is, of the same shape though of different size? Because the corresponding sides are in the same ratio. Clearly, observations of this kind contribute no more to our understanding of *Gestalt* seeing than to that of *Gestalt* hearing.

The problem is merely localized, as it were. Mach writes: "The question of why geometrically similar structures are also similar optically . . . contains the whole problem of *Gestalt* seeing." Mach takes it for granted that audible and visible *Gestalten* are closely related, and that inferences based on the analogy between the two are legitimate.

It is repeatedly astonishing how even the most perspicacious and conscientious researchers content themselves with the most superficial analogies when dealing with a question marginal to their own fields of study, and how easy it is to discover what makes such analogies misleading. If we consider the most elementary geometric figure, the triangle, we must ask whether the eye apprehending *Gestalt* identity or nonidentity is actually guided by the lengths of the sides rather than by their positions, that is, the angles they form. When comparing △ and △, it is not the lengths of the sides but their positions—that is to say, the angles—that I recognize as identical in both, affected by the difference in size between the two triangles. Conversely, I directly recognize that △ and △ are not similar, that they are dissimilar in shape, only because the corresponding angles are not equal, not because the corresponding sides are slightly different in length. When we look at figures of different shape, yet whose corresponding angles are equal, for example, ▱ and ▱, we do not notice slight differences in length unless they are associated with differences between the corresponding angles. That ▱ and ▱ have the same shape we can see only after we draw diagonals, mentally or on paper; that ▱ and ▱ do not have the same shape we can see at once, although the lengths of corresponding sides differ less than in the preceding example. Thus, more generally, it seems that in recognizing geometric forms, the eye is guided by the angles, by directional not dimensional ratios. (How else could circles, and all curves, be seen as similar, as being of the same shape? Here the degree of curvature performs the office of the angle.) As every reader of Euclid's *Elements* knows, the angle is an even more problematic entity than the straight line or the curve: half ratio and half magnitude, something that expresses the reciprocal inclination of two lines, the change of direction as we pass from one to the other. What corresponds to the angle in the tonal *Gestalt?* What guides the ear in apprehending the tonal *Gestalt* in the same way as the angle guides the eye in apprehending the visual one? Can we say, for example, that tones are "reciprocally inclined"? Does a change of direction take place as we pass from one tone to another?

Next objection: a figure must have two dimensions to be perceived by the eye; the order of tones according to pitch has only one dimension. If melodies are to be represented as figures, the time dimension—tone duration—must be added. Horizontal lines may indicate time, vertical ones the rise and fall of tones. Accordingly, the first step in the motif cited above, 𝄞, would look on paper approximately like this: ⌐ . The horizontal strokes represent the tones, with the length of the strokes indicating tone duration and their position indicating the pitch; the vertical line indicates pitch difference. The same step transposed to another key 𝄞 —same tonal *Gestalt*, the same numerical ratio, but different frequency numbers—would therefore be represented by a similar figure: same *Gestalt*, the same numerical ratio, but with different lengths. What is the vertical line supposed to indicate now—the ratio $3:2$ that obtains for both 𝄞 and 𝄞 or the reduction in frequency in the ratio $6:5$ that results from the transposition? In the former case, the figure would be the same, not similar, and the picture would not show that the motif has been transposed; in the latter case, the figure would no longer be similar because the vertical line would be shorter, whereas the horizontals representing tone duration would remain the same as before.

A neat geometric representation of tone relations can be achieved only if, instead of figures, we use vertical lines to indicate frequencies and the ratio between them. The step would thus be represented by | |, the transposed step by | |. The differences in pitch are here represented by differences of length, the equal ratios of their lengths expressing the fact that the two tonal patterns are identical. But is it still true that here, too, without using figures or angles, we directly apprehend the identity of the two patterns, or even apprehend it as directly as we hear the identity of melodies? In the diagram given below, can we *see* at once which of the three pairs at the right exhibits the same ratio of length as the pair at the left?

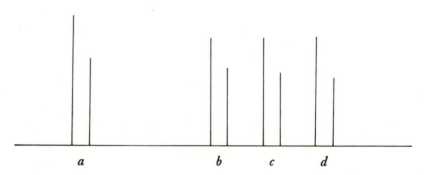

Can we *see* this as immediately and unmistakably as we *hear* that (pair *a*) is correctly transposed in (pair *c*) but not in (pair *b*) or (pair *d*)? The foundation on which comparability of the heard and the seen is supposed to rest proves on investigation to be anything but solid.

Last and decisive objection: it is by no means the case that the tonal *Gestalt* remains unaltered in transposition because the pitch ratios remain the same. The latter is certainly a necessary but not a sufficient condition. It is enough to listen to the major scale as to a melody. ♪ [musical notation] surely says something more than the same thing twice in different positions. And yet the pitch ratios in [musical notation] are the same as those in [musical notation]. For a tonal *Gestalt* to remain unaltered in transposition, it is not enough to keep the pitch ratios unaltered: we must also see to it that the dynamic qualities do not change, i.e., that the dynamic center is shifted with the other tones. Nor could it be otherwise, for a tone becomes part of a musical whole by virtue of its dynamic quality, not by virtue of its pitch, and the dynamic quality of each tone is determined by its relation to the dynamic center, not by its position or its frequency in relation to neighboring tones.

In the motif [musical notation] the step characterized by the frequency ratio $2:3$, the fifth, occurs twice. Is the fifth [musical notation] the same thing as the fifth [musical notation]? It is the same only in an abstract sense, removed from musical reality. After all, even the step [musical notation] takes place not in a vacuum, an empty tonal space, but in a dynamic field, which the step itself creates and defines. Only as an event in a dynamic field is it a musical event, does it *say* something, namely, $\hat{5}$-$\hat{1}$. But if this is the case, [musical notation] is by no means the same thing in another position, two different tones exhibiting the same ratio of frequencies: it *says* something else, namely, $\hat{2}$-$\hat{5}$, and it *is* something else; in music tones are what they say. For this reason there can be no such thing in music as *the* fifth [musical notation] or *the* fifth [musical notation], no more so than *the* tone [musical notation] or *the* tone [musical notation]. There can be only the fifth $\hat{5}$-$\hat{1}$, the fifth $\hat{2}$-$\hat{5}$, the fifth $\hat{1}$-$\hat{4}$, depending on what the fifth says (all intervals to be read downward). Just as music knows tones only as vehicles of dynamic qualities, so it knows intervals only as vehicles of dynamic statements. A tonal step transposed to another key remains the same for musical hearing only if it says the same thing as the nontransposed one.

What has been discussed in the foregoing was not melody proper, an extended sequence of tones, but the steps from tone to tone: the intervals. It is a matter for debate whether music's actual building material consists of individual tones or of intervals. Be that as it may, the tiniest musical unity (which is not susceptible to further subdivision into parts) is the interval. When Ernst Mach formulated the problems involved in tonal patterns, he was right to single out the interval as "the datum in its simplest form." Every psychological investigation into how we listen to music centers around the interval. Unfortunately, in most cases a faulty, nonmusical notion of the interval serves as the basis. All psychologists, including the Gestaltists, treat the interval as a relation between tones in tonal space, between pitches corresponding to a specific ratio of frequencies—in other words, as an acoustical phenomenon rather than a musical one. To this day the intervals studied by psychologists of music are dead intervals, just as the tones investigated by earlier mechanistic-minded psychologists were dead tones. The musical interval, however, is *alive* and, like the tone, derives its life from tonal forces, not from tonal positions. Only because it is alive by virtue of forces active in and through it can one interval be linked to another, can a sequence of steps give rise to a tonal whole of a higher order, a melody. , which begins Bach's Fugue in E$^\flat$ minor, is not "a fifth," $2:3$; it is $\hat{1}$-$\hat{5}$, the sounding of pole and counterpole, suggestive of the primordial tension which is the hallmark of our music. What follows, , is not a series of ascending and descending seconds, $15:16:15:13\frac{1}{2}:12:13\frac{1}{2}:15$; if it were, where would the bond, the meaning be? It is $\hat{5}$-$\hat{6}$-$\hat{5}$-$\hat{4}$-$\hat{3}$-$\hat{4}$-$\hat{5}$, which spins out the tension introduced with $\hat{5}$ by playing around the tension tone. Then comes , certainly not any fourth, $3:4$, but *the* fourth $\hat{1}$-$\hat{4}$, whose function here is to begin the gradual reduction of tension, . In this way the first interval's living statement gives birth to the musical idea:

In this sense, not in any other, as a chain of statements, is the musical idea apprehended and understood by the ear.

Only of the dead acoustical interval is it true that equal frequency ratios secure equal results when different pitches are used. The living interval is anything but indifferent to being shifted back and forth in tonal space, as though it were a dead thing. If I begin the fugue with directly after playing the prelude, I do not hear the same interval as before in a lower position: this time it expresses something very different, namely, $\hat{5}$-$\hat{2}$. Instead of stating pole and counterpole, the step sides exclusively with the latter, the aspect of tension. In the following we hear not a playing around $\hat{5}$, the tension tone, but $\hat{2}$-$\hat{3}$-$\hat{2}$-$\hat{1}$, a gravitating toward the center, that is, the pole—an entirely different statement. If I continue and play the whole theme

what I hear is doubtless the same theme as before shifted to a lower position; but I hear it as the same not because the pitch ratios are the same, but because my ear has been reoriented in the process and the dynamic center has been shifted with , so that the tones retain their dynamic qualities despite their new positions, and the intervals say the same thing as before. If I make a slight change, playing [♪♪] instead of [♪♪], my ear will not be reoriented: the transposed fourth [♪] will say $\hat{5}$-$\hat{8}$—that is, pretty much the opposite of the earlier $\hat{1}$-$\hat{4}$—and as a result the idea will be so altered as to demand an entirely different continuation. If the ear apprehends [♪] without having been prepared for it by the prelude, the interval will, for reasons to be stated below, be clearly heard as $\hat{1}$-$\hat{5}$. In this case, the ear has been correctly oriented from the outset, and the theme is actually heard in a lower position—an instance of perfect transposition.

Clearly, the musical interval is anything but insensitive to shifts in tonal space. On the contrary, it is highly sensitive to every positional change, save where accompanied by some corresponding dynamic change. By learning to convey very different things with the same interval, musical language since Bach has discovered one of its principal means of expression. To pick an example at random, a man who hears Beethoven's

merely as three equal steps, three gradually ascending fourths, and fails to hear how the same acoustical interval takes on a new meaning as it ascends from $\hat{1}$-$\hat{4}$ through $\hat{2}$-$\hat{5}$ to $\hat{3}$-$\hat{6}$—the concluding [♪] recapitulates the fourth $\hat{6}$-$\hat{5}$-$\hat{4}$-$\hat{3}$, read backward—such a man does not hear music. (The meaning of the first fourth, $\hat{1}$-$\hat{4}$, is defined by the context.) The difference between the acoustical and the musical *Gestalt* is even more apparent when not only the pitch ratios but also the pitches themselves remain the same, although the dynamic qualities are altered. To make such a transformation noticeable, it is most often necessary to add new voices or chords to the melody. In the following example

the change is effected within the melody itself. The interval c-b, $\hat{6}$-$\hat{5}$, in the first bar, says $\hat{2}$-$\hat{1}$ in the second. Intervals can say different things by using the same means as well as the same thing by using different means.

At first glance it might seem that Gestalt psychology is especially equipped to do justice to this fact. After all, the principle that the whole is perceived before its parts implies that the context of the given *Gestalt* will determine whether or not elements which are identical considered in themselves remain the same; it also implies that elements which are not identical by this standard may become the same within the context of the whole. Comparison with visual *Gestalten* immediately shows the looseness of this argument. The two vertical lines which are perceived as equal in ⊣⊢ are perceived as unequal in ⟩⟨ . In terms of the aural *Gestalt* 𝄞♭♭♭♭ and ♭♭♭♭ heard separately, heard as the beginning of the fugue, are "the same in different positions." But heard within the context of the *Gestalt,* in this case the connection of prelude and fugue, 𝄞♭♭♭♭ and ♭♭♭♭ are no longer the same: ♭♭♭♭ is something else than 𝄞♭♭♭♭ transposed. More generally, then, whether repetition of an interval is to be taken as conveying the same or a different musical sense depends on its function within the *Gestalt* as a whole.

But is it actually the *Gestalt*—for, after all, this question must be asked—that gives the interval one sense or another, that determines its musical meaning? Is it the *Gestalt* of the E♭-minor Prelude which accounts for the fact that 𝄞♭♭♭♭ says $\hat{1}$-$\hat{5}$ at the beginning of the fugue, whereas ♭♭♭♭ would say $\hat{5}$-$\hat{2}$? Actually, any prelude will achieve the same result provided that it concludes in the same key. Indeed, once the center has been made clear, by whatever means, the intervals will be heard to convey just what they convey at a given point. The structure from whose context one or another meaning of the interval is derived, therefore, is not a *Gestalt* but a *system*. What an interval says—i.e., what it is as a musical event—is determined not by its position in the tonal *Gestalt* or the tonal space, but solely and exclusively by its position in the dynamic field. All intervals of all diatonic tonal *Gestalten* derive the meanings of their statements from the seven dynamic tone qualities in the diatonic system, which are always the same. To be sure, the dynamic qualities are heard only in tones within musical contexts as tonal *Gestalten*; however, they originate not in the *Gestalt* but in the tones themselves, in so far as they belong to a system, and tones, like numbers (it does no harm to repeat this), exist only "within the system." The dynamic tone quality—the audible incompleteness of tones, their pointing beyond themselves—is not directed toward other tones within the given *Gestalt*, but toward other tones of the system to which they belong. Sounds without audible dynamic quality, sounds as purely acoustical phenomena, too, form aural *Gestalten*. Chiming bells, birdsongs, screaming sirens—they, too, are dynamic structures, for a *Gestalt* comes into being whenever a "force" gets hold of "matter." In the musical *Gestalt*, however, "matter" itself is "force": the musical *Gestalt* is a dynamic structure of a higher order. Tonal forces are not *Gestalt* forces. Actually, musical *Gestalt* dynamism presupposes tonal dynamism; and a theory of hearing that can adequately account for *Gestalt* hearing still has a long way to go before it can adequately explain how musical *Gestalten* and dynamic qualities can be heard.

So far as Gestalt psychology is concerned, musical hearing cannot be basically different from other types of hearing or, for that matter, from any other sense preception. Since our senses always perceive the external world in the form of *Gestalten*, this theory looks upon the tonal *Gestalt* as one of several aural *Gestalten*, one among the many *Gestalten* of the sense-perceived external world. Consequently, the basic concepts of this theory apply to musical phenomena only in so far as the latter are not essentially different from other auditory phenomena, that is, only in so far as they are acoustical, not specifically musical. But to hear music, to hear dynamic qualities, is to hear what tones *say*, for tones are meaningful, audibly meaningful; a musical context is a meaningful context, and at bottom, even as a phenomenon music is not a *Gestalt* but a vehicle for conveying meanings. By the same token, musical hearing is essentially different from any other kind of hearing. The sound of bells (an aural *Gestalt*), too, has meaning—not in itself or for the ear, but only by being associated with something else, the source of the sound, for example. The spoken sentence, another aural *Gestalt*, has meaning not just as a sentence: each individual word, like each tone of a melody, has a meaning of its own. But the meaning of a word must be given, must be known, is not directly present to hearing, whereas in musical tones the sound with its meaning is present to hearing. Only musical sounds are directly perceived as meaningful; only in them does pure apprehension of meaning occur: here meaning is sense-perceived. This is the special, unique characteristic of musical hearing, the "breakthrough" in the realm of perception. Every kind of perceiving, every kind of hearing, including the musical kind, involves the apprehension of a *Gestalt*, but in music meaning is apprehended before the *Gestalt*. Here and nowhere else, the ear functions not merely as an organ that apprehends *Gestalten*, as any other sense organ does, but as an organ of comprehension. In hearing and distinguishing dynamic tone qualities the organ itself rises to the spiritual level of comprehension without the aid of other, "higher" functions. Kant's maxim that intuition without concepts is blind does not apply to the ear's musical intuitions. Here the intuited is meaningful as such; intuition is apprehension of meaning. Here the "bare" fact so beloved by theoreticians—bare of meaning, bare of sense—is simply nonexistent.

(Needless to say, all the foregoing is true only of tonal music, i.e., music whose tones and intervals are audibly related to a superordinate center; it is not true of the twelve-tone music of this century, the tones of which are no longer subject to this order or to its implied characteristic differentiations. In this new music, the twelve tones of the chromatic scale are treated as full equals. Without relations to keys, there is no context for the succession of tones: the latter can be related only to each other. No radical break with the past was involved, for in the last stages of tonal music there was an ever more rapid shifting from key to key, no one key allowed to provide a fixed point of reference for very long. With the new music, the key changes with every step; each interval has, so to speak, its own center of reference. The interval becomes absolute, stands wholly on its own, and expresses nothing but the relation between two tones of different pitch. Links between successive intervals can be created only through the formal pattern given these intervals: this supplies the only structural principle. Thus, very logically, each composition is based on its own tone row, a particular arrangement of the twelve tones in a definite order, but never the same in successive works. The row now serves as systematic principle, replacing the key in tonal music. As must be evident, the patterns of twelve-tone music are based purely upon relations of pitch and are fully consistent with the teachings of Gestalt psychology. Indeed, they serve to illustrate the theory. However, the development of atonal music has no bearing whatever upon the very different problem of accounting for the structural principles of tonal music.)

THE PSEUDOTEMPORAL *GESTALT*

We have noted above that Gestalt psychology fails to account for another aspect of musical phenomena, namely, how time is perceived in a sequence of tones. We have also noted that the school, for very good reasons, first tested its equipment with spatial patterns and on this basis developed its concept of *Gestalt*. It was natural to go on to think of temporal patterns as being pretty much like the spatial ones, only involving a "before" and an "after" of successive spaces. This approach proved fruitful as well. Gestaltists did not just "reduce" time to space, in the old mechanistic way. Gestaltists actually dynamized space—"Visual space is a dynamic event rather than a geometrical pattern"—thus linking it to time, which for its part was dynamized anyway. The traditional antithesis between space and time here seems to lose its sharpness: spatial and temporal patterns could now be viewed as two manifestations of the same basic *Gestalt* phenomenon, differing only in the way the parts of a whole are perceived—all at once, as simultaneous, or separately, as following one another. A spatial pattern is apprehended directly as a whole; a temporal pattern is built up step by step, by a process of accretion, each new element being added to the preceding, which is somehow preserved as echo or recollection. After all, many spatial structures (sculptures, big buildings, a whole city) are taken in by the eye bit by bit; their components are not perceived simultaneously, but as a sequence of partial views. The difference between the two seems to amount to no more than that in one case all the elements are present at once, whereas in the other only some are actually present, the remaining ones being represented more or less consciously by echo or recollection. In either case, the whole of the *Gestalt* contains all the parts—if not actually, then at least for the mind.

Initially, succession in time posed a real problem to the Gestalt school: how can the whole determine its parts where no more than one part at a time is ever present to perception? But very soon the problem diminished considerably in importance. That the parts are perceived one after the other does not require an essential modification of the concept of *Gestalt*. Gestaltists often seem to think that this way of apprehending things as wholes can be attributed to extraneous factors, that it is forced upon us by some limitation of our own constitutions;

were we equipped with an all-encompassing eye, no doubt our apprehension of sculptural and architectural *Gestalten* would be much more satisfactory. In the case of purely temporal patterns, too, we can observe how the *Gestalt*, which unifies the parts apprehended one after another, breaks away from and rises above them to achieve a reality of its own. The meaning of a spoken sentence, in which the individual words are heard consecutively, is formed by all the words together: it breaks away from the temporal sequence of words and exists in the mind as an autonomous *Gestalt*. We can imagine that we hear melodies in a similar way, as though we were watching a figure being drawn on a board and as though each line, after being traced by one hand, were erased by the other before the next line was started—erased, that is, from the board but not from the mind, in which each line is stored, so that in the end after the last line has been erased and *nothing* remains to be perceived, a figure built up out of all the parts together is present to the mind.

Such analogies between space and time are so natural, so seductive, that they easily obscure the impossibility—indeed, the absurdity—of the conception on which they are based. To clarify the situation we shall go back to the elementary process of the interval.

Until now we have discussed only intervals between tones sounded successively, not simultaneously as in a chord. Gestalt psychology is merely being consistent when it fails to distinguish sharply between the two (this is, by the way, true of all other psychological theories of music). It is also consistent in exhibiting a certain predilection for the chord: indeed, two tones of different pitch sounding simultaneously provide a far more striking illustration of the quasi-spatial character of the tonal pattern than two tones sounding in succession. For this reason, Gestaltists treat the tonal sequence ♩ as the chord broken up into two successive tones. They use the terms "horizontal" and "vertical" (derived from the way symbols are arranged in our notation) to designate the difference between the step and the chord, because in their view this difference is as inessential as that between two figures in geometric space. A simple rotation of ninety degrees is sufficient to turn a horizontal into a vertical—the line itself remains the same as before. According to them, the whole difference between [♪ notation] and [♪ notation] comes down to this: in the chord the unity of the *Gestalt* is based on the link between two tones actually present to the ear, whereas in the step it is based on the link between one tone actually present and another present only as a lingering echo or as a recollection. Now, this may be true of the interval viewed as a purely acoustical event, but the situation is very different in the musical event. Here the difference between [♪ notation], a two-tone sequence, and [♪ notation], a chord, cannot be overemphasized. The horizontal step $\hat{1}$-$\hat{5}$ is anything but a folding out in time of the vertical interval $\genfrac{}{}{0pt}{}{\hat{5}}{\hat{1}}$. In the sequence [♪ notation] the tone [♪ notation] is audibly related back to the tone [♪ notation], a tone, however, that is *absent*. The tension of $\hat{5}$, its pointing toward $\hat{1}$, is here perceived as a tendency, a yearning, i.e., a privation; the dynamic quality of the tone expresses a lack, the nonpresence of $\hat{1}$. But according to the Gestaltists, the moment $\hat{1}$ is present to the ear, whether actually or only in the form of an echo or a recollection, we hear the opposite: fulfillment instead of privation, completion instead of yearning. Similarly, the first tone of the sequence, $\hat{1}$, is first heard as an urgent demand, a striving for and an expectation of fulfillment, whereas the sound [♪ notation] proclaims *both* demand and fulfillment. Were [♪ notation] a temporal version of [♪ notation], [♪ notation] would be the same thing in reverse, the mirror image of [♪ notation], and [♪ notation] would be a strictly symmetrical configuration. To the musical ear, however, ♪♪♪ is not just a back-and-forth movement, but is first and foremost a progression, a story; the concluding tone, though the same as the opening one, is as different from it as an expectation fulfilled is different from an expectation not yet fulfilled. To the eye, ♪♪♪ may be symmetrical; to the ear it is at most symmetrical only as question and answer are. But an answer is never a question in reverse. Succession in time cannot be interpreted in terms of spatial or quasi-spatial symmetry.

The pseudotemporal *Gestalt* of ♪♪♪ viewed as the temporal unfolding of the chord ♪♪ which the mind abstracts from the sequence is construed as follows: when the first tone is sounded, the second is anticipated, expected; and when the second is heard, the first is present as a recollection. Here no negative character is recognized, either in the "not yet" of the future or the "no longer" of the past. Both tones are interpreted as present, one actually present and the other as anticipation or recollection. This is a false structuring of time, a denial or, indeed, an abolition of it. By contrast, in the authentic temporal *Gestalt* of ♪♪♪ the sequence in time is not some sort of translation of an extratemporal content; the meaning of the interval is the very essence of time: time is its lifeblood. The dynamic quality of $\hat{1}$, of the first note, which expresses a demand, is simply an audible "not yet," and the second expresses an audible "no longer" (and an audible "not yet" in relation to the next interval). The reality of the interval consists of progression from an audible "not yet" to an audible "no longer." The dynamic tone quality taken by itself— directed tension originating in the tone's incompleteness, its privation, its striving to be completed—is precisely this: the very presence, audible existence of the "not yet" and the "no longer" as such, i.e., as *non*existent. It is the exact opposite of what occurs in the pseudotemporal *Gestalt*, in which anticipation and recollection imply a stemming of the forward flow of time, a denial of any difference between a thing's being present and its not being present to awareness. Yet a serious conception of how time is, in fact, structured must begin by postulating pure nonbeing as something real, something that can be perceived—the audibility of time. An ancient paradox for the intellect, it is no problem for musical hearing. Abolish the paradox and you abolish music.

Of course, there are chords in music; indeed, the discoveries and conquests in the field of simultaneous sound are the great achievement of Western music; and one chord, the triad, has even been regarded as a kind of Platonic idea of all music. Sequences of the type of  can only be perceived as chords broken down into their components; their very designation as "accompaniment" suggests their nature of chord. Great composers have, in passages of some length, created melodies simply by arranging the notes of a chord in temporal succession:

In other words, there exist tonal configurations to which the "quasi-spatial" interpretation of Gestalt theory can be applied.

As for the triad, it must first be repeated that in music there is no such thing as *the* triad, no more so than *the* tone or *the* fifth. Music knows triads only as harmonic degrees, as triads of the I, II, III, etc., degrees—as chords each defined by the position of its root in the dynamic field, which relates it to a superordinate dynamic center. In harmony, the elementary event is not the chord but the chordal step, as the tonal step is in melody. Here, too, it is utterly misleading to distinguish between melody as the horizontal and harmony as the vertical dimension of music. Music knows only the horizontal. Just as melody is tonal progression, tonal motion, so harmony is chordal progression, chordal motion. Even though the individual chord has greater auditive value, so to speak, than the individual tone, here, too, musical hearing proper is characterized by direct perception of relations. We need only think of the triads of degrees I and V to realize how much the difference between dynamic states outweighs the identity of the acoustical states, as far as hearing is concerned.

For all that, it is undeniable that the triad, even considered in itself, is a musical phenomenon because we hear it not merely as the conjoint of three tones arranged in a definite pitch pattern but as a dynamic organization, as the conjoint of three tones dynamically related to one another as $\hat{1}$, $\hat{3}$, and $\hat{5}$. The triad is what no individual tone can be: demand and fulfillment, striving and consummation in one. For this reason it is self-contained, perfect. Separation and union, initial conflict and final reconciliation, are here embodied in one sound, which may be said to symbolize, to contain in germ, everything that art music offers in fully developed form. As a symbol, the triad is situated outside time, yet not in space—at least not in the usual sense of the totality of loci where all things are situated—but in a form of supertime, which ancient and modern mystics call "the moment of eternal duration." Reversing the Platonic saying that time is the moving image of immobile eternity, one might call the triad the eternally immobile image of moving time.

Needless to say, the ear will stay longer with a sound that is an event in itself than with an individual tone which becomes an event only in a sequence of tones; and the inner event of the chord can also express itself outwardly, in a sense, as a sequence of sounds, as motion—and not only as pseudomotion, in the form of accompaniment, but also as true tonal motion, in the form of melody. There are triadic melodies, chordal melodies, tonal patterns which can be interpreted as quasi-spatial, as breaking up—delaying, stretching, tightening—an "all at once" into a before and an after. The theme of Beethoven's *Eroica*
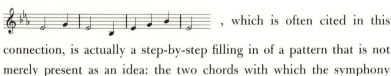 , which is often cited in this connection, is actually a step-by-step filling in of a pattern that is not merely present as an idea: the two chords with which the symphony

opens are a compact version of the triad that the following theme resolves into motion, and are reconstructed from the motion. Here, every new tone actually takes its place next to the lingering echoes of the preceding tones; a whole in which all parts are present simultaneously is here developed as a temporal sequence:

However, attempts to extend this quasi-spatial view of Gestalt theory beyond the narrow boundaries within which it is valid fail when confronted with the facts. In the Weber melody cited above, ♩♩, the quasi-spatial principle of organization is dominant in the first three bars; this dominance ends with the tone ♩ when we realize that the preceding sequence of tones lived only on borrowed time, so to speak. The new tone certainly does not align itself with the lingering echoes of the preceding tones; if it did, the result, ♩, would be the opposite of the one intended at this point, judging by the accompaniment. Rather, it obliterates every echo of them. The moment ♩ is heard, the preceding sound ceases to be present in any form whatsoever. It certainly does not cease to *be;* rather, it enters upon, as it were, a new mode of being; it begins to be *absent.* In saying $\hat{2}$, the tone ♩ keeps everything preceding alive with all its strength, but precisely as something that is *not present.* Much the same is true of the second partial phrase of the melody, ♩ . Even this type of melody, which consists largely of a progression of chords, cannot be interpreted as a whole unfolded in time, all parts of which are simultaneously present. We realize at once that such an interpretation is absurd when we consider any melody that is not a progression of chords:

would be chaos, not *Gestalt.* In such a melody, every new tone obliterates the presence of the one preceding it, in order to refer the more securely to its *absence.* (Nor can every melody that progresses in triadic steps be interpreted as a temporal extension of a quasi-spatial *Gestalt.* Bach's

Lob	und Eh - re	und Preis	und Ge - walt
Praise	and glo - ry	and might	un - to God

is certainly more than a C major triad unfolded in time. The very opening ♩ ♪ ♪ ♪ is a genuine third, an away-from, a leap, an exertion, new and surprising, in contrast to Beethoven's third ♩ ♩, which effortlessly copies a form that is not new, not an away-from; and whereas Beethoven's fourth ♩ ♩ says nothing we do not know already, Bach's ♪♪♫ rises with tremendous force to the highest step.)

Not only in respect of the "not yet" but also in respect of the "no longer" is it possible to detect a difference between the two types of melody. In either case we hear a melody, tones as vehicles of forces, each tone incomplete in itself, pointing beyond itself, striving to be complete. In either, hearing is anticipatory, directed toward the tone not yet heard. Now, in the chordal melody, this anticipatory hearing is guided by the tonal pattern prefigured in the chord: the ear is in a sense directed by the latter, its anticipation to some extent foreknowledge. Each new tone serves merely to confirm what the ear has anticipated: interest and suspense center on *how* the pattern given beforehand will be filled in step by step, not on *what* will fill it. If even this interest is lacking, foreknowledge becomes certainty; the sounds have nothing to confirm. What we hear is merely "accompaniment" or bad melody. By contrast, in nonchordal melody, i.e., in melody pure and simple, this anticipatory hearing reaches into a void. Here nothing is given in advance: there is no pattern, no whole that might guide the ear. In this case, hearing is not guided; it has to find its way. It is foreknowledge neither of a *how* nor of a *what*, only of a *that*. Every new tone is both expected and unexpected, each an event, a discovery, a surprise. This is true even of the concluding tone: many things can still happen before the end; often, indeed, surprises occur before the final tone is reached, surprises not only for the listener but even for the composer (a well-known example: the two versions of Prelude no. 1 of *The Well-Tempered Clavier*). The tone pattern is actually built up step by step, wrested from the void; it discovers—uncovers—itself to the ear tone by tone. Strictly speaking, we can never hear such a pattern as a whole, as we do a chord unfolding in time; we can only have heard it.

It must be noted, however, that only in respect of pattern does hearing of this type reach into a void, has *nothing* given to it beforehand; in another respect, everything—a complete tonal system—is given to it: in mechanical terms, the keyboard with its white and black keys, and in musical terms, a dynamic field, an order, a law. But the difference between the two types of melody is not merely quantitative, between the three or four tones of the chord and the seven or twelve tones of the system. The difference remains fundamental. In the chordal melody, what is given beforehand is *already* pattern; in the other, more general case, it is not pattern but system, law: the *possibility* of pattern, the matrix of every possible pattern. Whatever is given in this way will not direct the ear toward any specific pattern. The ear's foreknowledge of the law governing tonal energies—its knowledge of the *what*, manifested by its ability to identify dynamic tone qualities—is closely connected with nonknowledge, a mere knowledge of the *that* as far as patterns are concerned, and consequently with an urgent will to discover the pattern. Audibly bound to the system, audibly subject to the law, the tone is at the same time audibly wholly free for an infinity of possible tonal patterns.

Gestalt psychology can explain how we hear quasi-spatial, pseudo-temporal patterns, but so far has been unable to explain how we hear authentic temporal patterns. In other words, its theory of sense perception leaves out of account specifically musical hearing, the aural perception of dynamic tone qualities. The Gestaltist can explain how an extratemporal or supratemporal whole is gradually built up in the mind, as the past (deposits of memory) joining with the future (anticipation or foreknowledge) shapes the present. He has an explanation for the whole determining its parts, even when the former is never fully present to perception, the latter only one at a time. This is equivalent to saying that each single tone's dynamic quality is more or less consciously determined by recollections of the past and anticipations of the future: that I hear what there is to hear because I have heard what there was to hear and will hear what there will be to hear. This is a false description of the role of the ear in music. This is just what does not take place. In point of fact, though it strains grammar to put the experience into words, I hear what is, I hear what was, and I hear what will be. What takes place when we hear tones with their dynamic qualities cannot be described in terms of past, present, and future. Those who, by means of the grammatical tenses, divide time into different kinds of time put themselves outside time, let time flow by. But to hear music is to be flowing with time, is to know the past and the future only as characteristics of the flowing present, as its two directions, away from and toward. Thus we can understand how tonal forces can be heard and tonal patterns apprehended. The Gestaltists cannot grasp musical structure save as an extratemporal merging of past, present, and future; only by invoking recollection and anticipation can they combine the successively heard parts of the pattern into a whole. To them music must be as incomprehensible a phenomenon, as much of a breakthrough into another realm of sense perception, as it was to the academic psychologists of the nineteenth century.

Paul Valéry has given us an accurate and eloquent description of this breakthrough:

"As a result, music possesses a realm that is absolutely its own. The world of musical art, a world of sounds, is quite separate from the world of noises. Whereas a noise merely evokes in us some isolated event, *a produced sound in itself evokes the whole musical universe*. If in this hall where I am speaking, where you hear the noise of my voice together with various other auditory events, a note were suddenly heard—if a tuning fork or a well-tuned instrument began to vibrate—the moment you were affected by this unusual noise, *which cannot be confused with the others*, you would immediately have the sensation of a *beginning*. A quite different atmosphere would be immediately created, a special state of expectation would be felt, a new order, a *world*, would be announced, and your attention would be organized to receive it."

Pieces of music have been expressly composed to provide just that "sensation of a beginning" that Valéry evoked. Beethoven's improvisations may have been a case in point. The finest example, perhaps, is the overture to Weber's *Freischütz*. The first tone rings out, unaware of where it has come from or where it is going, but it has a kind of *striving* about it, and in a mighty push forward finds its octave. Encouraged by this, it ventures a step backward, then a step forward, then again gropes cautiously back and tries to start all over again—at which point the counterpole is discovered. This, too, has its octave, with its neighboring tones alongside it; again there is a groping backward, a waiting, and then the purest triad rings out, from which the purest melody is developed. Music is being born into the world. Here music writes its autobiography: the tone, otherwise and always no more than an element of a pattern, turns back into itself, inquires into its own nature, seeking and finding its own answer.

PHYSIOLOGY AND DYNAMIC
TONE QUALITY

And now physiology. The following discussion does not deal with the present state of our knowledge concerning the organic processes involved in auditory sensation—processes of incredible complexity. Its sole purpose is to show that they are today viewed from a new angle, and that the change of perspective has some bearing upon the question of how we apprehend dynamic tone qualities.

"I hear a tone." Most people today interpret this statement as it was interpreted a hundred years ago. The tympanic membrane in the ear is set vibrating by a sound wave, the vibration spreads to the inner ear, and, once communicated via the auditory nerves to the brain, produces a sensation of sound. Neither the first nor the last link in the chain is in question here, only the intermediate. What takes place between the tympanic membrane and the brain center? In view of the ear's unbelievable intricacy—in comparison the eye is as a bicycle to an automobile—the question involves overwhelming difficulties.

The classical answer was given by Helmholtz in his *On the Sensations of Tone* and, outside a narrow circle of specialists, is held to be valid to this day. The gist of this theory is as follows: In the innermost recesses of the ear, inside a snail-shaped passage, the membranous labyrinth, a delicate, tautly stretched membrane is embedded in fluid. This membrane is composed of more than ten thousand fibers varying between .04 and .5 millimeters in length. It communicates with the external world through a tiny window, whose elastic pane vibrates in unison with the tympanic membrane. Only fibers of a specific length and a specific degree of tension respond to specific vibrations spreading in the auditory canal: the fibers act like the strings of a harp or piano with raised pedal. Each fiber is connected with the brain by a nerve which, stimulated by the vibration at one end, produces a state of excitation at the other. To every tone of a given pitch (i.e., frequency) thus corresponds a vibrating fiber in the internal ear, a nerve acting as conductor, and a specific spot in the brain, the excitation of which appears to be the "cause" of the auditive sensation. The harmonics normally accompanying every tone similarly touch off organic and nervous processes corresponding to their frequencies; but harmonics are normally too weak to produce auditive sensations of their own. They do, however, "color" the fundamental tone in various ways (flute tone, trumpet tone, and so on). When several tones resound simultaneously, the corresponding fibers, nerves, and brain cells are activated simultaneously but each independently of the others: this is why a trained ear can easily analyze a chord into its components.

As can be seen, the theory of hearing we have characterized as traditional is closely related to this classical, so-called resonance theory. According to this, we always hear single tones, either one after the other or combined into one sound. That the sounds are heard separately is accounted for by the structure of the ear and by the arrangement of the parts of the brain connected with it. Each tone in itself is like the string of a piano. What links one tone to another, what takes place *between* them, cannot be apprehended by the ear, but only by some other "higher" function.

The resonance theory as originally formulated by Helmholtz immediately ran into considerable difficulties and was eventually abandoned by physiologists. It is based on the assumption that when one fiber vibrates, all others (except, perhaps, those adjacent) remain at rest. Arbitrary to begin with, this assumption proved untenable. The image of the harp inside the ear has a certain aptness, but to bring it closer to the facts one must suppose that all the strings of the harp are linked to one another by tautly stretched wires, and that the whole instrument is immersed in a mercury bath. Resonance will still take place, but with this difference, that now not just one string will vibrate but the entire system, or at least a sizable portion of it. The vibrations will spread to areas whose size and location will vary depending on the tone's pitch. If the process is interpreted in this way, the original theory is no longer incompatible with the results of experimental research. According to Helmholtz, sensations of sound are localized in definite areas of the brain; thus, if it were true that the sensation produced by a tone of definite pitch corresponds to the excitation of a definite area of the brain, an injury to this area would make it impossible to hear tones of that pitch. It has been established that this is not the case. Destruction of limited parts of the auditory brain center does not, as a rule, produce the gaps we should expect on the basis of the theory. In contrast, if we assume that a vibration of a specific frequency spreads to sizable areas of the auditory brain center and involves whole complexes of nervous filaments, this particular objection to the theory is eliminated.

This and other objections raised against the resonance theory eventually led to the formulation of an entirely different theory, known as the "frequency" or "telephone" theory. According to the latter, the physiological cause of the sensation of tone is not a vaguely defined stimulation of nervous filaments; instead, it is assumed that the vibrations of the membrane are transformed into as many electrical impulses, which are transmitted to the brain. As a result, nerves and brain actually "vibrate" with the same frequency as the tone. What takes place is as follows: The fibers of the membranous labyrinth—the strings of the "harp"—are equipped with tiny hair cells which carry electrical charges and are connected with the ends of the auditory nerves. The hair cells vibrate with the membrane; with each vibration, the distribution of the electrical charge on their surface is altered, and the resulting fluctuations of tension produce electrical impulses in the nerve. The impulses traveling along nerve filaments reach the brain. According to the resonance theory, only one fiber of the membrane, one nerve, and one spot in the brain must be activated to produce the sensation of a specific tone; according to the "telephone" theory, every fiber, every nerve, every spot in the auditory brain center can produce the sensation of any tone. What particular tone will be heard depends solely on the number of nerve impulses (similar in frequency to the sound vibrations) transmitted to the brain.

This theory, too, came into conflict with the facts. Experiments prove that the auditory nerves can receive and transmit no more than 1,000 or 2,000 impulses per second, not the 5,000 or 10,000 or 15,000 impulses corresponding to the frequency numbers of high tones. Attempts have been made to circumvent this difficulty by assuming that the electrical impulses are spread, by means of complicated couplings, over sheaves of nerve filaments, and also by combining the "telephone" theory with the resonance theory, the former accounting for perception of low, the latter of high tones. The discussion is still in a state of flux.

Surveying the physiological and psychological theories of hearing, we note that both developed along the same lines—from the primacy of the individual part to the whole, from the elementary datum to the *Gestalt*, from mechanistic to dynamic interpretations. The classical theory of hearing treated the individual sound wave, defined by a specific frequency number, as an isolate from first to last, right down to the moment when it excites a particular spot in the brain; in the later theory, the individual wave in process of being transmitted to the brain affects a sizable area, so that the physiological end result is not the excitation of a specific area but a specific distribution of electrical tensions over an extended portion of the brain, a specific overall tension or, if you will, a tension pattern. The latter will vary for each tone, each chord; more than that, even one and the same tone will result in different tension patterns if it has not been preceded by identical tones. The change produced by a given tone in the overall tension will obviously depend on what this tension was before. Similarly, waves produced by a stone thrown into a calm stretch of water will differ from those produced when the stone is thrown into a turbulent stretch. The classical resonance theory, whose greatest achievement was to explain how the ear could analyze a chord into its component tones, was unable to explain how the ear blends the component tones into a whole—and not just the notes of a chord but also a sequence of notes, a melody. It is absurd even to suppose that the ear can perceive whether an individual sound wave corresponding to the tone d, for example, was preceded by a sound wave corresponding to the tone c or c♯. The vibrating medium has no memory; it vibrates with a specific frequency, not with another: that is all. But if the tonal whole itself, of a chord or of a progression, affects the overall condition of the ear and the auditory brain center, it is no longer incomprehensible in principle how a tonal whole, a relation between tones, can be heard as such. Thus it is by no means absurd to look for characteristics corresponding to the audible relations between tones, the dynamic qualities—e.g., the characteristic that distinguishes the tone $d = \hat{1}$ from the tone $d = \hat{2}$ or $d = \hat{7}$, or the characteristic that the tone $d = \hat{1}$ shares with the tone $e = \hat{1}$, or $d = \hat{2}$ with $e = \hat{2}$—if not in the physical phenomenon, i.e., the sound wave, at least in the physiological phenomenon, the overall tension of the auditory center.

Here we are obviously suggesting a new program of experimental investigation—or, if not a new one, a new version of an old one. For the problem was clearly formulated long ago by Ernst Mach in the most general terms when he wrote: "If we can break up B [B stands for sensation, N for nervous process] into several independent psychological components, we shall not rest until we discover similar components in N corresponding to those in B. . . . For all psychologically observable particulars of B we must find correlated physical particulars of N." So far this requirement has been only partially met. The acoustical components of tone sensations (pitch, loudness, timbre, and duration), the psychological components of the accompanying sensations, and the organic and nervous processes corresponding to them have been systematically investigated; but the component (if it may be so designated) that makes the sensation of sound musical, the dynamic quality, has been left out of account. The new physiological theories have not even touched upon the problem of musical hearing. The same is true of psychological theories of music: where they deal with the process of hearing, there is always question of pitch, loudness, timbre, duration of tones, and the accompanying sensations, the specifically sensory qualities of tones, that is, of acoustical and psychological phenomena. This is particularly striking where interaction between tones is investigated, and where one might have expected that the musical phenomenon could not be ignored; but here the subjects treated are confined to beat tones, combination tones, fading tones, and so on, that is, purely acoustical phenomena, and to the specific sensory qualities associated with tones heard in definite pitch ratios.

Investigators still concentrate on questions such as the one asked by Ernst Mach, "What is the sensory component that is stimulated by any combination of thirds?" To be sure, there is such a thing as the quality of a third as such, and it would be ridiculous to deny that it plays a part in music (e.g., Mozart's thirds, the "Italian" thirds), but it serves merely as the coating of the musical phenomenon proper, as a coloring, as an epiphenomenon. The musical quality proper is *not* what all thirds have in common; it is rather, for example, the quality that distinguishes the third $\hat{1}$-$\hat{3}$ from the third $\hat{2}$-$\hat{4}$. But this problem is never investigated. As for the triad, what should be investigated is not the sensory quality that audibly characterizes every major triad, but the sensory quality that distinguishes a major triad of the first degree from the same major triad of the fifth degree—the last chord of the sequence from the last chord of the sequence . What should be looked for is the N corresponding to this B. A difference in the dynamic state of the same chord, so pronounced that it communicates itself to the whole body, a sharp increase in tension in the second case and the relaxation of tension in the first, must somehow be reflected in a corresponding physiological process. Certainly not so that a plus or minus of tension in the auditory center corresponds to one or the other chord—such an idea would be naïve—but surely in such a manner that the tension produced by the same chord will be different if the preceding sound is different.

In this connection an older work of some interest may be mentioned. According to a theory formulated by the neurologist Walter Börnstein in his treatise *Der Aufbau der Funktionen in der Hörsphäre*, the human auditory function is divided into a basic function and a higher function.

The task of the former is to perceive noises and trigger corresponding motor reactions; it is common to man and animal. The latter function is subdivided into perception of spoken language and perception of music, and is specifically human. Its task is to apprehend sound patterns. The basic function is located in the primary auditory center of the brain cortex, which is not further subdivided. The two higher functions are localized in secondary centers of the cortex. Sounds "are transmitted through the auditory convolution [of the primary center]" to the secondary centers, where they are transformed into verbal or musical patterns. What is peculiar to the performance of the center where musical patterns are formed is this, that in it the patterns are apprehended within its own sphere; here apprehension is nothing but hearing, whereas apprehension of verbal patterns involves other functions that go beyond perception of purely sensory data. (Apprehending a noise, hearing *what* it is, also involves other functions.) The essential, crucial task of the musical function is to distinguish between pitches: according to Börnstein, musical patterns originate directly in pitch differences, and animals do not perceive the latter; where they seem to react to tones differing in pitch, they are actually reacting to sounds differing in sharpness, loudness, vocalization, and timbre. Thus, according to him, the line that separates the acoustical from the specifically musical phenomenon is drawn between the three qualities just mentioned and pitch. Having recognized that tonal patterns originate not in pitches but in dynamic tone qualities, we must shift the line by one step, so that pitch falls within the domain of acoustics, and we may safely assume that animals can perceive pitch differences. Otherwise nothing changes in the picture given by Börnstein; the center where musical patterns are formed is now the focus in the brain where dynamic qualities are transformed into auditive sensations.

Let us assume that the processes in the musical center of the brain could be recorded in films and diagrams, so that we could actually see how a I triad differs from a V triad. Could we then "explain" how dynamic tone qualities are heard? Would a riddle thus be solved? Would we have discovered the physical counterpart in the external world whose absence endows the dynamic qualities with a special status in the audible world? Would the reality of music have been demonstrated? Not at all. We would merely have come one step closer to the problem.

The electrical states of tension in the brain constitute the intermediate link between the mechanical-material processes inside or outside the organism and the psychological phenomenon, that is, the act of perceiving. An object perceived is held to be real when, and only when, we can ascertain the presence of all three links of the chain. What aspect of the object perceived as a whole can prove that the dynamic tone qualities are something real, not just imagined? The classical theory of hearing has no answer. The modern theories have one: not an aspect, but the whole of the object perceived, the pattern. In the individual tone we hear how the whole affects the part; we perceive pattern-structuring forces in action. And what we perceive as a whole determining its parts has its demonstrable counterpart in physiological processes, in states of tension in the nervous system.

This answer may be sufficient as far as visual patterns are concerned; it misses the problem of tonal patterns. To go back to the example cited earlier: in the figure 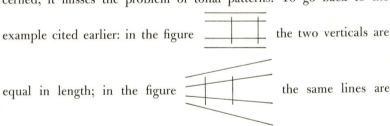 the two verticals are equal in length; in the figure the same lines are

unequal—but only seemingly so, it is usually added, for they are found to be equal when measured. But what matters here is precisely the seeming inequality, not the measurable equality. Here all three links of our chain are present: the physical phenomena of light distribution, the visual perception, and, between the two, the electrical processes in the visual brain center. The last named, if the states of tension

corresponding to them could be recorded in diagrams, would account
for the fact that measurably equal lines in visual patterns can be
perceived as equal in one case and as unequal in the other. An analogous
phenomenon in the domain of audible patterns occurs when the same
tone seems to have a different pitch in two different tonal contexts,

e.g., the next to the last tone in

and [musical notation]. In one pattern this tone has
the dynamic quality $\hat{4}$, in the other the dynamic quality $\hat{7}$. It is this
difference between the two dynamic qualities, the fact that $\hat{7}$ strains
toward $\hat{8}$, and $\hat{4}$ toward $\hat{3}$, that accounts for the seeming difference
in pitch. Seeing measurably equal lines as equal in one case and unequal
in the other is matched by hearing tones of equal frequency as differing
in pitch. And yet it is not true that the tone is for the ear what the
line is for the eye, because in the dynamic quality we can hear *what
the tone strives for*. In order to grasp the difference fully, imagine that
we can see the seemingly shorter line trying to grow longer, and the
other line trying to grow shorter. Only if we could see this would the
analogy with hearing dynamic qualities of tone be exact. Our surprise
at such a phenomenon in the visible world may express what remains
incomprehensible in the musical phenomenon even after the dynamic
character of the pattern has been recognized and intelligibly related to
dynamic nervous processes. If the dynamic tone qualities were rooted
in the tonal pattern, it would be possible to represent our three links
in the following diagram:

$$F \longrightarrow N \longrightarrow P$$
$$\downarrow$$
$$D$$

(*F* stands for the physical process, the frequency number, *N* for the
physiological process in the nervous system, *P* and *D* for the psychological elements of the chain, apprehension of pattern and of dynamic
quality.) In this way the chain would be complete, and dynamic quality

connected with material processes. But actually dynamic tone qualities are not rooted in the tonal pattern—the reverse is the case: tonal patterns are rooted in dynamic tone qualities—so that the diagram should look like this:

$$F \longrightarrow N \longrightarrow P$$
$$\uparrow$$
$$- - - - \rightarrow D$$

Here the places in the material process leading to D remain unoccupied; the gap remains open, and with it the question of the reality of D. Since in both cases we are dealing with dynamic processes, we easily forget that tonal forces belong in principle to a category different from the forces operating in our three-link chain. The latter manifest themselves in their effects, the former in their activity. D is not an effect caused by active forces; D is an active force, which produces the effect, namely P. Dynamic tone qualities cannot be reduced to electrical forces.

To sum up: Present-day theories of hearing, even as revolutionized by modern psychology and physiology, do not fit the facts of musical hearing. In particular, they fail to account for the extraordinary fact that the ear perceives dynamic tone qualities directly as forces in action and interprets their meaning at the same time. However that may eventually be accounted for, this much is certain: in apprehending musical tones we become aware of a unique, incomparable blend of reality, activity, and meaning.

XII. Hearing Motion

To HEAR MUSIC is to hear motion: interpretations of music have differed at all times, but on this score far-reaching agreement prevails. How the concept of motion in general must be revised in the light of musical experience has been dealt with elsewhere.[1] Here, we are concerned with its consequences for a definition of hearing. Since music exists solely and entirely to be heard, I must experience the kind of motion it is by hearing it. How are we to understand the kind of hearing that can perceive progressions of tones as motion?

"Hearing motion" usually refers to events very different from musical events. When I hear someone passing in front of my window in the dark, my ear functions as organ of spatial orientation: it determines the place and by the same token the change of place of a source of sound. In performing this function the human ear is not distinguished by any special accuracy; many animals are far superior in this respect. Still, the function is biologically valuable, for it informs the organism about events in its environment when light is absent and the eye of no use. Let us assume that our passerby is humming , and so on. Now I hear two motions—that of the singer and that of the song. Because the same verb, "to hear," serves to denote both, one might think that it denotes

---

1. *Sound and Symbol: Music and the External World*, ch. 7–10.

a single function apprehending two different events. But this would be to take language too literally. Nor can we argue that the same organ is involved in both cases. In view of the overwhelming complexity of the ear and its network of nerves, "the same organ" can denote many different things. Only in a crassly superficial sense can the function of apprehending a motion of the familiar kind, the displacement of a body, be "the same" as that of apprehending a radically different kind of motion, a motion *sui generis* in which nothing is moving, nothing is ever in a given place at a given time. In one case hearing, like other sense perceptions, refers to an organism's behavior in its environment, and thus serves its self-preservation in the broadest sense; in the other case, hearing serves no biological purpose whatsoever. It is, as has often been said, a luxury function; the information it conveys—concerning relations between tones—has nothing to do with the organism's self-preservation. On the other hand, if we consider the tremendous effort nature had to make in order to develop the ear's ability to distinguish pure pitches (without which no music could be heard)—its "harp" with ten thousand strings bearing electrically charged hair cells, and a highly complex network of nerves which (if the above-mentioned hypothesis proves correct) connects them with a brain center specialized in hearing music—if we consider all this, we will hesitate to call this function a luxury, unless we use the term in the same sense as when we say that man is a "luxury" product of the animal world, or mind a "luxury" product of nature.

To understand how tonal motion is apprehended, we must form as accurate an idea as possible of this type of motion.

There is such a thing as bodily motion, and there is such a thing as psychic motion: motion and emotion. Now, the soul, the psyche, is certainly not a body that occupies a definite place, that can move from one place to another; for this reason it is asserted that only in a metaphorical sense can the term "motion" be applied to the soul or psyche. Such motions, we are told, are actually nothing but alternating, changing states of mind, of a "self," though it remains very questionable whether the terms "mind" and "self" correspond to anything that exists independently of these states, whether the expression "states of mind" stands for much more than a concession to our grammar. Nevertheless, when I say, "I am deeply moved by a sight," I say something very definite, and very different from what would be expressed by the words "my state of mind" or "a state of mind has changed." Whatever the word "I" may stand for in sentences such as "I am glad," "I am afraid," "I am getting up," or "I am falling asleep," this much is certain: the term "change" is a highly inaccurate designation of what is happening to the "I." What distinguishes the motion from a mere change or alternation of "states" is the undeniable presence of an element of activity. The latter may be touched off by an external impression; even so, it originates in itself, in an inner force; it feeds on itself; its level rises and falls like that of water in a spring. Indeed, it is as though the doubts expressed concerning the existence of the self as permanent core and substratum of its changing states only served to confirm the realization that the term "motion" here denotes something real, is not a mere metaphor. It is enough to recall the career of the term "stream of consciousness" in psychology, and especially the fact that the man who coined it emphatically denied the existence of "self" and the reality of the soul. A stream without water, a streaming without a stream, have long since ceased to be dismissed as nonsense.

At any rate, this much is clear: tonal movement is psychic, not bodily motion, a motion without a material substratum, nonspatial motion, spontaneous or self-motion. The states of mind in psychic motion are matched by the continually changing and internally coherent dynamic states in tonal motion. The movement so heard is "emotion," not motion of bodies. In this sense, the proposition "To hear music is to hear emotion" is true.

It is well known, however, that this proposition is by no means always interpreted in this sense. To clarify its proper meaning and to dispel the confusion created by both proponents and opponents of the emotive theory of music, it is first of all necessary to spell out as clearly as possible what presents itself to us in music as audible motion. For simplicity's sake, a monophonic melody, that of the previously cited Hallelujah Chorale, will serve as our example. After all, music has this in common with a magnet, that even a tiny splinter of it exhibits all of its essential characteristics.

The opening has already been discussed. ♩ : the presence of a dynamic field is disclosed; one tone, , is placed in the center; repetition of the opening confirms this result. What next? rings out—the counterpole, $\hat{5}$, unmistakably directed toward , attracted by . The sequence of tones, yielding to the pull of the active force, makes ready to close the gap between $\hat{5}$ and $\hat{1}$, step by step. This is not to say that the tension will be reduced gradually: , $\hat{2}$, rather increases the tension most emphatically, disturbs the balance most perceptibly; and just at this point, before the last, crucial step in which the striving to reach $\hat{1}$ becomes so pronounced as to be almost tangible, the movement comes to a stop. It starts again with and now the opposite of what the tone has been striving for takes place: although the tension of $\hat{2}$ has not been resolved, the sequence moves away from $\hat{1}$, in a direction counter to that of the active force—the halting way in which each step starts suggests a continual struggle against the downward pull—until the counterpole is reached again, and with it the turning point. The direction is reversed, the tones yield to the pull of active forces, and the attempt that failed the first time succeeds the second time:

step by step, $\hat{1}$, the dynamic center, is reached, and balance is restored. Because the lengthened penultimate note, ♩♩, suggests for a moment the possibility that the goal might not be reached this time either, the final restoration of balance is all the more relaxing. (The line might also read ♩♩♩♩♩♩, but the effect would have been weaker.)

The second half of the melody is basically intended as a repetition of the first; unlike the first half, however, it begins not with ♪♪♪♩♩ but directly with ♩♩♩♩: to confirm ♩ as $\hat{1}$, after the tone has already been emphatically established as the dynamic center, would be pointless. The beginning with ♩ is all the stronger because $\hat{5}$ is now contrasted with a $\hat{1}$ which has been strengthened by repetition. Thus the second half of the melody is from the outset marked by heightened tension and countertension. The idea of repeating the first partial phrase is taken over from the first half. This implies that now we have two unsuccessful attempts to reach $\hat{1}$ and two disturbances of the state of balance, with the result that tension at this point is increased. Thus it is by no means "the same once again" that we get when the melody repeats the earlier sequence from ♩♩♩♩ on: here the upward movement, away from $\hat{1}$, must assert itself against a far stronger counterforce. Similarly, the reversal of direction from ♩ on marks a third start, the third attempt to achieve balance; and the concluding ♩♩ marks a real terminal point, for it resolves all of these built-up tensions.

What takes place in this melody can be represented in the following diagram:

What we see here, the dynamic process—tensions and counterten-
sions, the action and interaction of tonal forces—is precisely what gives
the tune inner coherence and meaning, what makes of it a melody,
this particular melody. The diagram traces the evolvement of this
melody in its own way. It shows how a dynamic field is set up; how
pole and counterpole are announced; how the tones first yield to the
pull of forces for a short stretch, then resist it, run counter to it, and
in the end surrender to it; how the first melodic line singly and then
both lines combined are determined by the fundamental tension $\hat{1}$-$\hat{5}$-$\hat{1}$;
and how the second half of each line is built upon the unresolved
tension of the tone $\hat{2}$, and then held together and carried by it. This
and nothing else is what we hear, what we must hear, when we hear
the tones as melody, for only this and nothing else makes of these tones
a melody. If to hear melody is to hear motion, it must be this meaningful
alternation of dynamic states that is heard as motion and understood
by the ear alone, without recourse to intellectual functions. We are
reminded of a line in a remarkable poem on the subject of music,
"Meaning motion fans fresh my wits with wonder."[2]

A diagram such as the one given above not only retraces the melodic
evolvement as such; it also discloses its internal order. It shows the
melody both as an individual creation and a structure governed by
certain laws. Moreover, as will be seen in the next chapter, a given
melody's artistic rank can be read from such a diagram. Here, it seems
first of all to confirm a feeling we have when we hear this or any other
good melody—a feeling that everything in it is absolutely necessary:
that not a single tone can be added or removed, that each tone must
be exactly what it is. Now, in order to gain further insight into what
makes tonal motion different from all other kinds of motion, we must
understand how this undeniable necessity always coexists with an

---

2. Gerard Manley Hopkins, "Henry Purcell."

equally undeniable freedom. No tone must be different from what it
is, yet each tone might have been different from what it is: were not
both of these propositions equally true, there would be no music.

In describing the chorale melody, we encountered, after the repetition of the introductory ♪♪♪♪, the question "What
next?" To grasp the nature of tonal motion, hardly anything is more
essential than the realization that before each step, before each new
tone, the melody is confronted with this question, this blank. Why
must the twice repeated ♪♪♪♪ be followed by the tone
♪? Some will say: because of the law governing this melody,
because everything in it has the character of necessity. But who knows
the law before the melody has been completed, before all the steps
have been taken? What would be "false," contrary to the law, if the
second ♪♪♪♪ were followed not by ♪ but by ♪
and continued thus: ♪♪♪♪; or if ♪ were followed not by
♪♪♪ but by ♪♪♪? Well, then we would have a different
melody, with a law and a character of necessity of its own. That the
second line of the melody should begin with ♪♪♪♪ is dictated by no law, prescribed by no necessity; it is the result of genuine
inspiration, a decision of which the melody knows nothing, so to
speak, until it has been completed and by means of which it actually creates itself. It is in this manner that it creates itself step by
step, wresting its form from the void; the law governing it is not given
in advance; the melody must discover it step by step, as it reveals itself
gradually; a melody can also lose its way and fail to discover the law.
In any case, its character of necessity is always recognized *post factum.*
Every step, as it is being made, is free; once made, it is necessary.
Freedom in prospect, necessity in retrospect: this duality is characteristic
of the type of law that governs tonal motion. The same type of law—

freedom in prospect, necessity in retrospect—is above all characteristic of living processes. What is distinctive of music is the fact that in it this law governing life (in a higher sense) becomes audible.

Just as we have distinguished earlier between bodily and psychic motion, we shall now distinguish between animate and inanimate motion, between moving oneself, or self-motion, and being moved by something else, or being in motion. An inanimate body is in motion either by inertia or because it has been acted upon by an outside force. Whether used to denote a reality or as an auxiliary term that provides a frame of reference for a rational inquiry into the cause of motion, "force" is "the other" in relation to "body." Body is what resists force, and force is what acts "from outside" against the body's resistance; a body is in motion when its resistance has been overcome by a force. A motion is inanimate when an active force has caused it to move with absolute necessity; this is why such a motion is always calculable in principle. In other words, a motion is inanimate in so far as it is a purely physical phenomenon. The principle of indeterminism which, according to modern physics, governs the motions of the smallest known particles refers to situations in which the distinction between body and force becomes fluid, in which the question "Why?" loses its traditional sense, so that questions and answers must be formulated in new terms.

Animate or living motion is anything but undetermined. It is true even of a body which moves itself that its resistance has been overcome by an active force. But in this case force is not "the other" of the body, does not act from outside. "I move myself" implies that the mover is the moved, that the force acts from inside. Physics is perfectly justified in rejecting this distinction, for there is no such thing as a bodily motion that is not in some way part of a closed system, that is not acted upon from outside; thus it is always possible to look for an outside cause of its motion. Motions of my arm together with the nervous processes that triggered them can certainly be regarded as produced by forces acting from outside or by electrical and chemical processes within the organism. But this does not do away with the distinction between this motion as "mine" and all motions that are not and can never be "mine." "I move myself": here "I" am the mover and the moved, and in so far as I am the mover, I make the choice, it is not determined for me: "I" determine the motion, which for this reason is what "I" cause it to be. Thus the motion is not undetermined but self-determined—determined only from the "self's" point of view, though undetermined from the "other's" point of view. At the same time, "undetermined" here denotes not "less" but "more" determined. The determination is fully there, but it is only accessible from inside.

It is this overdetermination, characteristic of all animate motion, that enables us to recognize it as animate (even in another "self") and to distinguish it from inanimate motion. The fact that it is possible to confuse one with the other, and that intermediate forms exist, does not invalidate the distinction. Compare a leaf driven by the wind with a flying swallow. The motion of the leaf is entirely determined by active forces from outside: the leaf has surrendered to them. How different the flight of a swallow. Here we can actually see that guidance, direction coming from inside; inner impulses are at work. To be sure, external forces are involved as well, and the inner force does not set them aside or ignore them; on the contrary, it bases its own action on them, comes to terms with them, now yielding, now resisting, as though playing a game. If the bird yields to the wind or to gravity, lets itself be driven or drops, this does not just happen; it happens with the bird's assent, which can be withdrawn at any moment. When it is withdrawn, when the motion is reversed, when the bird flies against the wind or rises vertically or spirals and circles—whatever it does results from a decision that might have been different, and for this very reason the bird's motions are never uncontrolled, accidental, arbitrary, but rather internally consistent, determined and guided throughout by the inner impulse. In comparison, the motion of the leaf—which is entirely determined, necessary, which could never be other than it is—strikes us as random, arbitrary, accidental.

Tonal motion is animate motion. If it were inanimate, if its course were exactly predetermined in each case, if the tones followed a path prescribed by active force as is the path traveled by lifeless bodies which are the subject of physics, they would have no choice but to yield to the pull of the forces; they would always drop to the ground like dead birds. But what takes place in animate motion is the very opposite—a playing with forces, a coming to terms with them, a yielding *and* resisting, each step freely decided upon, determined from inside, guided throughout by an inner impulse, the result a well-ordered, meaningful whole.

Living motion is self-motion: *who* is the "self" which moves itself in the tones? *Whose* life manifests itself in them? These are questions that turn back upon themselves, loaded questions; no matter how you answer them, the answer is false. For they are based on the weighty and untested assumption that the "self" of self-motion is an "I." Whose motion is audible in our chorale melody? Surely not the composer's or that of the hearer's, but precisely that of the tones. No doubt there is a living relationship between the melody and its composer, and between the melody and those who listen to it. But what makes the melody a melody, and what we apprehend as a living process, is not these relationships, but the relations of tones to one another. Tonal patterns are not essentially different from novelistic or dramatic patterns. The life expressed in a novel is not that of its author or that of its readers; the life expressed in a drama is not the playwright's: it is the work's own life. Indeed, many novelists acknowledge that the characters they create often get the upper hand of their creators, guiding instead of being guided. We are not taken aback when we are told this; after all, here we have a "self," even if fictional, that can be said to be alive. In the case of tones, however, especially the tones of instrumental music, there is not even a fictional self: the life of tones is not that of a self, but life as such, pure self-motion. The evidence of the tones is unmistakable: there is such a thing as self-motion, pure life, yet we are reluctant to admit it. Everything—intellectual habits, logic, language itself—seems to speak against it. We cling stubbornly to the notion that life must be "someone's" life; if it is not, it is not life in *any* sense.

In terms of this false alternative, the assertion that to hear music is to hear emotion can only be misunderstood, both by those who accept it and those who reject it. Just as in the case of life, we ask almost automatically, Whose emotion? Once again, the assumption implicit in the question prejudges the answer, which can only be: the emotion of the composer. Thus music comes to be regarded as the language of emotions, of affects. Just as spoken words are audible signs by means of which a "self" expresses and communicates ideas, so tones are supposed to be audible signs intended to express and communicate emotions. If this view is rejected, the only thing left is to deny any relationship between music and emotion. Tones do not stand for emotion, are not signs of this type of motion, but are themselves *in* this type of motion, *in* emotion; the emotion in this case is that of the tones, not that of a "self," and yet no matter how clear the evidence of music may be on this score, we cannot admit it. We are caught in a false alternative: either music is the language of emotions or has nothing to do with emotion. Thus begins and ends the sterile debate on whether music is autonomous or heteronomous, whether it refers to emotions or to nothing at all.

To clear up the confusion prevalent on this subject, we shall examine in some detail one of the arguments Eduard Hanslick put forward in his well-known treatise *The Beautiful in Music*, the classical attack against the emotive theory of music. He rejects the conception of music as "the expression of feelings" in favor of his own conception of "dynamic sound patterns," which, he declares emphatically, are totally unrelated to psychic motions, i.e., emotions. "Psychic movement as such, without any content," he writes, "is not an object of artistic embodiment." Among the prime exhibits which he cites in refuting the emotive theory is the famous aria "J'ai perdu mon Euridice, rien n'égale mon malheur," from Gluck's *Orpheus*, concerning which one of the composer's own contemporaries observed that it could equally well be sung to the words "J'ai trouvé mon Euridice, rien n'égale mon bonheur." The observation is quite justified; indeed, a listener who does not know the text would probably choose the second interpretation. Be that as it may, this argument is decisive: a language whose words can stand for the opposite of what the speaker intends to express would be a strange language indeed. Unfortunately, Hanslick takes it for granted that his argument against the emotive theory proves his own theory, that is, that music has nothing to do with emotions. Instead of relying on such pseudologic, he should rather have allowed himself to be guided by the melody itself. Then he would have admired Gluck's genius, his deep insight into the nature of dramatic truth, thanks to which Orpheus expresses himself in precisely this melody rather than in a melody anyone could at once recognize as "sad." He would have noticed that although it fits the words "j'ai perdu" just as well as the words "j'ai trouvé," it would not fit the same words if "mon Euridice" were replaced with "mon parapluie," unless it were intended as an obvious parody. He would have realized that something must be wrong with his assertion that music is "neutral" in relation to feelings. After all, the tones themselves tell us where they are and where they are not neutral. They are neutral where distinctions between such emotions as grief over a loss and joy over a find are concerned; but they tell us clearly what grief over the loss and joy over the recovery of a beloved person have in common, and what distinguishes them from similar emotions aroused by the loss or recovery of an object, namely, their depth and intensity, and the accompanying mode of self-awareness. The real subject of Gluck's melody is neither "bonheur" nor "malheur" but "rien n'égale." If you imagine that the melody is sung to words expressing happiness, you will discover that, under the influence of the tones, the emotion takes on a distinctive quality similar to the quality of Orpheus's grief. Tones do not express or represent specific emotions. Tonal patterns communicate their motions to the listener's emotions, and as a result the latter take on the character of the patterns. The melody stamps its character on the emotion, not the reverse.

Thus, the light of musical experience introduces a certain order into the confusion resulting from the indiscriminate use of the term "emotion." Music is not a language of emotions—the language of joy, grief, despair, fear, exaltation, rapture, of a feeling I have or someone else has. But at the same time music is far from being indifferent to feeling. It is neither the one nor the other. If you will, you may call it a language of feeling, but here the word is not used as the singular of the plural "feelings," does not denote any one of the emotions more or less accurately designated and distinguished from one another by the words "joy," "grief," and so on. "Feeling" here denotes a singular for which there is no plural—self-feeling, pure spontaneity, something no one "has" but everyone "is," not something that is originally attached to a self, rather something to which the self attaches itself, something which is "everything," as Goethe says. "Feeling is everything": if the word used here referred to any one feeling, the singular standing for the plural "feelings," this sentence would not express a truth but a profession of boundless sentimentality. That emotion becomes audible in music is true only in this sense of the term "feeling"—as pure spontaneity, nonmaterial motion, bound to tones, not to an "I." The emotion audible in music is that of the tones which communicate it to the listener.

SUSANNE LANGER

In two remarkable books, *Philosophy in a New Key* and *Feeling and Form*, Susanne Langer formulates, on a much broader basis, distinctions that are largely in accord with those discussed here. She rejects the sterile alternative between music as language of emotions and music as pure form totally unrelated to life, between the emotive and the formal theories, and suggests a new approach: music to be interpreted as "expression of feeling," "feeling" being used in the sense of inner life in contradistinction to "feelings," and "expression" in the sense in which we "express" an operation or relation by a mathematical or logical symbol, such as $\int$ and $\subset$, or a technical term such as "integral" and "implication." Tones stand for something; they are symbols, universals arrived at by way of abstraction from actually experienced particulars, and what they stand for is called "feeling," "inner life." "What music actually renders is nothing other than the morphology of feeling . . . the law of experience, the order of affective and self-feeling existence, which cannot be said in words, but is not for this reason unsayable." The concluding sentence of the passage reads: "Music is our myth of the inner life."

The theory of music outlined in these two books fails to mark an advance over the other theories in one essential respect: it shares with them their basic psychological assumptions. Susanne Langer does not reject them, or does not reject them explicitly. Although she rejects the trivial psychological interpretations according to which the meaningful content of music is purely "subjective" and only its acoustic content is "objective," she retains the basic division between the "external," sense-perceived aspects of music, as expressed in tonal patterns, and the "internal" aspects, as expressed in "feeling." According to her, music is form, expression, symbol, and that which is formed, expressed, symbolized in tonal patterns is the "inner life" of a psyche. "The morphology of feeling," "our myth of the inner life": these phrases imply that "feeling" viewed as a state of mind and the "inner life" viewed as a psychological reality are considered the subject matter of musical patterning, as the content about which tones think and speak. In the course of our foregoing discussion we have reached a different conclusion: tones are not primarily something external related to some inner life; the relationship between external and internal is wholly embedded in the tone itself. The inner life which music reveals behind

the external tones is the inner life of the tones themselves, not that
of a psyche. Or if we want to speak of psyche, it would have to be
the psyche of the tones, something psychologically external. The
musical tone is symbolic not because it helps us to perceive something
that is in principle unperceivable, but primarily because its pure dynamism is directly apprehended by the ear. In so far as it can be called
"expression," it is not expression of a feeling, but of the tone's own
dynamic quality. A concrete example will clarify this. If, taking the
psychological approach, we ask what Gluck's aria discussed above is
about, what is the idea it expresses, the answer Orpheus's feelings, his
psychic state, will sound plausible enough. If the same is asked with
reference to the Hallelujah Chorale or any instrumental work, the answer
cannot be very different, except that this time the psychic state will
not be that of a specific individual but of man in general. How different
is the picture resulting from our analysis of the chorale melody. There,
too, the question was what the tones were about, what subject they
treated, what gave them their meaning. Yet nowhere did our account
refer to anything psychic, to feelings, to states of mind; we spoke only
of tonal forces and their activity, the way the tones were related to
the forces, and the motion in which their life manifested itself. The
question on the meaning of these tones was fully answered by the
diagram that showed the network of their dynamic interrelationships.
The situation is only superficially different in the aria from *Orpheus*:
here, too, the tones are above all melody, a sequence of the same kind
as that of the chorale, an expression of dynamic relationships, pure
motion; and only because the tones are all that can they be regarded
as the expression of a psychic motion, the self-feeling of an "I." To
be sure, music is morphology—a morphology of pure forces. It can also
be called the myth of our inner life, but not the myth of a soul or
of the psyche in a broader sense; or, if it is the myth of a soul, it is
the myth of the world soul, the myth of the world's inner life.

THE SELF THAT HEARS MOTION

Our purpose in this chapter has been to understand how tonal motion is perceived. It was necessary first to form the clearest possible idea of what is perceived as motion in musical experience. To understand the act of perceiving, one must first know the object perceived.

Tonal motion is motion of the type of emotion, self-motion, living motion, but not that of a "self." Tonal motion is *audible* motion of this kind, is audibly alive. How is living motion audible?

To begin with, let us briefly recall how movement of any kind, whether self-motion or being in motion, is perceived. Perception of the latter, as well known, is problematical. As a rule, we do not perceive at all the movements of our own bodies. No perception informs me about the movements my body makes under the influence of the earth's gravitational pull; all I am aware of is that "something" is in motion. I need a good deal of persuasion that this something is myself, and even then I remain somewhat skeptical. Everyone is familiar with the illusions we are exposed to in moving vehicles: we think we are in motion when we are at rest, and vice versa, and the same is true of bodies other than our own. I do not hesitate to say that I see the motion of a body, but, strictly speaking, all I see is changes in the relative positions of bodies. Most often favorable circumstances exclude the possibility of doubt: the relative positions of apple and tree change because the apple falls, not because the tree rises. But the circumstances are not always favorable, and in principle the question remains open. Do we really see motion? Do we know more about motion than a blind man warming himself in the sun knows about light?

No such doubts arise concerning self-motion. Apart from pathological or extreme cases, self-motion is always perceived. He who moves is directly aware that he is moving. What he is directly aware of is not a change of place, not that he is at different places at different times, but that he himself is the cause of the motion: this is direct perception of movement as such. Nowhere more than here is the old saying true that like recognizes like. If we could not directly be aware of self-motion, if we knew only motions which can be seen and had no awareness of a living body possessing the power to move itself and an organ capable of perceiving self-motion, the term "motion" would be meaningless and superfluous: "displacement" would be sufficient.

The living body needs motion just as it needs light and warmth. At first glance it might seem surprising that this need is satisfied, and even especially well satisfied, when the body does not move itself but is moved, namely, by machines. This is not a symptom of degeneracy, to be laid at the door of modern technology: technology merely makes it possible to carry to pathological extremes a tendency deeply rooted in human nature. It is enough to recall the pleasure children take in such contraptions as the swing and the merry-go-round. Such machines do not serve to replace living forces with mechanical ones, but to extend the scope of the former: they realize the dream of a body capable of superhuman achievements. What we have here is self-motion through borrowed forces, the archetype of which is probably the horseman. This accounts for the fact that bodies moved in this way expose themselves to their environment as much as possible. Here the skin functions as an organ perceiving motion.

Only living motion can perceive living motion: self-motion can only be self-perceived. Here the perceiving agent is also the object perceived. Strictly speaking, I perceive only my own motion as living motion or self-motion. Perception of living motions of others, seeing them—the flight of a swallow, for example, which I see as animate motion—is mediated, is not perception in the proper sense: interposed between the motion perceived and the perceiving agent is another body whose motion is "its own." What I see is the trajectory of an animate motion, not the motion itself. There are words denoting the acts of seeing and hearing, but no word that denotes the act of perceiving animate motion;

we must be content with the ambiguous, vague term "feeling" of which we avail ourselves whenever we need a term to fill, at least provisionally, a gap in our understanding. At any rate, if "feeling" is taken in the sense of "emotion," i.e., self-motion, it would seem that this act, too, falls under the category of motion.

There is, however, such a thing as music, tonal motion, *audible* living motion. In music I experience an animate motion which is neither my own nor someone else's, and which I perceive directly, rather than through the intermediary of a body whose motion it would be—pure self-motion, bound to no body, no "self." The act of perceiving this motion must itself be a motion. What the eye cannot achieve—namely, direct perception of animate motion—can be achieved by the ear. In the act of hearing, living realities come into direct contact; hearing tones, I move with them; I experience their motion as my own motion. To hear tones in motion is to move together with them.

Thus, not just the tones I hear are "in motion"; hearing them, too, is "in motion." Not only the motion I hear but also the hearing itself is "emotion." What is wrong with the usual question about the respective shares of feeling and intellect in musical experience should now be very clear. The intellect—the faculty of abstraction and conceptualization—has no share whatever in structuring musical experience; the intellect does not enter the picture until later, as a reflection on music. Similarly, "feeling" in the sense the term is used in that context, as the singular of "feelings," enters the picture only afterward. Music is experienced solely by being heard. The act of hearing is itself an act of feeling and understanding—feeling in the sense of being in animate motion, "in emotion," because only in this way can the motion of tones be perceived, and understanding in the sense of perceiving the dynamic qualities which determine the movement of tones. The idea of "disinterested contemplation" which still haunts aesthetics is nowhere as far removed from reality as in the case of musical experience. A kind of hearing that would not be animate motion, that would be altogether divorced from living processes, that would merely serve as a mirror of the tones and treat them with "sublime indifference," would be deaf to everything essential in music. A motionless kind of hearing can never come close to tonal motion, just as a dog can never come close to a bird, at best only bark after it. The ear is not a reflector but a resonator of music. The more deeply I share in the living motion of tones, the more genuine, more valid, more informed my experience will be.

It is generally thought that the miraculous transmutation of physical events into sensations is effected by the sense organs (including the relevant parts of the nervous system), which link the physical to the psychic world in a completely unfathomable way. Accordingly, the ear's specific task is to transmute air vibrations into sensations of sound. Musical experience has disclosed the ear in the exercise of another function. In music, the ear is not situated between two radically different worlds, separated by an unbridgeable gulf: rather, the events on this side of the sense organ (if one may put it this way) do not differ in kind from the events on the other side. In transmuting physical events into sensations, the sense organs are inevitably deceptive, misleading: the pictures they give us of the world hardly resemble the originals. They translate electromagnetic waves into colors, movements of the air into tones or noises. Such observations may, of course, be rightly dismissed as irrelevant on the ground that sensory functions are not cognitive, and that their true purpose is not to give a true picture of the world but to help the organism survive in its environment. Musical experience, however, teaches us that human sense organs are not confined to the biological function. Hearing tonal motion is an act of cognition by means of which we actually perceive an event in our environment. We must not view our sense organs as serving only biological purposes, as receptors of signals, "information" from an essentially "other" world—a hostile or at least an alien one—which are transmitted to other parts of the organism, where they are translated into biologically useful reactions. No doubt, sense organs do serve as signal receptors, among other things, and this function may be by far the most important in animals. But not in man, whose senses are organs that serve not merely to protect him against dangers and to determine his behavior in his environment, but are first and foremost organs of cognition, of apprehending the true nature of the world and himself—not just barred windows that separate "world" and "self" from one another, but open doors through which the two can approach one another. The old definition of vision as an encounter between an inner light emanating from the eye and an outer light moving toward the eye is anything but "primitive," yet although it meets the highest intellectual requirements, it has become alien to us. We prefer to regard the eye as the prototype of all signal receptors. The human skin may be regarded as the prototype of a sense organ combining the functions of barred window and open door, which separates the organism from its environment and at the same time exposes it. The shedding of all natural protective covering of the skin, which distinguishes man from animal at least as basically as man's erect posture, may well mark the turning point in evolutionary history where self-preservation as the highest goal of a living being was subordinated to self-assertion in the encounter with the world, to knowledge of self and world as the highest goal of a spiritual being.

The ear has much more in common with the skin than with the eye: this is why, in deaf persons, the ear's function as organ of "musical" sensation is taken over by the skin, not by the eye. No graphic representation of sounds in the form of lines and curves on the oscilloscope screen can serve as substitute for sensations of sound. In contrast, when an area of skin sensitive to subtle vibrations is exposed to sound waves, it has sensations which, however shadowy, correspond to sensations of sound. Just as the skin is exposed to the surrounding air, so the ear is exposed to sound. Just as inner warmth and outer warmth, and inner and outer coolness, meet in the skin, so inner and outer living motion meet in the ear. Colors do not color us in the same way as warmth warms us, but tones "tone" us and tonal tension "tenses" us. Sound waves being transformed into sensations of sound: this is how we hear noises. Hearing music is something else. Like an infinitely sensitive hand on a tautly stretched membrane, the ear lies on the tensed surface of the tones—this time sensitive only to nonphysical tension, not to physical vibrations. The ear is like a hand that inner life holds out to outer life, expecting to make contact with it and knowing itself to be spiritually alive in the contact—a spiritual hand, the hand of my inwardness. This hand does not transform: it beckons, receives, welcomes, recognizes. The kind of hearing that moves with the tones draws me into their motion; by being heard, nonmaterial living processes characterized by states of tension become something perceived, something known.

Now, what about the "I" that hears music? In what respects does this "I" differ from the "I" in the sentence "I hear a spoken statement" or "I see a light"? When I hear music, my ear is not an organ I make use of for a specific purpose, rather the reverse—the organ makes use of me. The ear that perceives music makes demands upon me, takes hold of me, can function only if it is itself an "I," so to speak, capable of living motion. The situation is aptly expressed by the phrase "I am all ears." We use the same phrase to indicate that we are listening, or willing to listen, attentively to a spoken statement; but we do this because we intend to react either explicitly, by replying to it, or implicitly, by storing it in our memory. The listener to music has no such intention; his attitude is not that of a ballplayer waiting for the ball in order to throw it back or even merely to catch it, but that of a swimmer who allows himself to be carried by the current or the waves as he swims. We can also say, "I am all eyes," and then our attitude is that of the ballplayer, expectant, observing, countering. The phrase can also mean that we contemplate what we see in the same way as we hear music, e.g., when we contemplate a work of art and identify with what we see. We can hear spoken statements in the same way, as when we listen to the sound of the speaker's voice rather than to what he says—not critically, with the intention of making inferences concerning his character, but without any intention, purely out of sympathy or love. Conversely, it is possible to hear music in the way we hear spoken statements, listening, expectant, intending to reply, as one would listen to signals. In that case, the ear gives me information about an event in my environment. The ear is "my" ear; it communicates something to me—"I," "ear," and "something" being clearly distinguished from one another. But the moment I begin to hear music instead of signals, the situation changes.[3] The relation between "I" and "ear" is reversed: now the ear possesses me and I am possessed by the ear, which in turn is possessed by the music, becomes the tones' own ear. At this point language, being firmly tied to the subject-object-predicate structure, begins to fail us. The "I" is no longer something that "does" something (i.e., hears) and "has" the results of what it has done (sensations of tones); now it denotes only one of the three aspects (the other two are "hearing" and "tones") which constitute the living event. Here, having recognized that to hear music is to share actively in the life of a living reality, we are inescapably confronted with the difficult problem of artistic rank. Every tone in a musical context is, and is heard as, the vehicle of a dynamic quality; every musical sequence of tones is, and is heard as, living motion. Life, especially human life, has a hierarchical structure; its manifestations are always characterized according to rank and degree. It is differentiated within the fundamental orders of authentic and inauthentic, noble and vulgar; it is ordered according to stages of growth ranging from simple beginnings to final maturity. Since music is heard as something alive, it too must be audibly characterized according to differences in rank and degree, and the human ear must be able, by itself alone, to distinguish between authentic and inauthentic, noble and vulgar, mature and immature, rudimentary and highly developed musical works. That we

---

3. Striking effects are achieved when a musical signal is turned into pure music (cf. Beethoven's *Fidelio*) or when signals are fused with musical sounds, as in the third act of *Tristan und Isolde*.

do this, all of us know: all of us distinguish between works of art and inferior imitations, between folk music and art music. The criteria we apply in making such distinctions may be hard to formulate, unprovable in principle; definitive agreement concerning them may never be reached; wide divergence of judgment in individual instances may always be possible: all this in no way detracts from the validity of the distinctions, which are irreversible and independent of individual opinion.

These problems, here thus merely mentioned, will be discussed in greater detail in the next chapter.

A few words would not be amiss at this point as to why, in a chapter devoted to tonal movement, no mention has been made of rhythm, normally the first topic discussed in this connection. The answer is simple: here we have been concerned with kinds of motion perceptible only to the ear. Rhythm, notoriously, appeals to the senses of touch and sight as well; and, as far as hearing is concerned, some means other than tones in a musical context may be used to stimulate rhythmic sensations as effectively as, or often more effectively than, musical tones in a musical context: mere noises—nonmusical phenomena—or tones used as acoustical sounds, as signals. Moreover, the experience of rhythm is closely bound up with motor sensations within the body of the hearer that stimulate corresponding movements, either actual or merely intended, by triggering muscular responses which are frequently considered as the true core of the rhythmic experience. To separate what is specifically musical from the motor processes associated with our experience of rhythm would require detailed analysis, so as to establish it for what it really is: the experience of the movement of time. We did this in Volume 1 of this work. Here we have been concerned to stress the fact that motion in music can be accounted for solely on the basis of the audible relations between successive tones, a species of motion peculiar to music and perceived by hearing alone.

XIII. Hearing Organic Structure

THE ACT OF hearing music is by no means completed with perception of acoustical, dynamic, and motor qualities. It might even be maintained that, strictly speaking, what is so apprehended falls short of music in the sense of art music. On the one hand, composed music marks a notable advance over folk music, the former being music at its mature spiritual stage, the latter music at its primitive, nature-bound stage; on the other hand, musical works of art differ from shoddy fabrications as radically as creation differs from mere exercise, and the genuine from the spurious. We need not concern ourselves with the wretched opinion that distinctions of this kind—distinctions of artistic value—are a matter of personal taste. After all, before they can become a matter of taste, they are a matter of hearing, but no longer of the hearing of acoustic, dynamic, and motor qualities. The latter are perceived in any piece of music, in the simplest folk song as well as in a Bach prelude, in an étude by Czerny as well as in one by Chopin. That tones are audibly interrelated and give rise to tonal motion is equally true of vulgar hits and works by Mozart and Schubert. Not tonal motion alone, not the fact that it is motion, but the manner, the "how" of this motion, its internal, organic structure, identifies music as high art. Consequently, to hear music as the art of tones in the full sense of the term, we must hear not only tonal relations and tonal motions but also internal structure. This crucial task is performed by the highest of the ear's four component functions which together constitute the whole of musical hearing. Just as musical hearing first penetrates the acoustical surface of sound, apprehends the dynamic tone qualities, and rises to the level of comprehension, so now the process is repeated on a higher level: the dynamic/motor phenomenon becomes a surface, a foreground, which is nourished and articulated by forces from deeper layers. Once again hearing must penetrate it and rise to the level of comprehension, perceive and interpret the background meaning of the tonal pattern, distinguishing the complex from the simple, the rare from the commonplace, the true from the false.

To begin with, it is necessary to make clear in what sense we use the terms "surface" or "foreground," "deeper layers," and "background meaning." The tune of "Death the Reaper" will once more prove helpful for our purpose, thanks to its clarity, purity, and perfect proportions. In describing the melodic events we will proceed as we did in the case of the Hallelujah Chorale.

The tonal gesture conveyed by ▱▱▱▱, the opening—an away-from-and-back-to movement, $\hat{1}$-$\hat{3}$-$\hat{2}$-$\hat{1}$—declares the tonal center and the mode; but instead of coming to a stop at $\hat{1}$ (as it does in the Hallelujah Chorale, with ▱▱▱), the movement continues downward, passing through $\hat{1}$ and coming to a stop at $\hat{5}$: ▱▱▱. It starts again an octave higher, ▱▱, in order to make room for continued downward movement. $\hat{5}$ is directed downward toward $\hat{1}$, ▱ toward ▱, and the movement follows the same direction: ▱▱▱▱. Now something has happened. In the Hallelujah Chorale, after the first appearance of $\hat{5}$, the movement yielded to the pull of the active forces, tone following upon tone in single file, so to speak, ▱▱▱, $\hat{5}$-$\hat{4}$-$\hat{3}$-$\hat{2}$ (d is $\hat{1}$). In the song, too, the tones yield to the pull of the forces, but they do it no longer as simply and passively as in the chorale. They do it taken as a whole, but individually they take liberties, playing with the forces, diverging from the straight line:

We still see (and hear) the simple movement $\hat{5}$-$\hat{4}$-$\hat{3}$, but only in the background, as it were, whereas in the foreground the movement does not proceed directly from one main station to the next; the tones reach them by short detours, in roundabout ways, as though trying to conceal their destination. The successive tones are no longer equal in value; a differentiation has begun, a structural differentiation within the tonal sequence. First, individual tones form small groups, then one group is aligned with the next, and the whole becomes a sequence of groups rather than individual tones—and it is as a group sequence that the phrase says $\hat{5}$-$\hat{4}$-$\hat{3}$. The motion proceeds on two planes: in the foreground we have the succession of tones as they are actually heard, with their detours and paraphrases; in the background we have the succession of main stations toward which the tones move via the detours of the foreground. The ear perceives and interprets the phrase as such a two-layered structure: in the sequence of tones, as though behind them, it discovers the sequence of groups; in the movement proceeding in the foreground it discerns the succession of main stations indicated in the background, in the freedom of the pattern the law that governs it. (The opening tones of the phrase, 𝄞, taken literally $\hat{5}$-$\hat{4}$-$\hat{3}$, anticipate the statement of the phrase as a whole; the ear at once differentiates between this "seeming" $\hat{5}$-$\hat{4}$-$\hat{3}$ in the foreground and the "really" intended one in the background. We can see why such a phrase cannot be represented by a simple row of dynamic symbols, $\hat{5}$-$\hat{4}$-$\hat{3}$-$\hat{4}$-$\hat{3}$-$\hat{2}$-$\hat{3}$: this tone-by-tone, literal translation, so to speak, renders the meaning of the motion just as inadequately as its audible content.)

It might be objected that we are devoting too much space to what is, after all, a quite simple, easily understood process. But we are face to face with the simplest form of a process that in its ultimate enrichment has resulted in the greatest masterworks of music.

Returning to the tune: after the stop at $\hat{3}$, the movement starts again with $\hat{5}$ in a second attempt to reach $\hat{1}$. Its course is as follows:

The score clarifies what is taking place: once again the movement proceeds on two planes—groups forming in the foreground, a single-file sequence in the background. On reaching $\hat{2}$ the movement comes to an abrupt stop, skipping $\hat{1}$, which should come at this point, and dropping down to the lower $\hat{5}$. But the groups in the foreground have grown to twice their former size, thereby considerably lengthening the distances and increasing the tension between the main stations in the background. The groups have doubled in size as the result of a kind of organic growth: the earlier pattern now appears with its own sym-

metrical mirror image, 🎵 becoming 🎵.

Here, as previously, the rhythm contributes its share in making it impossible for the ear to miss the meaning of the motion.

The built-up tension at the end of the phrase is matched by heightened expectation—all this is to be understood in a relative sense, keeping in mind the proportions of this simple tune—of what will come next. What does come, after $\hat{5}$ has been taken to the higher octave, is a third attempt to reach $\hat{1}$, and this time the goal is achieved. This was perhaps to be expected. What was not expected is the way this is done—without any detours, without splitting the tonal motion, directly, concisely, in a single-file progression: 🎵, $\hat{5}$-$\hat{4}$-$\hat{3}$-$\hat{2}$-$\hat{1}$. The return from freedom to law at the crucial point is all the more emphatic because these are the tones sung to the refrain, "Beware, little flower" and "Rejoice, little flower."

To complete the picture, we must consider the motion in the background as a whole:

Clearly, this too must be interpreted as a sort of detour, as the expansion of an even more direct progression, as a first advance into freedom. which goes beyond the elementary law expressed by ![music], $\hat{1}$-$\hat{5}$-$\hat{4}$-$\hat{3}$-$\hat{2}$-$\hat{1}$. A third structural layer comes into view: we discover that there is a middleground, which serves as bridge between the background and the foreground. The latter now appears to be dominated by, determined by, dependent upon a background via a mediating middleground. Accordingly, the complete picture we get looks as follows:

As can be seen, this picture provides the key to understanding the final phrase of the melody. The short phrase directly and concisely sums up the overall meaning of the melody represented by the background. It is features of this kind that enable us to recognize the genuineness of a melody, the fact that it is something grown, not fabricated.

This simple example was intended to illustrate in what sense we have spoken of a tonal motion structured in depth, of foreground, deeper layers, and background meaning. What is in question here is not the horizontal articulation of the motion conceived of as parts succeeding one another in time, out of which the whole of a melody or a musical work is built, but the articulation imparted by a dimension which is, so to speak, vertical to the succession in time. The fact that tonal motion is heard as it is heard, as a complex process, as the result of a many-layered series of events, necessarily presupposes this vertical dimension. After all, there can be no doubt that the events in question are actually heard; we do not just imagine them, read them into the tones. The ear apprehends them directly; the intellect looks for appropriate terms or images of these events only after they have been apprehended. Nor is any special musical gift required to hear in this way. Everyone who really hears the tune of "Death the Reaper"—that is, who really shares in its motion when hearing it—will hear it as it has been described above: not taking it in tone by tone, as a motion in single file, but articulating it, combining meaningfully related elements, separating out others, forming groups, distinguishing between groups and then combining them into groups of a higher order, and combining the latter into still higher units which correspond to the organization at deeper levels. The ear does all this, directly, functioning in essentially the same way as when it apprehends the meaning of a spoken statement, with this difference, however: in apprehending a melody the ear is not assisted by the intellect which, in the case of spoken statements, supplies the meanings of words. The ear performs the complex task of differentiating and integrating musical sequences without any outside assistance, entirely on its own. Needless to say, this, like any other task, may be performed more or less efficiently: performance is improved by practice. The demands made upon hearing by the tune of "Death the Reaper" are certainly not beyond the normal listener's capacities.

If we now return to the Hallelujah Chorale, we see at once that here, too, the melodic motion proceeds on more than one plane. A diagram of its structure in depth, however, will show only two layers—foreground and background. There is no need for a middleground; the background can be directly inferred from the foreground:

Diagrams of this type—two layers, minimal distance between foreground and background—are characteristic of folk music. Music in the state of nature exhibits the simplest structure in depth. The tune of "Death the Reaper," with three layers, is somewhat of an exception. But even this fine folk song falls far short of the complexity of art music, as will become apparent presently.

These reflections have long since been following a path which was first discovered and explored by Heinrich Schenker, a great and truly brilliant thinker and visionary. His work has enjoyed steadily increasing recognition, but its epoch-making significance for the theory of music and art in general has not yet been sufficiently appreciated. Even an approximately complete exposition of his theory would require thorough familiarity with all branches of traditional musical theory, and would be outside the scope of this book. It is a construction which in its boldness and complexity equals the theories of higher mathematics. We shall attempt no more than to extract its core, in so far as it serves as the foundation and guide for the present reflections.

To begin with, a few words on the state of musical theory at the turn of the century, when Schenker began to publish his writings. "For a century," he writes, "a theory was taught as introduction to musical art, which is the opposite of what it purports to be." This statement is remarkably accurate on two counts. Of theory in the true sense of the term, as an effort to understand the nature of music, there was no longer any trace in traditional musical theory. It was exclusively concerned with practice, with the acquisition of certain skills in dealing with tones. At the same time, however, it was perfectly obvious that these skills had nothing to do with the art of composition as practiced not only by modern but also by classical masters. The link with the actual practice of the art had been lost; the so-called theory also failed as practice. Schenker could rightly observe, "It [traditional theory] permits in no way a practical approach to the art." And he goes on to say:

"Here I put forward a new theory, inherent in the works of great masters, which is the secret of their birth and growth, the theory of organic structure." Schenker was certainly concerned with practice, too; his theory was intended for interpreters as well as composers. But his conception of practice is firmly rooted in theory, theory in the true sense: an effort to grasp art music in its essence, to answer the central question about what makes a masterwork what it is. For this reason it is not tonal material but the finished work that serves as the starting point of his theory, which does not teach us how to build smaller or greater structures with a given material according to rules, but inquires into the forces and laws which make possible the finished work as it is actually heard. It is not to be assumed, of course, that composers must be familiar with the theory to be able to create musical works: the theory flows from the experience of the works; the works do not flow from the theory.

Its gist may be paraphrased as follows:

Tonal life, like all other life, is primarily characterized by the alternation of polar states: systole and diastole, breathing in and breathing out, away from and back to. In the domain of music, this process has the form of a leaving behind and a returning to an audible state of balance, of positing a tonal tension, then a seeking and finding of its resolution. Reduced to its essentials, the process can be represented in symbols of tonal dynamics, e.g., as $\hat{1}$-$\hat{2}$-$\hat{1}$ or $\hat{1}$-$\hat{3}$-$\hat{2}$-$\hat{1}$ or $\hat{1}$-$\hat{5}$-$\hat{4}$-$\hat{3}$-$\hat{2}$-$\hat{1}$. Schenker's pictures are more complex; they take into account polyphony and harmony, the distinctive characteristics of Western art music. As a minimum they require a top part and a bottom part, and at least the suggestion of a chord. For example:

The top part is called the fundamental line; the whole is called the fundamental structure. (The Roman numerals refer to the chords.)

A fundamental structure of this type must not be mistaken for a primitive piece of music, for example, or an "atom" of music. As a matter of fact, it is not even meant to be perceived as music is, that is, to be heard: it is present to the mind's eye. It is "idea" in the same sense as Goethe's *Urphänomen*, the primal form, the fundamental law governing the organization of living things, which gives them meaning but has no tangible existence of its own. Every living thing exists by grace of this primal form, but no single thing is this form itself. As an audible reality, as a piece of music, a fundamental structure is nothing, a bit of trivia. It exists only as a potentiality, as the dynamic nucleus, the embodiment of countless possible patterns.

Every musical work, every finished tonal pattern, grows out of a seed that lies hidden and yet reveals itself in the pattern, which constantly leaves it behind and at the same time carries it forward. Although the "seed"—the primal form—is entirely dissolved in the pattern, it is the fundamental law governing the organization of the pattern. One and the same law determines the form and place of each of its parts and the way they are knit together into a whole. The process by which the finished pattern is gradually produced from the seed is called "transformation."

This process is vividly illustrated by Schenker's "layers." The discovery of the layers, of the fact that tonal motion is structured in depth, is Schenker's crucial achievement. What the ear perceives in the tonal pattern, in the finished work, is "foreground"; the primal form of the pattern, its seed, is "background." What lies between the two, and where the transformation takes place, is "middleground." Our diagram of "Death the Reaper" shows these three layers. But Schenker is concerned with art music, that is, with foreground patterns far more complex than those of folk songs. This greater complexity is expressed in greater distance between background and foreground, which allows for a greater range of transformations. One middleground layer is no longer sufficient; new layers must be added, corresponding to additional transformations, to greater complexity. A simple example will illustrate this. (If here, and occasionally later, simplification seems to be carried farther than is strictly compatible with Schenker's theory, this is justified by our intention to explain the gist of this theory with a minimum of technical references. So long as we do not violate the integrity of the patterns and do not misinterpret their meaning, the truth can suffer no damage.)

The example we have chosen is the theme of a fugue by Bach. We shall try to show how its sharply outlined pattern is, so to speak, developed from the background: the transformation of background into foreground will be retraced step by step. The two notes in the background merely set up the tension, $\hat{1}$-$\hat{5}$, ; the resolution of the tension cannot be part of this simple pattern, because only one theme is involved. First the seed begins to unfold itself; an intermediate station makes its appearance: , $\hat{1}$-$\hat{3}$-$\hat{5}$. Then the little unit is divided into two distinct parts: , $\hat{1}$-$\hat{3}$ and $\hat{1}$-$\hat{5}$. Next each of the parts displays a modest life of its own: . The gap between the two first notes of the first half is filled: . The corresponding gap in the second half, , is too wide to be filled in a similar way. The only thing to do is to stick with the jump. But where the transition in the first half was gradual and effortless, the leap in the second half is an effort. Note the firm foothold offered by the tone that serves as springboard, ▬▬▬, how the motion is accelerated by the rhythmic differentiation before the leap and reposefully slowed up after it:

♪♪♪♪♪. This is the foreground, the theme of the fugue. The whole process is represented as follows:

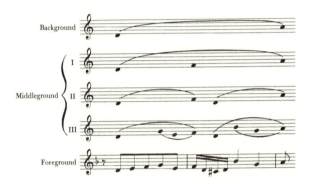

What everyone who hears this theme feels—the characteristic expressiveness of the musical idea, the rich promise it holds—is accounted for by its internal structure as shown above. The foreground pattern does not simply emerge from the background: we see that it is the result of a series of transformations. In comparison with folk-song tunes, such a pattern discloses greater depth of structure and generates richer tonal relationships and greater complexity. This is a difference in rank, not in quality: taken in itself the melody of the Hallelujah Chorale is not inferior to the Bach theme, but the theme belongs to another world, a world of higher tensions, a spiritual world, that of composed music proper. Composed music has no room for the simplicity of folk music—or rather, perhaps it has too much room. The "simplicity" so many great masterpieces are praised for merely seems simple: it is all the more admirable for the greater complexity it embodies.

We will illustrate this by a somewhat extreme example which at the same time allows us to familiarize ourselves with the internal structure of a really ambitious conception. At first hearing, can anything sound simpler, easier to grasp, than the theme of Beethoven's "Ode to Joy"? When we learn how much trouble the composition of this "simple" melody caused its creator, we are frankly baffled. Yet the diagram illustrating its structure in depth will help to clear up our doubts. This time we begin with the foreground. (Here, and in the following diagrams, half, quarter, and eighth notes stand for structural rather than time values; structural units are indicated by beams and ties.)

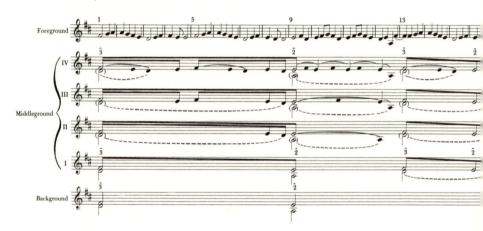

The pattern is certainly a simple one; but how complex is its structure in depth, how great the contrast between the background idea and its foreground realization. The task: to postpone time and again the resolution of the step $\hat{3}$-$\hat{2}$, to annul the step $\hat{2}$-$\hat{1}$ immediately after it occurs by repeating the $\hat{2}$, not to allow $\hat{1}$ to follow the repetition of $\hat{2}$ over a long stretch (measures 9–12), but on the contrary to announce stubbornly, even victoriously, that at bottom nothing has so far been achieved, that we are still at $\hat{3}$ (this is the sense of the surprising syncopation of the f♯ in measure 12); to accomplish all this with a minimum of motion, with the smallest steps in the narrowest possible range, save only for the one unexpected outburst in measure 12, the extravagant leap to reach the triumphant syncopation—even this, however, was prepared in the earlier structural layers. The seed $\hat{3}\text{-}\hat{2}\text{-}\hat{1}$ unfolding into $\hat{3}\text{-}\hat{2}\|\hat{3}\text{-}\hat{2}\text{-}\hat{1}$—generating new offshoots from layer to layer, firmly integrating them into the whole—the upper part of the background, $\hat{3}\text{-}\hat{2}\text{-}\hat{1}$, reappears in diminished form (corresponding to the first half of the melody, measures 1–8) in middleground II; the transformation effected as we move from the background to middleground I is repeated as we move from middleground II to middleground III (first half); the transition from middleground I to middleground II (first half, corresponding to measures 1–9) is repeated in the transition from middleground III to middleground IV (first quarter, measures 1–4)—until at last with the transition to the foreground the structure in depth is concealed in the final pattern: for what can evoke the step $\hat{3}\text{-}\hat{2}$ *less* than , the beginning of the melody, which attempts an upward movement, though actually a downward motion is intended, and the seemingly full relaxation of $\hat{5}\text{-}\hat{4}\text{-}\hat{3}\text{-}\hat{2}\text{-}\hat{1}$ where tension is intended? (The diagram also helps us to understand why $\hat{1}$ does not denote resolution in this case: because it belongs to the lower part of the fundamental structure, namely, as the initial note.) Schenker at one point quotes a remark of Hofmannsthal's: "Depth must be concealed. Where? On the surface."

To avoid possible misinterpretations which may be suggested by the diagram, let it be stated emphatically that foreground, middleground, and background do not form a succession in time. The individual structural layers do not represent so many stages in the process of creating a melody. This melody has never existed as background or middleground, nor has any music. Music exists in only one way, as foreground. Just as the primal form, the *Urphänomen*, is "idea," so are the transitional middleground forms; the foreground pattern alone is "reality." This is true not only of the work as we hear it or read it from the score but also of the musical idea in the composer's mind, whether it flashes upon him in finished form or he develops it step by step. Precisely where a composer's sketches bear witness to the way his work was gradually developed, we find that the process has nothing to do with the work's structure in depth. It must not be imagined that the composer works his way step by step from the background via the middleground to the foreground: what he sets down on paper is always foreground; the preliminary stages are not middleground but unfinished foreground. Thus the tonal pattern is derived from the primal form in the background ideally, not in actual fact; when we speak of the work as it is heard, we refer only to the foreground; everything else refers to the meaning expressed in the work; the structural layers must be understood as a logical, meaningful sequence, not as a temporal, genetic sequence. Close examination of the diagram will demonstrate at once that an actual emergence of the foreground from the earlier layers is not depicted. The graphic signs used show that background and middleground on the one hand and foreground on the other belong to different realms of existence. Music exists as temporal pattern, and can exist only in the dimension of time. Only the notational symbols of the foreground represent time values; the signs used in the other layers lack all temporal significance, thus indicating that they belong to the realm of ideas. Imagine that you are to solve the following problem: given the background and middleground patterns of the "Ode to Joy," find the theme. You will realize at once that even the last middleground pattern is so far removed from the theme to be found as to offer no clue whatever. It is as though we were given an ingenious biochemical diagram and certain chemical substances, and told to produce an actually functioning living organ.

This settles the frequently raised question whether the composer "knows" everything that goes into such a melody—the primal form, its transformations, the way the stages are internally related to one another and to the whole, and how the pattern is derived from the background and middlegrounds. The question is an idle one: whether the composer knows or does not know all of that is irrelevant. No practicable road leads from background to middleground and foreground; the road can be traveled in only one direction, starting from the foreground. As mentioned above, a great deal of work went into the composition of the "Ode to Joy": what would it have availed Beethoven to know that its middle section, measures 9–12, is primarily an extension of the tone $\hat{2}$ of the background? To extend a tone over four measures by figurations is a task for a first-year student of composition; anyone will discover a number of possible solutions, all of them equally trivial. Beethoven's problem was not to extend $\hat{2}$, but to find the one foreground pattern which correctly picks up the motion of the opening and leads into that of the end. That the pattern happens to require the extension of a tone from a deeper structural layer is, so to speak, no concern of his; one might almost say that it is up to the tones to solve this problem. On the other hand, one hesitates to say peremptorily that a master composer knows nothing about the internal structure of his patterns: after all, it is precisely his ability to open the foreground to the action of forces originating in deeper structural layers that distinguishes him from a mere hack. "In their compositions," Schenker writes, "the masters have displayed an ability, expressed in the work as foreknowledge and afterknowledge, which testifies to a clear overall knowledge of the laws of art, a knowledge that has dispensed them from commenting on their own compositions; indeed, every artistic achievement . . . is inseparable from the artist's intuitive grasp of internal relationships." As knowledge in the full sense of the term, as clear awareness of the goal to be achieved, this intuitive grasp refers to the foreground. Where the deeper layers are concerned, it would be more correct to speak of instinctive knowledge in the form of promptings from the subconscious, hunches, or presentiments. This is why Schenker observes that the secret of a perfectly coherent musical work is to be discovered in the deeper structural layers; the composer is instinctively aware of their presence: "This instinctive awareness is always in the back of his mind, otherwise every foreground would inevitably degenerate into chaos" (or into a barren waste, one might add, though this too is but a form of chaos). Schenker also refers to "the *miracle* of the transition from the fundamental structure to the foreground and back." The composer of genius has the primal form not as a schema in front of him, but as a force behind him. All this will be discussed later in greater detail.

The Bach and Beethoven themes analyzed above are parts of tonal wholes, are not themselves wholes. A diagram showing the structure in depth of a whole, no matter how large, does not differ essentially from that of a part. In either case, foreground pattern can be seen as the end result of gradual transformations of a primal form of tonal life; in either, the same threads run from background to foreground via intermediate structural layers. As the pattern expands, the threads may become more and more ramified, the inner relationships more complex, and their range progressively broader; accordingly, the diagram will grow more elaborate. But whether we are dealing with a part or a whole, it is always the same forces, operating according to the same principles, that secure the inner, organic unity of the pattern. Because the picture of the structural layers shows all this, we need no longer content ourselves with vague references to the internal coherence and self-sufficiency of musical works. The diagram clearly accounts for these characteristics. This is illustrated by a tonal whole of modest dimensions, the little tripartite structure (facing) which supplied the theme for the variation movement of Beethoven's Piano Sonata op. 26 (n.n. = neighbor note, an adjunct note or neighboring tone which moves to the next higher or lower tone, e.g., ≣≣≣≣≣, often abridged ≣≣≣≣).

To use Schenker's terminology: the upper part of the fundamental structure shows the motion of a third, $\hat{3}$-$\hat{2}$-$\hat{1}$; its lower part, the typical broken ground, I-V-I. In middleground I, the motion is shown in a more developed form, achieved not as in our previous example, by

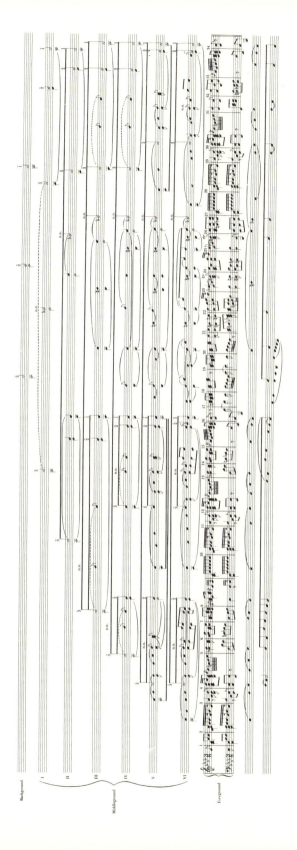

splitting up the motion, but by introducing a neighbor note,

$\hat{3}$ [musical notation], where the starting tone $\hat{3}$ comes alive. In middleground

II this tone generates of itself the pattern of the fundamental structure
by repeating it on a reduced scale, and the neighbor note produces

a higher neighbor note of its own, [musical notation]. In middleground III
the unfolded fundamental structure shown in middleground I is repeated
in abridged form. The central section of the whole now seems to act
on its own: the higher neighbor note asserts its independence: it is
reached by a stepwise ascent via its own leading tone (supported

by the correspondingly harmonized lower voices): [musical notation]. In
middleground IV the pattern is expanded; the motion of a third is
split up and instead of $\hat{3}$-$\hat{2}$-$\hat{1}$, we now have $\hat{3}$-$\hat{2}\|\hat{3}$-$\hat{2}$-$\hat{1}$, while in the central

section another neighbor note is added: [musical notation]. Middleground
V is marked by a decisive step, which gives us the first glimpse of
the foreground pattern: as though picking up the idea expressed in

the central section of middleground III, [musical notation], the melody now
gradually ascends to the starting tone in the motion of a third
[musical notation], which for its part is the mirror image of the same motion

in the fundamental structure [musical notation]. The neighbor note

ascends in a similar motion, [musical notation]. The idea of reaching the
actually intended tone from below is also taken up in the central

section: instead of [musical notation] we now have [musical notation]. In the last
middleground, the ascending motion of the beginning [musical notation]

is expanded to [musical notation], and the neighbor note [musical notation]

becomes [musical notation]; this expansion was obviously suggested
by the central section of middleground IV. The appearance of the
ascending thirds in the central section—one might almost speak of a
blossoming—can be read from the score.

The last two lines of the diagram, placed below the foreground, are intended to make clear how the two main active forces of the transformation process, the motion of a third in the background and the neighbor note in middleground I, contribute effectively to the end result, i.e., the foreground pattern—in other words, how the primal form is present in the melody as actually heard. In the first of these two lines, the melody is reduced to a series of motions of a third, in which a given impulse is picked up, carried forward, responded to, and expanded. We can see here how the central section—a single ascending motion of a third beginning with the starting note $\hat{3}$ (d♭ transformed into d)—is fitted into the whole; we can also see why the melody reaches its peak precisely at this point, at the center. The last line shows how the neighbor note [♪♪], now expanded to [♪♪♪♪♪], having found the resolution it looked for in [♪♪♪♪♪], ties all the parts together, indeed, actually unifies the whole. Thus the diagram of the structure in depth discloses that the entire second half of the melody, including the central section and the repetition of the beginning, is an enriched version of the first half. In this and all analogous cases, the traditional formal theory takes only the foreground into consideration and speaks only of its tripartite division into A (measures 1–16), B (measures 17–26), and A (measures 27–34), thus overlooking the essential fact that the tripartite A-B-A structure of the foreground is based upon the bipartite structure of the deeper layers. It points to the repetition in the foreground, which is a stylistic convention; it knows nothing of the repetitions in deeper layers, which disclose that the work has a genuinely organic structure.

It is especially interesting to observe how the pattern of the central section is produced by the combined action of the two motive forces. The sequence of the neighbor notes [♪♪♪], in conjunction with the pull of the third, first leads to the condensation [♪♪♪], which is immediately expanded to [musical notation]. But with

the latter—since the center of gravity has in the meantime been shifted

from a♭ to e♭ (by virtue of [musical notation])—a demand for continuation

has declared itself: [musical notation] is dynamically the same as the earlier

neighbor note [musical notation], 4̂-3̂, and like it demands to be supplemented

so as to become 4̂-3̂-2̂-1̂. Middleground VI shows how this demand

is satisfied. What takes place in measures 24–26—the deceptive cadence

of measure 24, the expansion of the period from eight to ten measures

(breaking the eight-measure norm so far in force)—cannot be accounted

for, say, by the composer's wish to expand the period in order to

increase tension at this point. This expansion is rather accounted for

by a situation in the deeper layers, which is in turn the result of the

combined action of the neighbor notes and the pull of the thirds,

operating in still deeper layers. It is this demand expressed in the deeper

layers that the composer—that a Beethoven—feels as a desire to expand

the period. And because this desire is rooted in deeper layers he feels

bound to satisfy it.

We shall mention one more detail, which perhaps more than any

other illuminates as though in a flash the threads running from middle-

ground to foreground and background. At first sight, probably no one

would think that the foreground figure [musical notation] is more than an

ornamentation. We discover only in the deeper layers what it really

is: the exact replica, transposed up one step, of the ascent to the starting

tone in middleground VI, [musical notation], which in turn derives

from the mirror image [musical notation] of the motion of a third in the

fundamental structure. The figure in question is not an accidental

formation: it recurs in measure 15, which ends the first half, and in

measure 33, at the end of the melody, this time in the same tonal

position as at the beginning of middleground VI [musical notation]. The foreground pattern offers no reason (such as the requirement of a melodic and rhythmic parallelism) for the repetition of the figure at these points. In fact, every external aspect would seem to rule out such repetition. The corresponding passage in measure 7 is [♪], which would suggest [♪] for measures 15 and 33; moreover, the figure [♪] has a pronounced upbeat character: it occurs in the last eighth of the measure, and from a formal point of view it simply makes no sense to use it as substitute for the stressed [♪] in the first eighth of the measure. And yet this is exactly what Beethoven did, and the fact that the figure sounds completely natural, "as though it could not be otherwise," is accounted for by the way it is related to the deeper layers. A hidden symmetry links [♪] in middleground VI to [♪] by way of [♪], also in the foreground. Yielding to this symmetry together with the directly following [♪] marks the partial close of the first half and the complete close of the whole. A circle has been closed: the last word of the statement recapitulates the essence of the whole melody: [♪ $\hat{3}$ $\hat{2}$ $\hat{1}$] —that is, [♪], ascent to $\hat{3}$, return to the origin. Concerning hidden links of this kind, Schenker says: "As a rule, they are so tenuous, so subtle, that even the most sensitive artist does not consciously perceive them. We can assume without further ado that they are produced by a kind of spontaneous generation. Curiously enough, their hidden nature testifies to their organic origin more convincingly than would any systematic play of repetitions." Elsewhere he says: "In so far as the term 'repetitions' can be applied to the successive transformations of a musical pattern, these transformations are 'repetitions' (parallelisms). Their mysteriousness serves a biological protective purpose: by remaining hidden to consciousness they have a better chance of thriving."

The concept of the organic plays a dominant role in Schenker's thinking. The term occurs on the very first page of the preface to *Der freie Satz*, where Schenker calls his new theory one of "organic structure." He continually speaks of musical works as organisms, and of musical processes as spontaneously alive. "Even the simplest reflection would long since have led to the inevitable conclusion that what is true of the human body is also true of a musical organism: its outward aspects are determined from within. . . . Whatever form a foreground structure may take, its spontaneous, organic life is always rooted in the fundamental structure of the background and the transformation layers of the middleground. . . . The fundamental structure tells us that a living natural force has given birth to living tones; the primal force, once it has initiated the motion, will strive spontaneously to sustain its life, taking on momentum until it realizes itself fully, like any force of nature." It is important to remember that Schenker does not use such language merely for rhetorical effect, metaphorically (as so many writers on music have done). He has a very precise sense in mind, one that greatly advances our grasp of the nature of musical works, of music generally.

First of all, let us make clear in what sense musical works can be compared to organisms. Judging by the most conspicuous features, music has nothing in common with organic life: it does not breathe; it neither ingests nor digests food; it does not preserve itself by adapting to its environment; it cannot heal its wounds by its own unaided efforts, nor does it propagate itself. Only in two respects can a musical work be likened to an organism: the way the parts are related to the whole and to one another, and the way they grow out of a single "seed" by successive transformations. In the case of musical works, however, these transformations, as we have seen, are not to be understood as real but rather as purely ideal. Even on the score of internal organization, moreover, the differences seem to outweigh the similarities. In living organisms, the relation of the parts to the whole and to one another is primarily functional, not formal; each organ has, of course, a form of its own, but heart and brain, blood vessels and nerves, eyes and ears are functional, not formal, parts of the organic whole. By contrast, in musical works it is precisely through its form and its specific dynamic pattern that each individual part is related to the other parts and to the whole. The endless flow of energy, the infinite striving to maintain a state that is the very opposite of balance, a state in which every element continuously dissolves and reconstitutes itself—all the amazing processes that take place within living systems and that have been discovered by the most recent biological research—none of this would seem to argue in favor of a close similarity between the laws governing living organisms and those governing music. And so we must ask whether an expression such as "the organic character of musical works" can be anything more than a poetic metaphor, suggested by strong but far from clearly definable impressions the living unity of musical masterpieces inspires.

Obviously, in terms of formal and functional order, formal and functional wholes, there is no basis for comparison between musical works and living organisms. Yet, although the organism is without doubt a functional whole of the highest order, it is not this that makes it an organism, not this that distinguishes it as an organism from other well-ordered systems. A clock, too, is a functional whole, and it may also be a formal whole. It may be beautiful; its appearance may give us the greatest pleasure. However, the mechanism by which the parts of the clock are assembled is not a matter of form but purely of function. The spring, for example, is a part of the clock not because its form is spiral but because it is a source of energy, and as such it can readily be replaced by a differently-shaped source of energy; the whole would not thereby cease to be a clock. In respect of function, clocks and living organisms are as far apart as possible. The advent of the electronic computer, however, has made us all aware of the fact that the functional range of mechanisms is not always so narrowly limited, but rather is capable of highly unexpected extensions. Today, electronic "brains" are programmed to react to environmental stimuli, "favorably" to friendly stimuli, with "hostility" to unfriendly ones; they are capable of finding sources of food to draw upon when their own fuel is exhausted, and then of moving on once their "hunger" has been stilled. Electronic brains can both learn and remember what they have learned, and their observable behavior is not in principle different from that of living things. However primitive, however laborious and clumsy their operation may be, they have opened the possibility of constructing mechanical models of organic functions. Since we no longer take it for granted that a given machine must be less complex than the machine that has produced it, since a machine capable of manufacturing machines more complex than itself, a machine that "propagates," even "develops" itself, has become conceivable—to be sure, no more than conceivable, but even so!—the gulf between the organic and the nonorganic, in respect of the type or order embodied in each, now seems to have been bridged, at least in theory: it seems possible to reproduce every organic function in a mechanical model.

The above developments cast a new light upon the problem under discussion, that is, the differences and similarities between a musical work and a living organism. Granted that a musical and an organic whole, the one being formal, the other functional, provide no basis for comparison; but if the type of order governed by function is not the crucial characteristic of organic life, the one that distinguishes it from inorganic, mechanical systems, the question remains open. To be sure, whether such a distinguishing characteristic of the organic exists at all, whether we should not rather recognize that the worlds of the organic and inorganic form a continuous series, and that living and mechanical things differ only in degree of complexity, has long been and still is a matter for debate. But there is no need to take sides in it to admit that organic and mechanical organized wholes differ in one essential respect: each functions according to a different kind of plan.

That machines function according to a preconceived plan is self-evident; whether the same is true of living organisms is the central question of biology.

Every machine is the product of human planning. Even the hypothetical machine of the future, capable of propagating itself, would still be dependent on the original plan drawn up for the first construction of such a machine. Machines are, then, comparable to organisms in the sense that both are products of a plan, an organizing principle, but in the latter the principle is inherent in the organism, whereas the organizing principle of any machine exists solely in the constructor's mind. The organism produces itself at the same time as it realizes the plan that governs its internal order. The plan is located within the organism; some specific part of it may determine the plan, perhaps in the form of a genetic message encoded in the chromosomes, which the organism gradually decodes in the course of its life-span. How the plan originates, however, and just where it is located, whether it can (were it only theoretically) be decoded from outside the organism, and whether we have as yet reached the point where, as it has been most strikingly put, "modes of behavior and qualities can no longer be described, but are themselves their simplest description"—these questions still remain unanswered. All we can be sure of is that some sort of plan does exist. The argument that not every system necessarily presupposes a plan but that an order may result merely from some chance combination of elements is self-defeating. For if some systematic principle of organization could be produced by chance, then we should be obliged to suppose that it could just as readily be broken up and disappear on the same assumption. Chance is the principle of nonorder, implying the nonexistence of form and function. To suppose that a principle of organization emerges in the first place, sustains itself, and moreover creates comparable principles of organization around itself "purely by chance"—this is patently absurd. Only theoretically is it possible to suppose that the theme of Bach's D-minor Fugue could be produced by picking at random from a set of twelve hundred cards, each inscribed with a note of the proper duration (half notes, quarter notes, and so on). Mathematically, the random selection of the cards would have to go on for about five million years even before the six

notes corresponding to had been reproduced

—an effort out of all proportion to the result. To go further and reconstruct the entire theme by this method would take hundreds of billions of years, more time than the universe as we know it has at its disposal. And even then all we should have produced would be the first two measures of the fugue, and only one voice of it, at that. What about the rest of the fugue? Obviously, the argument degenerates into pointless speculation.

Thus, the line separating organisms from machines can be drawn with a reasonable degree of accuracy. The machine is pieced together according to a pre-existing plan; the plan according to which the organism is built and functions is inherent in the organism and inseparable from it.

We have now reached the point where organisms and musical works can be meaningfully compared. Like the organism, the musical work is not constructed to some plan extraneous to itself. How would a composer proceed to construct a piece of music according to a plan? Obviously he could not proceed in the same way as a chemist, who collects the substances needed to manufacture a complicated product, taking the correct amount of each, and so on, all the while being guided by a plan without which he could not even begin his task. Taking the example of the melody by Beethoven discussed above, would a composer first of all collect his raw material, tones, values, and so on? How could he know what he must choose, and in what proportions, to produce his melody? Where is the plan that could guide him? It does not exist; it must be discovered in the first place. How? By discovering the melody. Discovering the plan and discovering the melody are one and the same thing. That the plan could exist prior to the melody, as a kind of schema to be filled with tones, is too absurd an idea even to be envisaged. Conventional forms are empty frames; stylistic features are merely linguistic material; they characterize all melodies. The plan of the individual melody is the melody itself. The essential, specific feature of organic life, namely, the fact that the plan inheres in and is inseparable from the living organism, is here present in its extreme, so to speak, its theoretically purest form.

Something that is not constructed, not pieced together according to a plan—an organic whole, in other words—can come into being only by a process of growth, beginning with a germ or seed of a musical idea and continuing with a process of development, self-duplication, and successive transformation until the work has been fully realized. Thanks to Schenker, we no longer need think of all this in terms of abstract speculation: it can be studied as a living phenomenon. The pictures of "transformation layers" are those of the process of growth. They show us the seed present at the beginning, the gradual unfolding of it through successive transformations, and the mature form as disclosed at the end: the unity and coherence of the whole as rooted in the primal form and the manifold inner interrelationships of the parts and their relations to the whole, which are the distinguishing characteristics of everything grown. Just as in the case of organisms, the order governing musical works is not arrived at prior to their actual unfolding; rather, it unfolds concurrently with the successive transformations of the primal form, and is completed at the same time as the finished form. Thanks to Schenker's pictures of structural layers, the characterization of tonal patterns as "organic" is no longer just a metaphor but the expression of a genuine insight.

How is this to be understood? After all, a musical work does not just grow, it is created. It is a work of art, a product of skill, of technique in the broadest sense, not a work of nature. Can it be both—both something created *and* something grown, never to be created? This question is answered by the above-mentioned distinction between the mode of existence of the foreground and that of the deeper layers: the reality of the former, the ideality of the latter. The phenomenon is unique, seems to elude comparisons. The composer builds his structure with real sounds, having in mind their foreground meanings; the result, if successful, then turns out to have been built upon the foundation of an entirely different meaningful context, and to have received its order from the latter. Think of a bridge: its various parts are pieced together mechanically, but what keeps them together is not just the mechanical bond but also the forces of gravitation acting from the center of the earth. Or the healing of a wound: the incredibly complicated process on the surface, which knows nothing of organic structure; yet the end result is in accordance with a plan that satisfies the demand of the organic structure. Made of real matter and real time, the musical work exists as foreground; but it has grown out of the seed of a fundamental structure to which, in the last analysis, it owes its meaning, the unity and integrity of its pattern. It is here, at the deep level of the fundamental structure, that the plan operates: this is why it is not available for purposes of "construction." All this will be clarified in the next section.

The following diagrams, one representing the process of growth of a biological organism

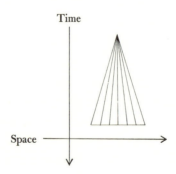

and the other of a musical organism

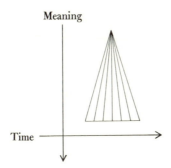

Meaning

Time

differ only in their co-ordinates. In both cases, the beginning is puncti-form; growth is an unfolding. The biological organism unfolds in space, the musical in time. The spatial growth of the biological organism is a temporal process, needs time; the temporal growth of the musical organism does not take place in time but in a dimension perpendicular to "time," just as in the first diagram "time" is perpendicular to "space." This dimension is here designated as "meaning"—perhaps not quite aptly, for after all meaning is present also in the foreground, in the dynamic tone qualities. What needs time in the tonal work is not the growing but the thing grown; and what needs growing is not time but "meaning." (It is true that the grown biological organism, too, unfolds in time, has a history. To what extent this history itself has "grown" in a dimension perpendicular to time, i.e., is meaningfully organized according to the type of its growth, cannot be gone into here. Surely, the primal phenomena of life are not confined to space alone.)

One particular objection has repeatedly been raised against Schenker's theory: What is gained by reducing the fascinating, marvelously rich world of musical patterns to a handful of empty formulas, the so-called fundamental structures? If we could be made to believe that Beethoven's theme of joy ultimately says nothing but , and that

a similar bit of trivia is all that is expressed in the melody of the variation movement of his A^b Sonata, and so on, we would not be richer but poorer. Such a theory, it is claimed, does not give us greater insight into music; it only serves to expose its insignificance. The mountain has given birth to a mouse. The objection would not keep recurring so stubbornly against all reason had it not been rooted in a deeper intellectual commitment, the nature of which is easily discovered. We refer to the traditional interpretation of the relation between idea and phenomenon.

We have said that Schenker's fundamental structure is the "idea" in Goethe's sense. But Goethe's interpretation of the idea was sharply opposed to the idealistic tradition. According to the latter, we "go down" when we proceed from the idea to the phenomenon: ideas are higher in truth, dignity, existential rank. Phenomena are mere masks that obscure and deform the ideas "behind them." In penetrating through the phenomenon to the idea, thought progresses from appearance to reality, from half-truth to truth, from darkness to light. In terms of this traditional interpretation, Schenker's foreground, being a manifestation of the idea present only in the background, is but an outer coating, a paraphrase, or, if you will, an embellishment of the idea: the actual meaning of the foreground pattern must be sought in the background; the truth of music is the fundamental structure. Hence that ridiculous objection. The distorted picture of Schenker's theory is eliminated the moment we replace the traditional interpretation of the relation between idea and phenomenon with Goethe's. His *Urphänomen* is invested with the full dignity, truth, and existential rank of the idea, but the path that leads from it to the phenomenon is not a descent; the phenomenon does not diminish or obscure the idea, but reveals and fulfills it. Against the "idealists of ancient and modern times," and their thesis that "the cause must have greater excellence than the effect," Goethe argued that "a spiritual form is in no way diminished when it manifests itself, provided that its phenomenal form is produced by a true begetting, a true act of procreation. The begotten is not inferior to the begetter; indeed, it is the advantage of living creation that the begotten can attain greater excellence than the begetter." Schenker's theory of how the foreground grows out of the background must be understood precisely in this sense of "begetting." Transformation of background into foreground does not diminish or obscure the idea, but on the contrary develops it to full realization. In showing the path from foreground to background, the theory does not seek to strip the surface pattern of its appearance, but to catch a glimpse of the miracle of living procreation, of transformation. The motto Schenker quotes, "Semper idem sed non eodem modo"—("Always the same but not in the same way")—is totally misunderstood if it is taken in the sense that all masterpieces of tonal music in the last analysis say more or less the same thing, as though the *idem* were referring to the fundamental structures. What it actually refers to is not the sameness of the begetting agent, but that of the *process* of begetting, the miracle of successive transformations, which is always the same miracle, and which produces the entire world of musical patterns from a few fundamental structures. The latter are indeed characterized by their utmost simplicity: since they give rise to countless patterns differing in content and expression, how could they be anything but undifferentiated, "empty"? What they stand for is hitherto unrealized potentialities, powers, not pre-existing things. The only way we recognize a power or potentiality is when we see or hear it at work. Schenker's decisive contribution to music theory is not his discovery of the fundamental structures, but that of the process by which one and the same fundamental structure gives rise to ever different, ever new foreground patterns. Knowledge of the background alone contributes nothing to our understanding of a foreground. In this case, "to understand" means to gain a clear idea of how, in what way, a given background can be

transformed into a given foreground. The field of action for this understanding is the middleground.

Without exception, Schenker's diagrams, intended to render intelligible the deep structure of tonal works, their organic unity, show only
the middleground, and in most cases, whether illustrating an entire work
or only a part of it, the middleground is represented by only one
structural layer. Schenker developed a system of symbols which makes
it possible to show in a single layer, as though in cross section, how
the process works in direction both to the foreground and to the
background. To show all transformation layers in the case of longer
works would entail an endless task (seven pictures of layers were needed
even for the short melody of our last example), but actually this task
can be dispensed with. From the diagram of one correctly chosen—so
to speak, strategically situated—layer, those familiar with the theory and
its symbolic language can make out what takes place in the preceding
and following layers. When the complexity of some passages in the
foreground raises special problems, or different structural interpretations
of a given passage seem possible, diagrams of such passages can be
added. The following diagram of a very simple "part-writing sketch"
(as Schenker calls it) is of this type. We remind the reader that
the metrical symbols—eighths, fourths, halves, wholes—are used here
not to denote relative duration values but relative structural values. This

is Chopin's Etude op. 10, no. 12. (The numbers at the top refer to measures; they show how the sketch is related to the composition, and the main sketch to the partial sketches.)

We have given the foregoing account of Schenker's theory not for its own sake but rather for the purpose of finding out just what the ear is capable of when we listen to music. Schenker answers the question of what actually goes on when we hear a piece of art music as such. A piece of music is what it is, a particular meaningful entity made of tones, because its deep structure is organic in the exact biological sense of the term. To hear a composition is therefore directly to perceive organic structure; the act of hearing itself is organic. Without any advance knowledge, without any contribution from the analytical faculty, the ear perceives both overt and hidden tonal relations, integrates and differentiates according to the given organic structure, distinguishes between superordinate and subordinate elements. To be sure, not every ear does all this in the same way, nor does any individual ear do it in the same way at all times: still, the human ear itself does it in one way or another. Those who distrust the testimony of a highly developed and refined ear because they cannot keep up with it beyond a certain point by the same token demonstrate the reality of what prevents them from going beyond this point: the reality of a resistance which can be accounted for only by the fact that musical works differ in their structural complexity, and by a particular ear's ability or inability to keep pace with increasing complexity.

In asserting that Schenker's theory demonstrates what is "truly" heard in music, what the "real" foundation of its patterns is, I realize that these statements must be backed up by solid evidence, the more so because they entail important theoretical consequences. If the claim to validity of Schenker's theory can be upheld, then it is possible to measure the artistic rank of musical works: rank is audible, inherent in the work itself, not a matter of personal taste. Obviously, such a claim is so completely at variance with currently accepted ideas that it cannot be taken seriously unless it is secured against any reasonable doubt. Until now this has not been done here. The point of the theory exposed to radical doubt is obvious, too. Who would not feel ill at ease if he compared the score of Chopin's first étude in C minor with the "part-writing sketch" shown above? True, we have referred to the gulf between foreground and middleground, between being and meaning, and we have said that this gulf cannot be stepped across but only leaped across. But how are we to leap across it starting from the foreground? It might be supposed that Schenker has something to say about this, that he indicates a method of discovering the fundamental structure. But he never does this; apparently he sees no problem here. If he were asked how he arrives at his diagrams of layers, he would only be surprised: "Why, it's quite simple," he would say. "We hear this." But suppose someone else hears something entirely different and, starting from the same foreground, arrives at a different deep structure? Where no predetermined method exists, such disagreements are always possible. Who will decide, and on what grounds? One person hears one thing, another person another: how are we to get beyond that fact? What creates the problem is not that one person hears nothing where another person hears structure: a blind man's testimony against the reality of the visible has no value, but when two seeing men cannot agree on what they see, then the reality of the seen and the truth of their statements about it become questionable.

We would not be living in this century and breathing its intellectual air if we did not know that to speak of truth is meaningful only where one can also speak of falseness, where the true can be separated from the false as unmistakably as light from darkness. The claim to validity of any statement must be supported by an irrefutable proof, which by the same token proves that the negation of the statement is false. Such a proof can be given only by two methods: the logical method, either by directly inferring the statement from other statements known to be true, or by proving that the negation of the statement involves a contradiction in terms; and the factual method, by showing that an event predicted by the statement actually took place, and could not have taken place if the negation of the statement were true. Every statement tested by one or the other method may lay claim to universal or objective validity, i.e., to express a truth independent of person, place, and time. The two methods of verification belong to two different worlds, the logical to the intelligible world, the factual to the tangible-visible world of bodies. That the sum of angles in a triangle is equal to two right angles cannot be proved by observation any more than Mendel's laws of heredity can be proved by logical deduction. When the two worlds meet, we speak of a miracle: even today, the discovery that geometry determines the trajectories of moving bodies will deeply impress any attentive reader of Newton's *Principia*. The same Newton, however, said, "Hypotheses non fingo," with the emphasis on *fingo:* "I do not *invent* hypotheses." In other words, he abstained from making statements whose claim to validity, to truth, cannot, because of their very nature, be confirmed by logical deduction or by empirical observation. The distinction between true and false is meaningful only if it can be so confirmed, at least in principle. Otherwise this distinction is meaningless and "knowledge" is impossible—not in the sense that it is impossible for us, here and now, or for us as human beings, but in the sense that to speak of knowledge in this case is as meaningless as to speak of the temperature of a molecule or the color of an electron. But "unprovable" does not necessarily imply "meaningless." Statements such as "God created the lion," "Man should be noble, helpful, and kind," and "Yellow is a beautiful color" are certainly anything but meaningless; they may take on a momentous significance and determine the fate of an individual, even of mankind. But they certainly cannot be called true or false. What is meaningless is to try to prove or disprove them, to assert or deny that they express something "known."

In the light of the foregoing, what are we to think of the truth not only of Schenker's theory but also of many statements we have made in the course of these reflections on music? Clearly, they cannot lay claim to objective validity. They are neither provable logically nor can they be verified by the occurrence or nonoccurrence of observable events. Since music belongs to the audible world, not to the world of concepts, any attempt to prove our statements about music by logic, by deducing them from unquestionably true propositions, must sooner or later trail off into a void. It cannot compel assent (as will be felt by any reader of *Der freie Satz,* in which this very attempt was made, that is, to expound the theory logically and deductively, *more geometrico:* it directly provokes doubt). As for proof by observation, there are certainly many elements in music that can be observed—the acoustics of tones, the mathematics of tonal relations, the techniques of treatment, the characteristics of stylistic types: all this provides sufficient opportunity for verifiably true or false statements, for "knowledge" in the domain of music. However, we have asserted that all these elements are only peripheral to music, and that the central phenomena, which constitute the very foundation of music, are here only superficially touched upon or taken entirely for granted. We have also asserted that these central phenomena are of dynamic nature, that the dynamic tone qualities elude observation: one need not be deaf not to hear them and the oscilloscope does not register them. Thus, everything we have said about the essence of music is unprovable in principle, is neither true nor false, has nothing to do with "knowledge." Our statements say something or say nothing at all, according to whether the person to whom they are addressed hears or does not hear dynamic tone qualities. They certainly cannot be termed universally or objectively valid. They can be valid only subjectively, that is, accepted by some persons, rejected by others.

The expression "subjective validity," however, must not be taken too literally here. If perception of dynamic tone qualities really depended on individual whims, moods, idiosyncrasies, music would be impossible.

The foundation upon which an edifice as imposing as that of music rests must surely be more solid than that. The composer who expresses himself in the language of dynamic tone qualities can be certain that at least in its essentials his statements are understood as he intended. If this were not the case, we would not hear them as music. Those who cannot hear what makes a sequence of tones a melody—tensions and relaxations, tightening and loosening, striving and attaining, demands, postponements, evasions, surprise, fulfillment—we might call tune-deaf, deaf to music: this designation implies that we are dealing with something anomalous, a defect. What we say about dynamic tone qualities thus has meaning and validity wherever our music is perceived as music. To be sure, this validity is not objective in the sense mentioned above, that is, completely independent of the listener's personality; yet it is not purely subjective either, is not dependent upon any individual's whim. Rather, it extends to a group, a collective personality, and is binding within the group.

The term "intersubjective" has been coined to denote this kind of validity, but so far as music is concerned this has not really illuminated the problem involved. How can anyone feel compelled to perceive something that lacks the character of physical or logical necessity? How can anyone accept a statement as valid rather than feel free to reject it if it cannot be verified? There are two ways to establish intersubjective validity. First, by the existence of logical and psychological laws governing the thinking processes of all normal individuals, of all "subjects," whether in the Kantian logical sense (as when Kant says that space and time are "the subjective conditions of our intuition") or in the behaviorist sense of similarly operating psychological laws. We have already shown, in our discussion of dynamic tone qualities, that the psychological theories of aural perception do not fit the facts of musical experience. The second way of justifying intersubjective validity is to regard it as a matter of "convention," in the broadest sense. Thus, validity that is based upon neither logical necessity nor empirical observation is simply a matter of "convention"—that is, is based upon a consensus of habit or usage. Verbal languages especially lend themselves to this sort of "conventional" explanation. Apart from a few exceptional cases, there is little or no link between the word and the thing signified. From this point of view, what turns a mere sound into a carrier of sense is something purely accidental or arbitrary; hence different languages have different words for the same things and also (often enough) employ the same word for different things. There is no trace of objective validity, yet the claim to validity can be no problem. And the validity is coextensive with the convention. We may be born into a linguistic community or join it voluntarily, or we may deny the validity and thus exclude ourselves from the language. Now, all this appears to apply equally well to the language of music. The meanings of tones, just like those of words, can be correctly understood only within a definitely circumscribed community. The music of other communities is as unintelligible to us as an unknown language, mere sounds where others hear meaning. Musical language can be learned, its meanings appropriated through usage, or its claim to validity can be rejected: we can exclude ourselves from its music. There definitely is some excuse, therefore, for extending the "conventional" theory of language to music.

However, in one crucial respect the parallel is misleading. Sounds become words by being arbitrarily associated with things; sounds become musical tones by being audibly related to other tones. Here convention simply does not come into the picture. Convention merely creates arbitrary links, whereas tonal relations develop out of themselves, out of inner necessity, the particular necessity that governs the elements of a particular tonal system. There is nothing accidental or arbitrary about this; nothing can be otherwise than it is. A word can change its meaning from one day to the next, but no power in the world can alter the fact that the tone $\hat{2}$ in the diatonic system is audibly oriented to $\hat{1}$, and that precisely this is the sense it makes. This is what makes learning languages so different from learning music. Learning languages is a matter of familiarizing oneself with the sounds designating things, is to acquire a kind of knowledge that can be codified in a dictionary. But who can conceive of a dictionary of tones? To learn the language of tones is to exercise and train one's sense of hearing. You close your eyes and open your ears, letting the patterns of sounds gradually reveal their inherent sense. What is revealed in this way is not convention: it is nature, with all the validity of a natural phenomenon.

Clearly, to view musical language as comparable to verbal languages raises more problems than it solves. Music confronts us with a claim to validity at once unassailable and yet dependent neither on logical proof nor on experimental verification, nor indeed on convention. If in view of these facts we still insist on the alternative of objective and subjective—including intersubjective—validity, we preserve a way of thinking and make understanding impossible. Understanding the phenomena in question must begin with the realization that this alternative does not apply here. Although statements about music are not objectively valid, although they are in principle unprovable, they do not cease to be true or untrue. In this case, although the traditional criteria of verification do not apply, the distinction between true and false is not meaningless. A theory of music which, alleging scientific humility, confines itself to the surface of the objectively verifiable and surrenders everything beneath the surface to the arbitrariness of convention or personal taste has been overhasty in its capitulation. But a theory of music which attempts to *prove* its aesthetic judgments is just as mistaken. We must realize that it *is* possible to make valid statements about music even where it is impossible in principle to prove or disprove them. That our thinking is here subject to special conditions is obvious. Contrary to current opinion, thinking on these matters has to be more, not less, rigorous than empirical or logical thinking, which, so to speak, relieves the thinker of personal responsibility for his decisions. Thinking here becomes a perilous venture: with every assertion he makes the thinker takes a leap into the unknown. No matter how convinced he may be of the truth of his assertions, he can never prove—not even to himself—that truth is on his side.

Now, we find it natural enough when a religion claims that its unprovable dogmas are true, for they refer to supernatural experiences, inaccessible to unbelievers. Musical experiences, however, are sensory; they presuppose no particular faith, illumination, or dogma; they are merely experiences of the normal human ear. That statements about sensory experiences should not be verifiable objectively by means of sensory experiences seems inadmissible. How could an unverifiable sensory experience be anything but some sort of hallucination or delusion? Yet everyone knows that musical experiences are not delusions. I do not imagine dynamic qualities of tone; I actually hear them in a text. This text is the music. Only because I hear what I hear and only when statements about dynamic tone qualities are recognized as valid, only then does a text exist. A text can be understood or misunderstood. And because I understand or misunderstand I am justified in my claim to validity vis-à-vis the critic who maintains there is nothing to be understood, there is no text, there are only bare facts. Now, the claim to objective validity is based on the certainty that others must observe or think the same as oneself, whereas statements about music will point out that they make understanding possible where without them there would be nothing to be understood. The criterion is not how many understand—this would be universal validity—but how much there is to be understood. Here the truth is measured by the enlargement of the additional areas it makes accessible to the understanding, by the increment of text.

This may be clarified as follows:

Suppose I am playing a radio for four listeners. A voice speaks on the set. I note expressions of puzzlement on the faces of the four listeners. So I try to explain. I take the set apart, naming the functions of the individual parts, and I demonstrate how an electrical vibration produced by a sound from a distant source is retransformed into a sound here and now. One of my listeners gets up and walks out. He has understood. The puzzlement of the others has not, however, been cleared up. So I go on trying to explain. I go into wave theory, frequencies, electromagnetic fields, and I explain their mathematical foundations. Now a second listener gets up satisfied, and goes out. But the two other listeners remain, obviously as puzzled as they were before. The question in their minds is: What was that voice *saying* in that foreign language? So now I go into the meaning of the individual words and explain the grammar and syntax involved. I translate for them, finally, word for word. At this point another listener gets up and goes out. But there is still the fourth listener. What can be bothering him? Well, as it happens, the sentence I translated was, "Time is the moving image of eternity." I discuss the meaning of these words with my remaining listener.

The attitudes of my four listeners illustrate four different senses in which we may say we "understand" something. The first two listeners "understood" in the sense of exact observation: science and mathematics. The other two "understood" in interpretative senses: the first in the ordinary sense conveyed when we say we "understand" a language, the second in the more complex sense involved in exploration of profound matters.

Now, to get back to Schenker's theory. In the light of the foregoing it must be clear that the undemonstrability of his propositions and the unverifiability of his deductions really have no bearing on their truth. Quite to the contrary: had it been possible to show that they are objectively valid, this would prove that his theory does not refer to what is most crucial and most specific in musical experience. Although the deeper layers (middleground and background) cannot be logically deduced from a given foreground, and although the deeper layers do not permit any verifiable prediction concerning the actual course of events in the foreground—in other words, although the possibility of distinguishing objectively between true and false is entirely ruled out—the theory's claim to be true or false, its claim to cognitive value, is fully upheld. It cannot be ignored, however, that the validity of its statements about the deeper layers is less firmly established than that of statements about dynamic tone qualities. In both cases we are dealing with interpretation: elementary—as it were, literal—interpretation where dynamic qualities are distinguished, and interpretation in a higher sense where deep structure is analyzed. In neither case is a given sensory material interpreted merely by the intellect: the ear functions as organ of interpretation in both—without assistance from the intellect in distinguishing dynamic qualities, and in conjunction with the intellect, though still in a leading position, in analyzing structural layers. But whereas to doubt the elementary interpretations would be to doubt the very existence of music, the same is by no means true of Schenker's structural layers. The latter rather share the fate of all higher forms of textual interpretation: namely, it is never possible to assert that one single interpretation is the ultimate or the only valid one; other interpretations, even mutually exclusive ones, remain possible in principle, nor can one always prove a given interpretation false. All this is the more applicable to Schenker's interpretations because, as we have said, they are mainly supplied by the ear, the intellect acting only in an auxiliary capacity. The point, however, is that the cognitive value of the theory is in no way impaired by the fact that each and every interpretation can be questioned, and another entirely different one suggested. If Schenker's theory is truly a theory of music, its individual results, as instanced by his diagrams, are nothing more or less than logically unprovable auditory inferences from objectively unverifiable auditory experiences.

This is certainly not to imply that the theory's claim to validity rests on the fact that its propositions are inherently unprovable and can always be challenged. As mentioned above, the truth of this kind of statements about music is measured by the amount of text they make available to interpretation. And this requirement Schenker's theory meets as fully as one could ask. Prior to Schenker, an investigation of music aiming at true judgments could deal only with surface aspects; anything beyond these was declared the domain of taste and feeling or magic and mystery, a vast no-man's-land inaccessible to the strict operations of reason. It is Schenker's abiding achievement to have reclaimed this territory for the mind. By his analyses he has demonstrated that the inmost core, the essence, of music, that which makes music more than mere sound, can be an object of thought and understanding. He has taken the miracles of the deeper layers—heretofore the murky playground of taste and feeling—and placed them under the keen light of the searching mind. Gone is the ignominious indifference (resulting from a misguided subservience to the criteria of science) that made the application of true-false judgments to the essence of music impossible, thereby denying that qualitative differences can be there, rooted in this essence. Schenker's theory has relieved us of our despair at the limitations of knowledge, a despair caused not by our inability to prove to the many who prefer *The Merry Widow* to *The Magic Flute* that they are wrong, but by the view that there can be no argument and that it makes no sense to speak of error since both sides of the controversy are equally valid, a despair caused not by the possibility that our judgments may be wrong, but by the claim that it is utterly impossible ever to be really wrong. In the last analysis, we have been liberated from the shackles of traditional musical theory not so much by Schenker's particular insights, but by his convincing demonstration that knowledge of the inner core of music is possible, that where serious matters of musical judgment are concerned we can be right and we can be wrong.

Does Schenker's theory supply us with an objective criterion by which we can measure artistic value? By this time I hope it has become clear how misleading this question is when so formulated. No truly objective criterion can be applied to any essential element of music as such: no authentic criterion of artistic rank can be objective. Schenker's structural diagrams can serve as such criteria precisely because they are valid without being objective.

Since Schenker was no philosopher, he never explicitly addressed himself to the problem of artistic value. He did not bother to analyze works he felt to be inferior because he knew that there was nothing to discover in their structure. However, his bold claims will not be readily granted unless we use his criteria and discover how they enable us to distinguish the merely fabricated from the organically developed, the spurious from the genuine.

That traditional musical theory is totally unable to account for the artistic rank of a work has never been more impressively demonstrated than in *The Power of Sound,* by Edmund Gurney; published in 1880, this book is still well worth reading. In a chapter on melodic forms, the author groups in pairs melodies which exhibit superficial similarities. Always he contrasts the work of a master with some popular hit or other musical commonplace. Gurney is frank to admit that although he is himself fully conversant with musical theory, he really cannot say anything of the one melody or tune that he cannot say of the other. Theory can make clear only what the two members of each pair have in common. He does not mention this in any spirit of skepticism: it does not even occur to him that the existence of differences in aesthetic rank can be questioned; he hears them just as clearly, they are just as real to him, as differences in pitch. His statement expresses the despair at the apparent inability of our knowledge to keep pace with our hearing.

Fortunately, Schenker has changed all that. His analyses in depth show clearly what the two members of each pair have *not* in common.

Below we attempt to illustrate his method, taking as our example one of Gurney's pairs, in which the melody of Schubert's "Forelle" is contrasted with something called "Kemo Kimo." Gurney's choice appears to have been dictated by the fact that both members of the pair exhibit the same contour line at the beginning  in conjunction with repeated returns to the opening tone g. (To facilitate comparison both melodies are here given in the key of C major.)

At first glance the melody of "Die Forelle" seems to be so simple in structure, its meaning so easy to grasp, as to make all comment superfluous. What could be said about it that the melody itself does not say in the language of tones? What traditional theory has to say—that the melody is composed within a narrow range of scale progressions and harmonic cadence, that in the middle section it modulates to the dominant and forthwith returns to the tonic—is completely trivial: the same is true of countless melodies, good and bad. Only the slight deviation from the metric scheme of the eight-measure period—the melody runs for 8 + 8 + 4 measures—might strike us as a peculiarity, but this too can be easily accounted for as conventional repetition of the last half-period. Where, then, is the special character of this melody to be found?

On the smooth surface of this foreground careful listening gains a first hold, discovers a first clue in the third measure. Why do we have here [♪ notation] rather than [♪ notation]? This would be so much more natural considering the melodic parallel [♪ notation] and the words of the text:

da schoss

(there shot)

Why is the motion arrested for two half-measures by the repetition of the tone g [♪ notation]? Obviously, the purpose here is to keep the listener in suspense and subtly direct his attention to the importance of the next step. The next step is precisely the delayed [♪ notation]. In this way the tone d, singled out by having been delayed and shifted to the weak part of the measure, is at once related to the previous highest tone e, which also occurs on the weak beat: a beginning $\hat{3}$-$\hat{2}$ progression in a deeper structural layer has become audible. But this progression is not completed; instead of continuing to $\hat{1}$, it rapidly slides down to $\hat{5}$ [♪ notation] (c is here an unstressed passing tone, dissonant against the harmony of the dominant chord). $\hat{1}$ in the fifth measure is heard as a repetition of the beginning, not as the conclusion of the preceding $\hat{3}$-$\hat{2}$. The repetition leads back to the highest tone e, $\hat{3}$; but this time the expected continuation leading to $\hat{2}$ is omitted: there is no preparatory arrest of the motion at the tone g, no leap from g to d. The tone $\hat{3}$ remains unresolved, hanging in the air, so to speak, and the entire rest of the melody hangs on the thread of this unresolved tone.

There follows the motif [♪ notation], which paraphrases the motion of the fourth [♪ notation], echoing the motion of the fifth [♪ notation] of measures 3–4, which it does *not* repeat. At the same time the dynamic center has been shifted from c to g, so that the last tone g of the motion of the fourth is heard as $\hat{1}$.

Here the first partial phrase comes to an end. What happens next is disclosed in the diagram of the deeper layers.

With the unresolved highest tone $\hat{3}$ left behind, the melody first repeats the motion of the fourth ![music] in an expanded version, but now, after the original center has been restored, this motion has a different dynamic meaning. (The shift of the center cannot be read from the melody alone; it is the harmony that caused the shift with ![music] [measures 6–7] and then canceled it with ![music] [measures 9–10].) Not until the last tone of the motion of the fourth, g, which now has recovered its original dynamic quality $\hat{5}$, has been reached (measure 14) does the melody remember its unfulfilled obligation. For a while, as though accidentally, it hangs on to the tone g ![music]; the link with measures 2–3 is established, and so at last, as if nothing else could be expected, there follows ![music], taking up the thrust of the tone e, which had been left behind but not forgotten, and the motion is concluded with d-c, $\hat{3}$-$\hat{2}$-$\hat{1}$. That the last four measures are more than a mere appendage, a conventional repetition of the last half-phrase, can also be read from the diagram. An inconspicuous change, which casual hearing perceives merely as an ornament, conceals the fact that these last four measures are a condensation, in terms of both duration and form, of the entire second part of the melody.

A similar, barely noticeable detail, which shows how the deeper structural layers account for even seemingly accidental melodic turns in the foreground, is found in measures 11–12. ![music] seems at first nothing but a variation of measures 9–10 ![music]

—intended, as we can often read, "to avoid monotony." The diagram shows that there is more to it than that. Whereas measures 9–10 serve to retrieve the opening note c of the motion of the fourth, measures 11–12 are part of this motion. This is why the upbeat before measure 11 does not lead up, as it does to measure 9 ♪♩, but down ♩♪! This in turn leads two measures later to ♩♪. We may also mention that apart from all this ♩♪ makes it possible, as though accidentally, to continue the motion with ♪♩ —after ♪♩, in terms of motion ♩ would be awkward—and in this way we are reminded as discreetly as possible of the existence of a higher position where something still has to be resolved.

Clearly, the "simple" melody of "Die Forelle" is by no means simple in structure. Within the narrow span of twenty measures, it narrates a quite complex little story of tension and conflicts, expanded and condensed passages, and surprises. What a very different picture is presented by the deeper layers of the second member of the pair:

After $\hat{1}$ and $\hat{5}$ have been declared, $\hat{3}$ is reached by an ascending motion and is immediately led back via $\hat{2}$ to $\hat{1}$; as a result of the melodic turn ♩♪♪♩♪ in measures 4–5, the tone c in measure 5 is heard as a new start, in addition to being the conclusion of what preceded it. The first four measures are repeated literally; the partial phrase concludes with $\hat{3}$-$\hat{1}$ in measure 8: we have come to an end before anything has happened. There follows, without preparation or preannouncement, the highest tone $\hat{5}$, reached via $\hat{3}$, and once again we are smoothly led back from $\hat{5}$, via $\hat{4}$, $\hat{3}$, $\hat{2}$, to $\hat{1}$, and then the beginning is repeated: ascent to $\hat{3}$, breaking off with $\hat{3}$-$\hat{1}$. And that is all.

It is music, no doubt; it is melody. Dynamic tone qualities are present, as well as audibly related tones, tonal motion, and hence also a background, a structure in depth. But it says nothing, does nothing; the "depth" is a shoal. As musical expression of idiocy, it even has distinctive merits. What accounts for the melody's weakness is not the simplicity of its background—even the finest folk songs have simple backgrounds—but its incoherence, its meaninglessness. Here one thing does not lead to another or follow from another; instead of being properly built up and properly resolved, tensions peter out ineffectually. Nothing happens; there is no real pattern. What we have is a string of tones tacked together. To recall once more how all this looks in a genuine folk song, we show, without further comment, an old tune whose background exhibits a similarly simple ascent to $\hat{5}$ and return to $\hat{1}$:

Gurney's pessimism about theory was unjustified. True theory can discover that the well-composed members of Gurney's pairs contain things which are absent from the poorly composed ones. Knowledge keeps pace with our sense of hearing, which permits no doubt concerning differences in artistic rank.

Below we present another pair of melodies, this time taken not from a theoretician's book but, curiously enough, from the records of a court of justice in Vienna. In the 1920s the composer of a successful hit was sued for plagiarism by a less lucky fellow composer. After the judge had listened to the two tunes, he rebuffed both plaintiff and defendant:

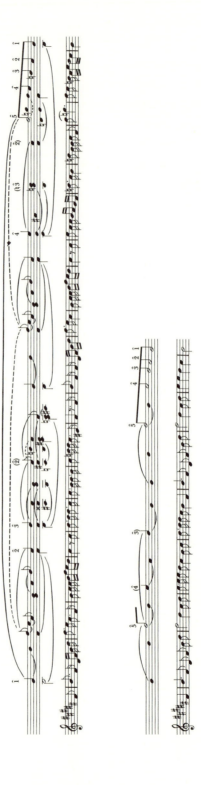

he saw at once—he may have practiced singing as an avocation—that both were plagiarists. The melodic turn that made the tune popular and was used by the two composers had been stolen from Schubert. On the facing page are the two melodies, each with the diagram of its substructure—the first that of Schubert's song "Die böse Farbe," and the second that of the hit.

We see how the impulse generated by the great gesture which opens Schubert's melody feeds and carries the melodic curve running through all the eighteen measures. The pause in the eighth measure has only surface value; it is bridged by the irresistible motion which from the outset aims at the event in measure 16, when the high tone f♯, as though inadvertently touched at the beginning, is at last legitimately reached. What happens on the way to it, and how the goal is reached, can be read from the diagram. The composer of the hit took over the opening gesture but did not know what to do with it—as if someone were swinging out his arm for a powerful blow and then suddenly changed his mind and walked away. In Schubert's melody the return to the beginning in the middle section marks a new effort to carry the movement to its end; in the hit it is merely repetition of a gesture already unmasked as meaningless.

As for other details of Schubert's melody, there is only this much to say: What makes the opening gesture [musical notation] so special is that the ascending motion $\hat{1}$-$\hat{3}$-$\hat{5}$ is carried out not in the usual way but like this: [musical notation]. The crucial point, however, is that here the motion did not aim at f♯, $\hat{5}$, but at e, $\hat{4}$! The piano explicitly stresses the step d♯-e, $\hat{3}$-$\hat{4}$, not d♯-f♯, $\hat{3}$-$\hat{5}$. The original impulse carries the motion beyond its goal; f♯ is "too high" and is to be understood as a suspension, delaying the actually intended tone e. And yet the step has been made and cannot be taken back: f♯ has resounded and would not be robbed of its right; even though $\hat{5}$ was not really intended at the beginning, it pulls the entire melody to itself at the end. The "mistake" of the beginning becomes the truth of the end, and thereby of the whole.

That we are dealing here with a kind of conflict is also suggested by the fact that $\hat{5}$ is finally reached by main force, so to speak, by the unnatural expansion of the second eight-measure period to ten measures. Normally, that is to say, if the period had eight measures, the melody would end with measures 15–16—that is, precisely *before* the last ascent to $\hat{5}$—like this: ; also the stanza of the poem ends here. Instead of this we now have

, a last-minute victory, and as though because of overpressure, the motion is carried beyond its goal. As a result the full close is related to the half close in measures 7–8: there it was

; here it is . The part

played by the major-minor alternations in this story deserves at least to be mentioned.

(It might be asked why in this instance, where after a preparation of sixteen measures, the tension is resolved by $\hat{5}$-$\hat{4}$-$\hat{3}$-$\hat{2}$-$\hat{1}$ in one single measure, we do not speak of a "petering out." To ask such a question would be to display incomprehension. What matters is not whether the resolution takes more or less time, but what happens between tension and relaxation, and whether anything happens at all. Nor must it be forgotten that although the passage in question concludes the melody, it does not conclude the song. The diagram of the entire song would show that the invested force has been anything but spent at the end of the melody. A great deal still happens before the road from $\hat{5}$ to $\hat{1}$ has been definitively traveled!)

The few examples discussed above are intended to convey only a general idea of how differences in artistic rank can be read from Schenker's diagrams of deep structural layers. A comprehensive treatment of the problems involved lies beyond the scope of this book: as we have said, our main purpose is to elucidate the part played by the sense organ in the act of hearing music; to understand the nature of hearing we must know what we hear. All our references to theory serve only this purpose. After all, musical theory (perhaps any artistic theory), unlike scientific theory, does not seek to discover the order, the law governing the confused and often misleading data of sensory perception; its task is not, as it was classically formulated, "to save the phenomena." In music, especially, we do not need theoretical thinking to discover the law governing its manifestations; the ear takes care of this. The task of theory, then, is to transform the implicit certainty of perception into explicit, communicable knowledge, to raise thinking to the level of hearing. This is why, in matters of artistic rank, the diagrams of structural layers cannot serve as criteria enabling us to decide doubtful cases, in which no decision could be reached on the basis of direct perception. Rather, the diagrams prove helpful only after everything has been decided, decided by hearing alone, and there is nothing left to doubt. What the diagrams can tell us is not whether the decision made by hearing is justified or correct, but how such a decision is possible, what must the nature of hearing be in order to be capable of such decisions. If artistic rank cannot be found anywhere but in the organic order characteristic of musical patterns, it follows necessarily that a kind of hearing able to distinguish rank must also be able to apprehend this order unaided. Anyone who has gained insight into the substructure of tonal events cannot help feeling that there is something amazing, something miraculous, about this ability: that where such events are understood and their meaning is grasped, a highly developed intelligence is at work. The musical ear, both a sensory and an intellectual organ, is equally proficient in both these functions. It might be objected that not everyone hears in this way, that quite obviously most people do *not* hear in this way, for otherwise most people would not prefer inferior products to genuine works of art. Such an objection is groundless. Differences in rank must not be confused with differences in taste. Failure to distinguish between these two largely accounts for the sterility of modern aesthetics. It is not enjoyment that determines what is or is not heard; rather, it is hearing that determines what is or is not enjoyed. A person whose ear is incapable of apprehending complex organic structures cannot possibly enjoy musical masterpieces and would prefer works that make lesser demands on hearing. The fact that great music does not appeal to most people, while inferior works draw crowds, bears witness to the reality of differences in rank just as clearly as does the fact that only a minority—which is not as small as one might think—prefer great music. And the few can enjoy great music only because they understand it by hearing it, i.e., grasp the meaning of what they hear, for otherwise there is nothing that can be enjoyed. Precisely because musical hearing is not mere recording of signals, reacting to environmental stimuli, but living, understanding, interpretative sharing in a living motion, because it involves the whole man, there must be as many ways of hearing a piece of music as there are listeners. Each hears what he is. And this is why the nature of human hearing cannot be discovered by questioning individual listeners, but only by studying its greatest creation, music.

MUSICAL THOUGHT

Introductory

"WASSERFLUT," the sixth song in Schubert's *Winterreise* cycle, is an exemplary model of a concise, self-contained musical pattern. Carried by one impulse, sustained by a single breath, its melody swings in a double arc from the beginning through the caesura and a new beginning in the middle to its inexorable conclusion. Its drive, germinated by the first melodic cell, leads the motion toward the predetermined goal, the final phrase, which is as unexpected as it is convincing and crowns and sums up all that has gone before.

However, a glance at Schubert's manuscript provides a surprise. As might be expected, it looks as if it had been written without hesitation, but the melody originally had a different ending! The very part the composer seems to have had in mind from the first simply did not exist. Traces of the erasure can still be made out: the perfect ending familiar to us came to the composer as an afterthought.

The wonder we feel at such a discovery could and should be of the kind which, according to Aristotle, inspired men to philosophize. For surely the change was not prompted by the composer's "critical intellect," was not due to his decision to "revise" the original "idea": in other words, we are not dealing with a normal, ordinary instance of collaboration between inspiration and reflection. The step from the first to the final version of the melody's conclusion—a step in which the meaning of the pattern he has already created is revealed to him, and which no critical intellect, no reflection could ever have suggested—is, rather, a paradigm of the creative act and, in this sense, an *act of thought.*

The third part of this book is intended to demonstrate that this assertion fits the facts of musical experience. And if we succeed, we shall be obliged by the musical evidence to revise a number of ideas concerning the nature of thought and thinking, just as we were earlier obliged to revise current notions concerning the nature of hearing and of the listener.

xiv. What Is the Nature of Thinking?

AT FIRST GLANCE it might seem that music is the last context in which to look for something basic, let alone new, on this topic. The musical work of art is looked upon primarily as the product of the imagination, of the faculties of feeling and expressing feeling, rather than that of thought. It is well known that every composer must study and master the theory of music, and we assume that every musical work contains an intellectual ingredient: we do not suppose that no such thing as reflection has entered into it at all. At the same time we assume—I think rightly—that in the process of creating a musical work the intellect serves in subordinate capacities, as in outlining an overall plan or framework to be filled in. The twelve-tone music of our century, for all its emphasis upon the constructive elements, has not really altered this relationship. Schönberg assures us that he never wrote a single note that was not dictated, justified by the requirements of "expression," and Alban Berg himself considered it a measure of success of *Wozzeck* that the extraordinary amount of construction is not noticed in hearing the opera. On what grounds, then, can we expect that music, of all things, will provide special insight into the nature of thought?

A similar question arose in connection with our discussion of the specifically musical experience of space.[1] Here, too, it hardly seemed likely that music, the least "spatial" of the arts, could ever supply new

---

1. Cf. *Sound and Symbol: Music and the External World.*

insight into the nature of space. But such skepticism turned out to be unjustified. It was based on the assumption that what is currently known of space is all that there is to space. So far as geometric space is concerned, the assumption works well enough, and music has indeed very little to do with it. It would appear that skepticism concerning the role of thinking in music springs from a similar prejudice, namely, that the nature of thought has been defined once and for all by logicians. And again: at best, logic enters into music rather minimally.

Still, these two preconceptions—as to the nonspatial and the non-intellectual character of music—are very different in one essential respect. The opinion that geometry deals with space pure and simple or that space is essentially identical with geometric space can plead that its validity stands largely uncontested. Not so the opinion that all thought is logical, that thought is identical with the definitions of logic. Although Kant said men could think only logically, only in concepts, and that any other kind of thought was beyond the range of the human intellect, he nevertheless admitted that some "superhuman" being might be capable of "intellectual intuition," that is, a kind of thought not subject to the laws of logic (which would nonetheless be *thought*). Goethe, a reflective artist if there ever was one, rebelled against the limits Kant set, and asserted emphatically that man, too—or at least one man (himself)—may be capable of a kind of thinking that is not tied to concepts, to the laws of logic. It has often been claimed (not only in modern times) that artists, especially poets, think in images rather than concepts, that their works are governed by an intuitive, visionary species of thought, that there is such a thing as a poetic logic, a logic of the imagination, though admittedly the proponents of such views most often contented themselves with the mere assertion, without making clear precisely to what they were referring. Anthropologists, too, have been led to assume the existence of a kind of thought different from the logical-conceptual kind. Mythical thought, the mentality of so-called primitive peoples, was at first defined as "prelogical"—that is, as existing at a stage historically precedent to "true" thought or thinking—but has eventually come to be regarded as a thinking *sui generis* involving processes remote from abstract conceptual thought. To be sure, logicians still insist that one can speak of a non- or extralogical thought only in a superficial, metaphorical sense, but their views have been challenged by one philosopher with some qualifications to speak on this matter: "If only we were not deceived by logic, and ceased to maintain stubbornly that we have long since known what thought is." In the same work by Heidegger (*Was heisst Denken?*) we find another telling phrase: "Science does not think." So what are we to make of our knowledge of thought when a leading thinker maintains that the very domain in which we usually look for essential information concerning the nature of thought is actually devoid of thought? And indeed it seems there is hardly anything we know less about—in any exact or comprehensive sense—than just this matter of thought or thinking. This being the case, we are entitled to set aside all preconceptions (including skepticism about the role of thinking in music) and find out for ourselves whether there is anything to learn about the nature of thought, this time addressing ourselves not to science—least of all mathematical science—but to another creation of the human mind, music.

Since the path we propose to follow will be somewhat laborious and some matters will have to be treated in detail, it may be well to indicate the main articulations of our argument. Our point of departure is the supposedly unassailable position of those who believe that the nature of thought is what logic says it is. Let us assume this to be the case. It follows, then, that no musical work can be begotten by thought. Does thought play any part at all in the creative process? The answer to this question is in the affirmative: thought does play a part, but one that must be regarded (still on the assumption that we know what thinking is) as secondary, the main impetus coming from some other creative source. We proceed to confront this hypothesis of two creative sources with the actual facts, drawing examples from musical masterpieces. They will oblige us to conclude that the hypothesis does not fit them and that the assumptions leading to the hypothesis of two creative sources are false. To account adequately for the facts, we must assume a single creative source. We are inevitably led to identify the nature of this single creative source of music as "thought," and to conclude that the term here denotes something entirely different from what we assumed at first. The belief referred to above—that the nature of thought is defined by logic alone—proves untenable. Thinking is *not* synonymous with logical thinking. The above discussion will bring us to the end of chapter 16, and in the remaining chapters we will attempt to define more closely the nature and laws of this other—musical—kind of thought.

xv. The Two Creative Sources

Music is the only one of the arts which is officially, so to speak, based upon theory. Unlike the aspiring painter or poet, the composer must begin by familiarizing himself thoroughly with the theory of his art. To be sure, what is called musical theory actually amounts to practice in manipulating the materials of music, yet it is significant that this practice is called "theory": theory, after all, has something to do with thought. Although the student of theory is primarily supposed to be learning a skill, he will not achieve skill before he has acquired a considerable amount of knowledge. This is the reverse of the actual practice of any other art: there knowledge follows skill. Nor is the student of music given the works themselves to practice on—at least, that is, in so far as the two traditional disciplines are concerned, counterpoint and harmony, which even today are most often the core of the teaching. The student is given, rather, highly artificial examples of musical theory. The problems which are set him to solve are a sort of music in the abstract. It is well known that no special musical talent is required to achieve considerable proficiency in these disciplines; indeed, with adequate training a deaf-mute could solve most of the problems. The fact that he is operating with tones is by no means essential; he might operate just as well with dots placed at set intervals: strictly speaking, he addresses himself to topological, not musical, problems. This is why, as has recently been discovered, electronic computers do not do so badly when given tests in musical theory. Here we are not criticizing musical theory in any sense, merely describing the situation the composer faces when he starts out; we are, rather, pointing out the considerable extent to which the musician's skill is based on knowledge, on the kind of skill the ancient Greeks called *technē*—as in the expression *technēn epistasthai*, "to have thorough knowledge of a skill."

As for composition proper, the study of which comes after theory has been mastered, its very terminology is revealing. The student is taught musical imitation, counterpoint, fugues, harmonization, variations, development—terms which denote methods of treating something already given. What is to be treated in these various ways is a "theme." When musical theory presupposes the theme as something given (or borrowed), it acknowledges that the source of the theme lies outside the part of music that can be taught or learned: knowledge and skill. A musical theme, however, unlike the theme of a realistic or naturalistic painting, has no external counterpart: it is itself music. This is why the musical work appears to be derived from two very different sources, one of which, technical knowledge, lies within the domain of thought, whereas the other seems to be spontaneous, something that might be called inspiration or genius. How to treat a theme, what can be done with it, is learnable, teachable, but not how to compose a theme; the explanation for this is that a theme is not made, but is simply found—it "occurs to one," all at once. How could something like this:

exist save as a "gift," the product of some force outside time, springing into being all at once, not bit by bit? This explanation involves a paradox, however. After all, a theme *is* a succession of notes that take time to write down or play. In the light of the foregoing, we would have to conclude that the creation of a musical work presupposes two things, thought and inspiration, and that both are indispensable if a musical work deserving the name of art is to be produced. The assertion that it has two sources implies a value judgment: the crucial contribution, what really determines the work's artistic quality, comes from a source at once unteachable and unlearnable—from inspiration. However indispensable, thought in the last analysis plays a subordinate part.

One good argument against this view might be to cite some especially sublime work, seemingly sheer inspiration and nothing else, into whose making neither teachable and learnable knowledge nor musical skill seems to have entered. Take, for instance, the Andante of Bach's A-minor Sonata for Unaccompanied Violin:

which is nothing but a single melody continually renewed, with scarcely any reference to what has gone before. The melody describes an ever broader curve, equally inspired in ascending or descending (never collapsing) passages without any sense of "necessary" development. At any point the melody could have taken a different turn; it seems to flow from some pure and inexhaustible source, sounding at once as free, as right, as convincing, as it is unpredictable. Arrest the melody at any point and ask yourself, utilizing all your knowledge, skill, and experience of music, to figure out how it should go on: you will not get far. The music is utterly unique, so much one-of-a-kind that no general rule, no experience of other music, will be of the slightest help to you in trying to find the next step. Of course, no ignoramus is ever granted such inspiration. It presupposes mastery of the highest order. Every step is infused by a knowledge and skill so deeply assimilated that they can be forgotten to let the other source flow unimpeded. A lesser man would have to give up after the first steps.

There is, then, such a thing as music that is all theme and nothing but. Is the converse also true? Is there such a thing as music that is nothing but "elaboration," music without a theme? One's first inclination is to say no. What would there be to elaborate were there no theme in the first place? And just where would inspiration step in? Music without a theme, one must suppose, would be a purely contrived music, some sort of exercise at best, not art. However, only those whose experience of music is confined to that of the eighteenth and nineteenth centuries could plausibly take this attitude. What we refer to as the theme—i.e., an expressive, self-contained tonal pattern capable of conveying a meaning, without reference to anything else—is a very recent (not necessarily very lasting) accomplishment in Western music. It did not make its appearance until the seventeenth century, in connection with the development of purely instrumental music, and in the music of our own century it seems to be disappearing. The whole of the great polyphonic epoch, from the fourteenth to the seventeenth century, is, in this sense, music without a theme; our familiar distinction between theme and elaboration is quite pointless where this music is concerned. Listen to some really long work of that period like William Byrd's *Great Service*, which takes nearly a whole hour: it is one powerful, irresistible, uniform flow of song, in the entire course of which no sharply outlined detail, nothing we might call a theme, ever emerges. Or take Palestrina's four-part motet *Super flumina Babilonis*. This is music as moving and beautiful as it is possible to find, but what does it contain in the way of thematic material? One short melodic phrase dominates each of the five parts into which the work is divided, like the psalm on which it is based. (See facing page.)

Considered in themselves these are trivial arrangements of tones which very nearly border on the amorphous. It would occur to no one to call them "themes" in our sense, not even to remark on their probable source in "inspiration." No one need await some specially privileged moment to produce something like this; all you have to do is to write it down, as anyone can do who listens attentively to the words, repeating

Su - per flu - mi - na Ba - - - bi - lo - nis
il - lic se - di - mus et fle - - - vi - mus,
dum re - cor - da - re - mur tu - i, Si - on:
in sa - li - ci - bus in me - di - o e - jus
sus - pen - di - mus or - gan - a no - - - stra.

(By the rivers of Babylon
there we sat down, yea, we wept
when we remembered Zion.
We hanged our harps upon
the willows in the midst thereof.)

them to himself with understanding, finding appropriate pitches and rhythms for them. Palestrina's melody seems to be little more than a saying of the words in tones. Only the third phrase with its two ascending fourths ![notation] rises somewhat above the level of simple stepwise motion, in keeping with the words, which at this point make the listener's heart beat just a little faster, "when we remembered Zion." But even if something like a "theme" appears here, no notion of inspiration has to be evoked to account for it. To be sure, many themes of classical instrumental works, too, look at first sight rather ordinary, not especially significant, but what is done with these themes or made out of them in the course of the work is all that matters, gradually disclosing all sorts of hidden strengths and meanings hardly to be suspected at the theme's first appearance. In Palestrina anything we might call a theme remains at the end just what it was at the beginning, a mere vehicle. The actual musical goings on are transpiring on another plane entirely—where the threads are woven, where the texture unfolds. The extraordinary, the unique character of the work, the creator's genius, and the inspired nature of his creation have to be looked for in the "treatment," in what is done with or made out of the given; the skill itself must be inspired. Not without reason was Palestrina celebrated after his death as the great cognoscente. Faced with such musical evidence, not just our distinction between theme and elaboration but all sense of a neat line to be drawn between two separate creative sources—theme as the work of inspiration, elaboration as the work of intellect—suddenly seems terribly naïve.

It will perhaps be argued that nonthematic music belongs to an earlier stage in the history of music, before musical sound had been emancipated from the word; that so long as music was composed to words, the latter performed the work of telling us what the tones mean, and that only at a later stage of musical history, in purely instrumental music, the musical theme itself takes over this labor and begins to be expressive of its subject on its own. Accordingly, the breakdown into theme and treatment and the corresponding distinction between inspiration and technique would mark the highest stage of musical development. After all, as mentioned before, the "theme" in our sense does not make its appearance until the advent of purely instrumental music. On closer examination, however, we find that even purely instrumental music is not necessarily bound up with a theme; there are many instrumental works in which a theme plays only a minimal part or even no part at all, and this is certainly not felt as a deficiency, let alone a deficiency of inspiration. These works, too, like those mentioned above, which seem to consist of nothing but "inspiration" are the glory of the greatest masters: extremes meet. At any rate, nonthematic music is in principle possible. Can the assertion that music has two sources, inspiration and intellect, be reconciled with such a possibility? How are we to understand the fact that there exist musical works of the highest artistic quality which the intellect cannot create unaided, yet no part of which can be attributed to so-called inspiration?

These and related questions can be dealt with sensibly only through careful analyses of musical masterpieces. To follow such analyses may impose a certain effort on the reader; however, no technical knowledge or thorough familiarity with the works is presupposed on his part (such as would enable him to hear mentally what he sees in the score). Since music is here treated primarily as a phenomenon of motion, technical terms can be largely dispensed with; a glance at the score, viewed as the visible record of audible motion, should give a sufficiently clear idea of the matter in hand.

There is no such thing as a clear-cut, black-and-white distinction to be drawn, to tell us in every case whether we are dealing with a theme or not. There are many transitional forms. In most cases, however, a theme is instantly recognizable as such, namely, as an expressive tonal pattern, meaningful in itself, as part of a whole yet itself with all the characteristic features of a whole—an organic whole, something more than just a bit of raw material. Think of Bach's fugues. After all, by definition a fugue is a specific way of treating a theme, and the theme is always presented perfectly plainly at the beginning in a single voice. The preludes to Bach's fugues are something else again. The very great freedom of treatment that prepares us for the "real thing," for the fugue which follows, leaves us uncertain as to what the preludes are actually about—indeed, whether they are about anything at all. A few preludes from *The Well-Tempered Clavier* will illustrate the transition from the presence to the absence of a theme.

PRELUDE IN G♯ MINOR (BOOK I)

This prelude opens with a series of notes, which, for all its brevity and unassuming character, is sufficiently original and expressive to be at once recognizable as a genuine "inspiration," as constituting a "theme": . Its originality and, one

might say, spontaneity are disclosed in the way the three opening
conjunct notes, 𝅘𝅥𝅯, are immediately followed by a succession
of thirds, 𝅘𝅥𝅯. The motion has overshot its mark, the tone
𝅘𝅥, 3̂, and so comes back to it by way of a leisurely descent,
𝅘𝅥𝅯. (Compare this theme with the conventional form,
𝅘𝅥𝅯.) From this point on, the theme is
treated in accordance with the rules of the art: the theme dominates
the whole piece; there is not a single measure in which it is not present
in one form or another. After its first appearance in the treble, it is
repeated by the bass in the second measure; the next two measures, in
the course of which the center is shifted from g♯ to b, work with
elements of the theme, 𝅘𝅥𝅯 and 𝅘𝅥𝅯. Then the theme
is stated in B major, 𝅘𝅥𝅯. Two measures later
it is so transformed that it can shift the center by itself, this time from
b to f♯: 𝄢 𝅘𝅥𝅯. When it reappears in the next
measure, the tone with which it begins is not 1̂ (as it was previously)
but 5̂. In the next measure but one (only the new elements are mentioned here) the theme, its motion reversed, seems to be standing upside
down: 𝄞 𝅘𝅥𝅯. And so it goes, on and on. A final
transformation is reserved till the end: 𝄢 𝅘𝅥𝅯
with its reverse 𝄞 𝅘𝅥𝅯. (Those who have
some knowledge of harmony will notice how this last form reproduces
the sound pattern of the conventional cadence, 𝄞 𝅘𝅥𝅯.)

　　In this prelude, then, the distinction between "theme" and "elaboration" can be easily perceived, and the hypothesis that music has two
sources—the theme originating in inspiration, and the elaboration in
expert knowledge—seems to tally with the evidence at hand.

PRELUDE IN C MAJOR (BOOK I)

This prelude presents a rather different picture. What theme is there to speak of here? The ear catches no clearly delimited pattern suggestive of one. What we are given is a lengthy succession of uniformly broken chords; at the end the chords are scattered up and down. Considering that until the middle section the harmonic progression remains entirely within the going musical conventions, one wonders what accounts for the unmistakable originality of the piece, for its peculiarly spellbinding quality. Listening more closely, we discover that it is accounted for by the special profile of the broken chords, the two upward thrusts and the sudden halt of the thrust on the top note, . Look at a more conventional such profile, , and the spell is gone. At the last moment, Bach's profile wishes, as it were, to recall the highest tone and make it re-echo in the ear; it leaves the chord behind, reaches out to the highest tone of the next chord, and the series of these highest notes hovers above the whole, as a hidden melodic line. Can the figure of the broken chords be called a theme? Certainly not, for its pattern changes, the intervals differ in each successive chord, and the phrase both contracts and expands—at the climax it stretches over two octaves; only the outline—the profile —remains unchanged. And yet the figure can be called a real inspiration: it is one of a kind, the hallmark of this particular piece; it inspires it, in the literal sense, i.e., breathes life into it.

PRELUDE IN F MAJOR (BOOK II)

This prelude, one of the major pieces in the collection, illustrates the next transitional stage, as between thematic and nonthematic music. Here are the first four measures:

No matter how attentively we listen, we can discover nothing in these measures that could properly be called a theme, or ascribed to "inspiration." Are these measures, perhaps, merely introductory, a kind of prelude to the prelude, the actual subject only appearing later? No, all that is to come is prefigured in these opening notes. It is impossible to discern a hidden melody, even, as was possible in the C-major Prelude. Here Bach did not wait for inspiration, did not trouble any higher power for a "theme" the elaboration of which would help him to complete the piece. Moreover, it offers practically no opportunity for displaying any special knowledge of composition. So we must conclude that it is impossible to account for the production of musical works as necessarily involving collaboration between separate faculties of inspiration and intellect. Were we dealing with some inferior work, this conclusion would carry no weight. But here we are dealing with a truly magnificent, artistically perfect work. How, then, was it produced?

What is in question here is not the actual circumstances of the work's production, but an attempt to reconstruct the essential process of its composition (which, emphatically, is not the way it was actually composed), to visualize what it might have been "ideally." Let us imagine our "ideal" Bach sitting down at the keyboard (sitting down actually or only in imagination). His finger strikes a deep note: 𝄢. He pauses a moment and then strikes the same note, f, three octaves higher: 𝄞. It is, as it were, an echo of the first note: across the distance the two recognize and salute each other, as though trying to get together. The higher note will go a long way to meet the lower, if only out of courtesy; after all, it is easier to descend than to climb:

This makes good sense in terms of motion; the poles of the dynamic field, $\hat{1}$ (f) and $\hat{5}$ (c), are being declared, but the result is not particularly satisfying artistically. Though meaningful as a whole, the pattern leaves much to be desired in its details. Suppose the higher note were to express its readiness to meet the lower with a wing-taking gesture, for example: ⟨notation⟩. This would be acceptable for a start. But what next? Merely to repeat the gesture would be to mark time: ⟨notation⟩; to keep going would involve further ascent: ⟨notation⟩. But suppose the direction of the gesture were reversed—not ⟨notation⟩ but ⟨notation⟩. Yes, now we are on the right track, downward, ⟨notation⟩, and we can descend all the way:

In this manner, a regular run of conjunct notes down the keyboard is transformed into a succession of notes, which plays its way around the main stations, each separated from the preceding by the interval of a third (before the last unit one note is skipped because the intended goal of the motion is c). Now, thirds form chords—triads and seventh chords—so we can, too. (Why not? After all, we are sitting at the keyboard.) We could simply let our fingers rest on the successively reached stations—not on all of them; the hand has not enough fingers for that—like this:

What we get now is a sensible series of chords, beginning with the dissonant triad ♯𝄞. At the first opportunity it is resolved (according to the rules) into the triad of the I degree (F major), 𝄞, followed at the end, as is to be expected, by the triad of the V degree (C major), 𝄞. The metric articulation too begins to take shape; it is more or less suggested by the motion itself. Including the lowest opening tone, we have altogether ten stations; if the last one is to coincide with the beginning of a measure, the motion must be in triple time $(3 + 3 + 3 + 1)$.

Had anyone else been sitting at the keyboard, this might have been all. Once the impulse given by the little gesture has been picked up in its reversal, everything seems to take care of itself; even the chordal element introduced by the held notes is treated according to the rules: everything takes place as could have been predicted, almost calculated in advance. But the man at the keyboard is Bach, a mind ever alive, who is not content with a first impulse or with letting things merely happen, who never ceases to create new events, and so something new occurs, this:

To make clear what has taken place, both the initial and final stages are shown here:

The exclamation point marks the crucial moment when quite unexpectedly, for no apparent reason, the profile of the motion reappears in its first form, before the reversal, ↗••, but only once, for it continues with its second form, ⌣•⌣. The change is unobtrusive, its effect delicate, but it has far-reaching consequences. What has been a mechanical, repetitive unwinding is now animated by a fresh impulse, a new start—after all, ↗•• was the form of the first impulse. Its reappearance is like a new inhalation after a long exhalation. We feel that here is the breath of life: at this moment the piece is born. The mere alternation between ⌣•⌣ and ↗•• will feed and sustain the whole prelude, manifest its vitality. In fact, its effects are perceptible at once. As though surprised by the unexpected event, the dissonant ♭𝄞 chord above it forgets to resolve at the proper place; it is carried over to the beginning of the next measure and is resolved belatedly. This event, too, produces consequences, begetting its own repetition with the new dissonant chord, ♭𝄞. The resolution of this chord, again, is delayed until the C major triad in the next measure; schematically represented, what we have is ♭𝄞𝄞. Play these measures without the crucial change in the second measure: at once the motion becomes inarticulate, lifeless. The substitution of ↗•• for ⌣•⌣ at this point converts the formless into form, into the kinetic pattern

⌢◡◡ | ◡◡⌢ | ⌢◡◡◡ | ◡◡◡ which recurs several times in
the piece. Is *this* the theme? At any rate, it is not too much to say
that ▱ here instead of ▱ makes the difference between
genius and mediocrity, between Bach and a talented pupil of his.
And to say this is not to exaggerate the importance of a detail, to
read into it things that are not there. It is in small things of this kind
that a work of art discloses greatness and authenticity; they decide
whether it is living or lifeless, and they are the prerogative of genius.
"Le bon Dieu est dans le détail"—this is one of the truest remarks
ever made about art: "God resides in the detail."

　　The table below sums up the whole development:

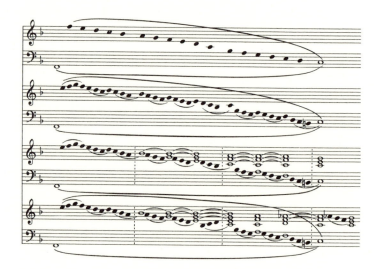

　　We shall continue our analysis for another few steps. At the end
of measure 4, the bass part, leading over to measure 5, breaks the
hitherto observed rule of reversing the motion after three ascending or
descending tones; with ▱ the circle is broken through
and a path is cleared for a new element, which is introduced at once

schematically: [musical notation]. This is nothing other than a succession obtained from the repetition of the initial formula [musical notation] —not from its reversal—resulting in an ascending line, its last link extended, its conclusion delayed: [musical notation]; below the extended link the reversed gesture slips in: [musical notation] —an exhalation under the inhalation (in nonphysical processes something of this kind is possible). At the same time, the dissonant chord held over into the next measure and its delayed resolution [musical notation] remind us of the analogous event in the opening measures.

The next two measures (7 and 8) repeat the two preceding ones at the next lower degree: [musical notation]. Once again something has happened. The fact that after the four-measure pattern of the beginning the pattern of measures 5–6 is repeated in measures 7–8—in other words, the fact that instead of hearing a four-measure unit, as in measures 1–4, we hear two two-measure units—has the effect (however discreet) of reducing the breath to half its span. And when the pattern of measure 9 is immediately repeated in measure 10 [musical notation]—that is to say, when the span of the breath is again reduced by one-half—one may feel a slight crowding. But then, in measure 11, there is a sudden loosening: the four-measure pattern of the opening re-emerges and continues unhindered. Crowding and loosening have a deeper meaning in the overall context of the piece: the crowding prepares the first shift of the center (from f to c); the loosening occurs at the moment when the new center comes clearly into view. But at the end of this four-measure unit, at the place where in measures 4–5 the lower voice freed itself from the strict rule with [musical notation] , the upper voice breaks through the circle with the opposite [musical notation], carrying the motion toward the tone c; one measure later the first point of repose is reached. But here, in measure 16, which marks a conclusion and a moment of repose, the pattern of the *first* measure—of the *opening*—unexpectedly reappears, reminding us that repose at this point can be only temporary. Measures 9–16 are repeated unchanged at the end of the piece (the center is f); in the last measure, however, we do not have [musical notation], as in measure 16, but [musical notation], the musical content being the same. Here nothing stirs again; the repose has become definitive.

However tempting and instructive it may be to continue our step-by-step analysis of this magnificent prelude, it would be beyond the scope of our reflections. Those who wish to study the pattern of the motion in detail and its relation to the larger tonal contexts can do so with the help of the table below. A schematic representation is possible in this instance because the entire prelude is practically "made" of nothing but repetitions (more than two hundred) of the four-note formula in one or another of its four versions, [musical notation] and [musical notation] occurring most often, and [musical notation] and [musical notation] used only in a few cases. Twice, in the stretto of a climax, the bass part gets carried away to [musical notation]; and directly before the few intermediate points of rest (there are three of them) the rule is entirely disregarded; but this marks the utmost limits of the freedom granted to the tones. In the table on the facing page the symbols are self-explanatory (the brackets above indicate the recurrent patterns).

The "given"—self-given—element, the theme with which Bach works here, what is it? [musical notation]: a nothing, a trifle. It would hardly occur to anyone to call something like this an inspiration. And everything else is work! What makes this piece so special, indeed unique, is not a "theme," a flash of inspiration, but the *work* that went into it. The term "work," however, must not be taken here in the usual

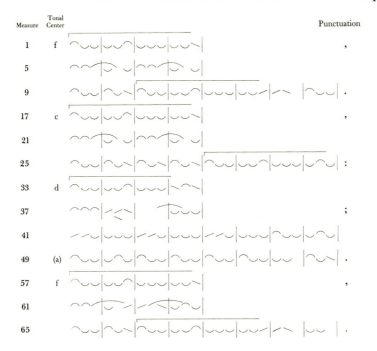

sense of an activity guided by knowledge and skill. For knowledge and skill cannot of themselves produce something unique, something that has never existed before; in the light of traditional ideas, such a piece can only be the result of inspiration. Should we say then that the whole piece is "inspired"? Statements of this kind are often made; even artists often assure us that a work was entirely present in their mind in a flash of inspiration, and that all they did was to reproduce the intuited whole as a succession of its parts. Such an interpretation would be faithful to the conceptual schema of inspiration plus intellect, or inspiration plus work, but would not add much to our understanding. What does it avail us to be told that Bach had a mental picture of this entire prelude in a flash of inspiration? What, in such a case, could be the whole apart from the details in which, out of which, it lives in the first place? What can it be but a vague foretaste of a certain interplay of forces and of the motion resulting from it until the work itself has crystallized out of this fog, step by step? After all, the individual steps in which the work's life unfolds, which are identical with this life, which *are* the work, cannot—not even as mere indications—all be present in the composer's mind simultaneously, in a single flash; each can emerge only at the right place and at the right moment, as it falls due in the course of the composition. How, for instance, could the melodic turn ♪♪♪ in measures 14–15 or the pattern ⌒ ◡ ◡ of measure 16 be present in the composer's mind before the music has actually reached this point? How could it have been produced without reference to everything that had come before it? Creation is a continual process; decisions are made from moment to moment, not in a single moment. It is a series of such flashes; work and inspiration are inseparable. The hypothesis of two different creative sources collapses, and if one wishes to insist that without inspiration no genuine work can be produced, then the composer's labors must be regarded as inspired. This, however, would imply a new concept of "labor," one that is not essentially linked to knowledge and skill, and one that, in the last analysis, must be associated with "thought"—or a new concept of thought.

PRELUDE IN C MAJOR (BOOK II)

This prelude represents the last stage in the transition from thematic to themeless compositions. Whereas in the F-major Prelude a "given element," however insignificant, was still clearly recognizable as the material which was treated by the composer, here every trace of something "given" has vanished: our distinction no longer applies. It would, however, be mistaken to expect laxness and diffusion as a result—as might be the case in free improvisation—since the link to a given element, a theme, is surely one of the most important elements that make for coherence. The C-major Prelude certainly has features suggestive of improvisation, but there can be no question of diffusion; quite to the contrary, the impression it produces is one of compactness and coherence hardly to be surpassed. Because of this impression, we will imagine on first listening to the piece that we hear continual references to definite tonal formulas, or tonal gestures, as they are heard in the F-major Prelude. Scrutinizing the matter more closely, we are surprised to discover that our first impression was deceptive. There are surely enough repetitions and variations of definite formulas, but they are short-lived and inconsequential: every time they emerge they quickly vanish, or else a formula is reduced to a falling half-tone, ,

something that cannot be called a form even in the most rudimentary sense, something that is merely musical raw material. Whereas the F-major Prelude was a tightly constructed chain of interlocking individual members with no gaps—though still discontinuous, because it was possible to distinguish between the links and the chain and count the links—here we have the unbroken continuity of pure flow. This is no longer a chain but a web that is spun on and on, a poem consisting of a single line that keeps growing longer. (A careful listener will discover that the "line" is articulated as follows: overture—2 measures; main section—$13\frac{1}{2}$ measures; interlude—$3\frac{1}{2}$ measures, running into the main section where the latter is in full swing, $2\frac{1}{2}$ measures past its beginning; then, repetition of the main section from here on with a different tonal center and an expanded conclusion—12 measures; and coda—3 measures. But this articulation is never stressed; on the contrary, it is blurred by the tonal motion. There are no caesuras, no rests until the end; a continuous flow is obviously intended.)

The improvised character of the piece is especially conspicuous in the two opening measures: the composer seems to be searching, experimenting, groping for the real thing. As in the Prelude in F major, the first tone to be heard is in the bass, the root (here c), which is picked up in the treble and transformed into motion, but, in contrast to the other prelude, here the motion does not crystallize into a specific figure, a specific tonal gesture to be worked with. Rather, tone follows upon tone; no definite form is outlined and preserved; everything remains in a state of flux, as it were. All we have is a single line which rises and falls as it gradually winds its way downward:

In measure 3, the line divides into four threads (the prelude is in four parts), and we discover that the real thing toward which the two opening measures had been groping is not essentially different from what was stated in these two measures; it is the same calm flow, tone by tone. Thus the opening measures are more than an introduction: they antici-pate the essence of the piece and supply a key to an understanding of it.

If, then, nothing is "given" here, no form, however rudimentary, to which subsequent motion could be related, if all we have is a succession of tones and intervals, why do we hear the prelude as a coherent, unified whole rather than as a random assembly of tones? For what we hear is not merely the overall unity given by the key (which would be audible in a mere scale), nor is it the overall chordal progres-sion embedded in the successive tones (present in any arpeggio), but this particular melodic line, this particular tightly knit, unique whole.

The piece begins with a gently ascending motion touched off by the root tone ("gently" because of the distribution of the metric accents; the beginning of the measure is empty, the central tone c the least accentuated): ♪♪♪, 1̂-2̂-3̂. However, the motion does not con-tinue upward, as it does, for example, in the theme of the Fugue in

C major of Book I, [music]. Rather, it breaks off abruptly; the next note is much lower: [music]. This *could* be looked upon as a definite form with which the motion would work from this point on—such as is the case in the D-major Prelude of Book I, [music]. Not so here; the tones ignore this possibility, so to speak, they pass it by, and the motion continues as [music]. Two things will be noted here: first, an alternation of steps and leaps—this will be recognized as significant only subsequently—and second, immediately perceivable, the presence of two motions, one at a higher, the other at a lower level, [music]. The crucial moment is the leap [music]: when the note [music] is played, the lower level is taken seriously, as it were (this is not the case in the D-major Prelude); the preceding g, $\hat{5}$, is set in motion via f, $\hat{4}$, toward e, $\hat{3}$. At the same time, through a kind of action at a distance, [music], too, is shaken out of its comparative state of repose, and drawn into a $\hat{3}$-$\hat{2}$-$\hat{1}$ motion. The motion at the lower level is short-lived and comes to a halt at its provisional goal, $\hat{3}$; as a result the ear is induced to concentrate on the motion that continues at the higher level; the course of this motion is shown in the following sketch:

After the initial $\hat{3}$-$\hat{2}$-$\hat{1}$, [music] is touched upon, alien to the key and referring to the center f; it has the dynamic quality $\hat{4}$—a tension tone—and is resolved in the presently following $\rlap{\underline{\smash{}}}\;\bullet$, $\hat{3}$. However, the shift of the center affects only this one step: the original situation with c as center is restored immediately, and the f that follows is heard as $\hat{4}$, with the concluding step f-e as $\hat{4}$-$\hat{3}$ in C major. In other words, what we have here is a regular alternation of tension and resolution, $\hat{3}$-$\hat{2}$-$\overset{\rightarrow}{\hat{1}}$-$(\hat{4}$-$\hat{3}$-$)\overset{\rightarrow}{\hat{4}}$-$\overset{\rightarrow}{\hat{3}}$. The lower line of our sketch, which indicates the duration of the motions in each stage, shows that the various steps are by no means of equal value. The fact that the step $\hat{2}$-$\hat{1}$ takes less time than any other suggests that it is the least significant: it does not mark the attainment of a goal; the motion continues beyond it. The next step—b♭-a—is lengthened, and the concluding f-e takes more time than all the preceding steps together. In this way it becomes clear that after the initial tone e, the motion tends toward the concluding f-e, and that from the outset it had aimed at $\rlap{\underline{\smash{}}}\;\overset{\circ}{\underset{\circ}{\circ}}$, $\hat{3}$ . . . $\hat{4}$-$\hat{3}$, motion through an adjunct note associated with a shift to the lower octave. The motion as a whole subtly indicates its purpose when it repeats the ascending motif of three notes leading to the initial e, $\hat{3}$, toward the end, *but not earlier,* where its goal is the tone f, $\hat{4}$, of the lower octave. : this is how the main note and its adjunct note reach out toward each other across the distance.

The sketches opposite are intended as the "ideal" picture of how such a completely nonthematic pattern is formed, and to show the connective element that links the successive steps into a unified whole. First there is the tone $\hat{3}$ above its root, which determines the dynamic quality (I). The tone's life is expressed in an away-from-and-back-to motion, $\hat{3}$-$\hat{4}$-$\hat{3}$, touching on the adjunct note (II). Next, the adjunct note strives to assert itself, to demonstrate that it has a life of its own: this is achieved by means of a second voice (III; the change of dynamic qualities in the main voice effected by the lower part—the adjunct note

takes on for a moment the appearance of a root tone—is indicated in the sketch). Next comes the shift to the lower octave (IV)—the main voice becomes the lower voice; the secondary voice is on top. To restore the correct situation, the second voice, too, must move to the lower octave (V). The last step marks a further unfolding and enrichment (VI). This is the ideal structure to which the melodic line of the two opening measures owes its solidity, its inner coherence. (In Schenker's terminology, II is the background, III–VI the middleground, the score of the prelude the foreground.)

As mentioned earlier, what is shown here is an "ideal" development, not a picture of how the piece was actually composed. It would be completely absurd to suppose that any musical work is constructed from a "background": the composer is always concerned with the "foreground." Indeed, how could ♪♪♪♪♪♪♪♪♪, and so on, be conceived except in the continuous motion itself, in the course of spinning out the line, the constant flow from tone to tone? Bach begins with ♪♪♪; there is a hint, a direction, a presentiment but no more, of what is to come: he is at once leading and being led. Because

his creative musician's mind is constantly focused on the primal forms
of tonal life, it is inevitable that one of these primal forms—here, the
adjunct note $\hat{3}$-$\hat{4}$-$\hat{3}$—should be embodied in the melodic line his mind
is developing as the meaning, the inner kernel, of this unique pattern
of motion.

Thus, what we have here is not any motion but a motion representing or expressing a meaning or inner kernel, an event at two levels,
a motion that says something, like any bodily gesture. But it is not
fixed in time (as gestures are bound up with a particular moment).
Rather, it spreads out in time, filling out and embodying time just as
a line or building fills out and embodies space. Are we, then, to speak
of a motion "structure" or "construction"? But what these terms—
"structure," "construction"—lack is the connotation of "about"; one
does not build or construct "about" anything, as one speaks or thinks
"about" something, as this particular musical line speaks "about" the
adjunct note, or as the man who conceives it is thinking "about"
$\hat{3}\ \hat{4}\ \hat{3}$. Again, this thinking is not of the kind that deals with
a problem in order to solve it; rather, it is a thinking that brings
something forth, that draws something hidden into the light—thinking
in motions of tones. Here too, of course, something is done, something
is made, but this doing consists in thinking. This thinking is not that
of a man who acts, this doing not that of a man who thinks. Doing
and thinking are wholly fused into one: thought that produces, producing that thinks. Not existence on one hand and thinking about it
on the other, but a thinking that by itself creates existence.

Here we might recall the starting point of these reflections—the assumption that a musical work is a collaboration between inspiration
and technical knowledge. We set out to test this assumption against
the musical facts. And, indeed, the assumption proves altogether untenable, tested against a work such as this prelude. Nowhere in it

can we point to elements derived from inspiration as distinct from elements derived from technical aptitude or training. The distinction appears pointless: the notion of two distinct sources contributes nothing to understanding the creative process.

CHORALE HARMONIZATION
AND VARIATION

Now let us briefly turn to two musical forms in which theme *can* be clearly distinguished from technical elaboration: here there is no doubt that both derive from different, most often externally different, sources. Chorale harmonization consists of devising suitable chords for traditional melodies. For all their simplicity, many traditional hymn tunes are exquisitely beautiful structures; if no composer is known, we readily ascribe their existence to some sort of anonymous inspiration. On the other hand, harmonization of these melodies is part of the elementary training of every musician. Not even talent is required: once the student has learned how to operate with the musical symbols according to the rules, he can solve the problems (even without reference to the ear) on a purely topological basis. Here then, the distinction between inspiration and technique as the two creative sources of music seems entirely justified, not least because here each is represented by a different person. To be sure, the case is a bit altered when it is a composer like Bach who supplies the harmonic setting. Bach's chorales have long been held in special reverence by all sorts of musicians because, for the first time, they revealed what music has actually gained by branching out into the dimension of harmony. Bach's settings are not mere accompaniments to, or supports for, the melody, not just a fleshing out; they demonstrate that harmony possesses the capacity to interpret melody. They bring to light the hidden facets of melodies. By themselves, in terms of dynamic tone qualities, these tunes seem utterly simple. It would scarcely occur to anyone to suppose there were anything to be interpreted in a hymn tune! But it was these simplest of all melodies that Bach transformed into the subtlest, most sublime of musical statements. Listening to the great Passions, one is not always aware that, thanks to the harmonizations, the same tune can be made to convey senses as diverse as "O great King, great at all times," "O great love, O love beyond all bounds," and "And yet how wondrous is this punishment," and convey each in a unique way. On closer scrutiny, these miracles of sound reduce to so many solutions of the technical problem, of finding three different bass parts for the one melody; both parts together will then suggest possible harmonies. In our example, the upper and lower parts begin as follows in the three harmonizations:

No one denies that musical skill of the highest order informs Bach's chorale settings, but when we are confronted with an invention like the third cited here, we begin to doubt that it could be produced by training, knowledge, or experience alone, of no matter how high an order—all the more when we recognize that the chordal sequence implied in the two parts expresses the questioning, marveling quality of the words in a way completely unfathomable. Our doubts give way to complete certainty when we listen to the famous chorale in the *Passion According to St. Matthew* following the Evangelist's words "And he died": too much more is involved here than just knowledge of musical composition. The same chorale has been heard four times in the course of the Passion, each time in a different harmonization, but in all four Bach kept the concluding phrase, ♪♪♪♪♪♪♪, perfectly simple, harmonizing it only with the normal chords of the cadence. So it is all the more surprising, indeed breathtaking, when now at the words "By virtue of thy anguish and pain" the familiar harmonies suddenly yield to unheard-of sounds, as if they rose from an abyss of uncertainty. The habitual world has vanished, a bottomless depth has opened, and the simple melodic turn suddenly serves to express the unfathomable. Were we ever asked whether it is possible to express the inexpressible, we could only point to this passage. To try it in words would imply a contradiction. No doubt, here too, it is the bottom part that, technically speaking, determines the chords:

But a bass line like this, together with the sounds it makes possible, does not derive from any sort of knowledge or experience; it derives from some "second hearing" (an analogy to "second sight") which detects undreamed-of things behind the notes of the melody. If anything ever deserved that name, this is a discovery of genius, a flash of inspiration, a brilliant idea, absolutely original, unique—not the inspired discovery of a theme, but inspiration "about" a theme; it is thinking, tone thinking, a thinking in tones about tones.

"Variation" or "theme and variations" is the technical term for a classical musical form in which a lengthy melody, often a borrowed one, undergoes a number of modifications, though the main features of the original melody are preserved. The formula "the same, yet not the same" is a fairly correct description of the result. (Bach's *Goldberg Variations* is not a set of variations in the classical sense: the work is based not on a melody but on the "background" of a melody.) Often enough the composer of such a work merely ornaments or paraphrases a given melody, presents it in a number of different scorings. The result can be very artistic, but the art involved here is certainly of a kind that can be learned: indeed, we must agree with students of composition that nothing is easier than writing variations. However, great composers have recognized that "the same, yet not the same" is not necessarily the same dressed up in a new garment, but can be taken in the deeper sense of metamorphosis. In this sense, writing variations is the most difficult of all tasks, namely, "transformation of the created," the conscious production of something that usually only nature can produce unconsciously. It is no accident that Beethoven, whose creative powers asserted themselves most strongly when restrained by self-imposed discipline, composed some of his greatest works in the form of variations. One day, as though having made up his mind to reduce ad absurdum the commonly held view that the theme is a matter of inspiration and its treatment one of mere technique, he chose a run-of-the-mill product of clever routine, a waltz by the music publisher Diabelli, as the theme for no fewer than thirty-three variations, thus creating a work rightly described as "the microcosm of Beethoven's genius, the quintessence of the whole world of music" (Hans von Bülow). The theme is conventional through and through, a product of average skill; the elaboration, thirty-three miracles of creative power, is a work of genius. After the Diabelli waltz has been heard, the first "variation" reveals at one stroke, with thunder and lightning, the face of Beethoven breaking through the mediocrity of the theme, and then anyone can tell where skill, knowledge, technique are at work, and where a higher faculty is operating.

It may be briefly mentioned here that in the two domains which twentieth-century music has explored most extensively, twelve-tone composition and jazz, the disappearance of the theme as the inspired element and vitalizing force of a work of music has been completed, at least for the time being. The tone row upon which every twelve-tone composition is based is not a theme in the proper sense, not an audible tonal pattern, but raw material prearranged in a specific way ready to be dealt with; it is not "inspired," but deliberately chosen in accordance with the composer's idea of how this specific bit of material can be elaborated. Inspiration can manifest itself, if at all, only in the treatment. Much the same can be said of jazz, which is indeed essentially an art of improvisation—not free improvisation, it is true, for it is ultimately bound up with a given theme. What jazz improvises is not the theme, but what occurs to the jazz composer to say about it: this is what determines the artistic quality of his production.

THE CLASSICAL DEVELOPMENT

The distinction between inspiration (responsible for the theme) and technique (responsible for the elaboration) was certainly not suggested by works of the kind discussed above, but rather by the great instrumental works of the classical epoch, whose form most clearly distinguishes between theme and treatment, the "given" and what is made of it, what happens to it. Their themes are recognized as authentic inspirations by every listener, and the treatment of the theme is governed by easily teachable and learnable rules. When we look more closely, however, we discover that here, too, the situation is not so simple as might appear at first glance. It is in the very passages of "treatment," where only knowledge of composition is supposedly involved, that we repeatedly run into musical happenings which in their unpredictability and uniqueness cannot have been derived from knowledge or experience, and immeasurably surpass anything merely contrived (in the sense of technique). Many a passage of pure elaboration, closely examined, utterly confounds our trained expectation: it is all too clear that in such cases so-called elaboration rises to the level of a creative act. Here, if anywhere, inspiration of a higher order must be involved—one might almost say higher than the one to which a theme owes its existence. It is easier to create something out of nothing than out of something given, easier to begin well than to continue well; hence the saying that one need not be a good musician to *have* a good idea, but one must be a good musician to make something good out of a good idea. In other words, genius does not need an inspired tune; an inspired tune needs genius. Those who neatly assigned inspiration to the task of inventing the theme, and knowledge plus technique to that of treating it, must have been rather obtuse. They could perhaps dimly conceive that an idea might occur to a composer out of the blue; that elaboration can be something entirely different from the mere application of rules was probably far beyond the reach of their imaginations. See what textbooks have to say about the development sections in classical music: you will find the implication that these could just as well have been composed by an advanced student or a good technician.

To understand the full meaning of these observations, we now shall turn to instances which they describe in general terms and study these instances in concrete detail. Cézanne's remark that God resides in the detail applies here in its full force. The Creator's hand reveals itself most convincingly in close-up. We have chosen two examples from the symphonic literature.

Our first example is the development section of the first movement of Mozart's Symphony in G minor (no. 40). Traditionally the first movement is in ternary form; the third section of it, in keeping with a latent striving for symmetry, repeats the first in outline as well as in many details; the function of the middle section is to delay with suspense the attainment of the goal of this striving, and in the end to attain it more or less dramatically, depending on the character of the work. The basic away-from-and-back-to motion which defines the meaning of the ternary scheme is expressed musically in the fact that in the first section the main key is relinquished in favor of a different one; in the middle section, detours which the composer is free to invent lead back to the main key; the latter is fully restored in the third section, but this time, in contrast to the first section, is not relinquished. The themes are stated in the first section, the so-called exposition;[1] the third section, or recapitulation, repeats them; the themes are elaborated in the middle section of the movement, the development.

To understand what happens to the themes in a development, one must first become familiar with what happens in the themes themselves. Here is the well-known theme that opens the symphony without any further preparation:

What might be considered as preparation is, so to speak, part of the theme itself, namely, the thrice-repeated start: ♪. (Something like this can only be the result of inspiration; no one would venture to contrive it.) This start, however, does not, as one might suppose, lead to a grand emphatic gesture, e.g., ♪. The gesture does in fact occur, but (this is the point) not where it is due; it is delayed, and as a result falls on the weak beat of the measure, ♪, thus disavowing itself, as it were, belittling the effort involved, as though suggesting that it must not be taken as seriously as all that, that what is actually intended here is not the high ♪ that has been reached, but perhaps the seemingly preparatory ♪, $\hat{5}$ (hence it has been repeated three times). At any rate, the motion at once descends in the same ♪|♪ rhythm of the beginning, and leads, via the opening note, to the next lower note, $\hat{4}$: ♪. The same steps are repeated as the motion proceeds from $\hat{4}$ to $\hat{3}$: ♪.

---

1. One of the conventions of the form is that the exposition is played twice; that no new formal element is introduced by the repetition is apparent from the fact that the interpreter is free to follow the convention or to ignore it.

The scheme of the whole, together with the obvious harmony, I-II-V-I, is:

The melody does not end at this point, but in what follows only this part of it is used as the "given" element to be elaborated.

Formally considered, the exposition is conventional. The development proper begins just as conventionally, with a few chords; the last of these is a diminished seventh chord, a sound that refers to four different tonal centers, here a, c, e♭, and f♯. Among the four paths open at this point of intersection Mozart chooses the one leading to the center f♯, which is the farthest removed from the main key (according to the cycle of fifths). A transitional phrase is played: It has been heard once in the exposition, where it led to the first restatement of the main theme. Here it is twice as long—a longer stop, a deeper inhalation before what is to come next. Then the main theme is stated in F♯ minor:

At first, almost as far as the middle, everything runs smoothly. But at the moment when the descending portion of the melodic curve is expected to reach the tone $\hat{4}$ (here), something happens: ; instead of we hear , a tone which does not exist in F♯ minor. Its effect is that of a discreet jolt: we have let ourselves confidently be carried along by the motion, and now we feel a shock; we are slightly apprehensive, bewildered—yet before we have the time to regain composure, the disturbance is removed. As though nothing had happened, the second half of the melody continues with the correct note $\hat{4}$, ♮ not ♯: . We decide that the jolt was but an accidental stumbling and, reassured, let ourselves be carried by the familiar motion. But three measures later, and once again exactly at the point where the descending part of the melodic curve, this time in the second half of the melody, is expected to attain its goal, $\hat{3}$ (here ♮), the same thing happens: . Now the effect is much stronger, not only because repetition of the "slip" suggests that it is not an accident but also because at this point the tone $\hat{3}$ was supposed to conclude the phrase and resolve the tension to some extent.[2] To be sure, the deviation is immediately corrected in the same way as before, but this means that the result, too, is the same: the "corrected" tone, ♮ instead of ♯, has the dynamic quality $\hat{4}$, not $\hat{3}$. Instead of having reached the end of the theme and a state of relaxation, we find ourselves once again in the middle of things, in a new state of tension, with a relaxing second half still ahead of us. *At the same time, however, the center has been shifted:* since ♮ is now $\hat{4}$, not $\hat{3}$, e has become $\hat{1}$ instead of f♯. From this point on the theme runs normally, , confirming the new center. The tones make a rush for it: without giving the theme a chance to reach its end properly, the violas and basses start it again in E minor:

In order to clarify what has taken place, we show at the top of the next page a schematic representation of this first stage of the development as compared with the theme itself. The theme: one melodic arc and its repetition, one degree lower; the first arc, leading from $\hat{5}$ to $\hat{4}$, heightens the tension of the start; the second, leading from $\hat{4}$ to

---

2. The harmony at this point makes it impossible to hear ♮ as $\hat{3}$ in F♯ major.

$\hat{3}$, resolves the tension. In the development, the idea of "shifting the melodic arc one degree lower" within its dynamic field is intensified to shifting the melodic outline *and* the dynamic field. Consequently, the correction of the "slip" which the second time leads to a new $\hat{4}$ instead of a $\hat{3}$ is not effected to avoid an awkwardness; rather, just as the seemingly accidental slip, it serves a still unrevealed higher purpose of the overall design (this will become apparent subsequently).

    The restatement of the theme in E minor marks a new stage in the development. The road hitherto traveled can be represented concisely by the stages   . Up to this point, the gradual shift downward of the overall motion has been carried out by means of inconspicuous detours; now the composer's intention asserts itself openly and vigorously. The moment the center e is reached, it is drawn into a new motion; the shift from e to d begins even before the second half of the theme has been given the opportunity to unfold: . As a result, the second half is omitted. Once the center d has been reached, the theme starts again from the beginning; this time we hear only its first half. The same happens two more times, when the center is shifted to c and then to b♭. After that, the motion becomes precipitous: no new center is fixed even for a moment; in the fray the melody even drops its first and last measures, and is reduced to its core,

The stages [notation] and [notation] are merely passed rapidly, and after the next step, [notation], something snaps: the motion comes to a halt.

The course of the development until this point, which marks the middle of the section, is schematically represented in the following sketch, where the characteristic interval of the ascending sixth indicates the stage reached at a given moment (the measure numbers show how the motion is gradually accelerated):

The idea of the gradual downward shift, contained in germ in the theme itself and brought to the foreground by the "accident" at the beginning of the development, has asserted itself, and in the end has become the dominant factor. The motion comes to a halt at the moment when the sixth c♯-a appears in the upper voice. The same sixth began the motion, but the dynamic meaning of the interval has changed: at first it was $\hat{5}$-$\hat{3}$; now it is heard as $\hat{3}$-$\hat{5}$. Consequently, the course of the development up to this point can be most concisely summed up in the formula [notation] : as a result of the motion, the dynamic quality $\hat{5}$ has been shifted from the lower to the higher note of the interval c♯-a. But since a $= \hat{5}$ implies d $= \hat{1}$, and since d is the dominant of the main key, in which the recapitulation is to be reached via the harmonic step D-G, we are here, though in the middle of the development, separated from its end only by one step.

The changed dynamic meaning of the sixth effected by shifting $\hat{5}$ from the lower to the higher tone has one direct consequence. The adjunct notes preceding the note $\hat{5}$ at the beginning of the theme, which elsewhere precede the *lower* note of the sixth and lead *toward* the leap,

now come *after* it, proceed from the

higher note, , and lead nowhere. What we

have now is not but . The motion

has come to a stop; the notes merely mark time. But

is nothing other than the begin-
ning and the end of the theme, without the middle. What had been
skipped in the fray—the first and last measures of the theme, so that
only its core, the actual vehicle of the motion, was left—is now suddenly
present again, present alone; now the core has been skipped, and we
shall not encounter it again until the beginning of the recapitulation,
when the theme will be restated in its entirety. And just as the first
half of the development is dominated by the element of motion,
so the second is dominated by the element of standstill
—logically, one might say, for how else can
one fill the long span of time available here for only one step, if
not with tones marking time? How Mozart succeeds in wresting, from
these tones, the inner motion that carries the tension of the preceding
outer motion forward—indeed, even increases it—cannot be shown here,
however fascinating this would be, for the task would involve detailed
technical explanations. The impetuous motion in the first half of the
development could be followed in the score, but only by listening can
one grasp the barely perceptible motion of the second half.

In the example just discussed, elaboration of a theme is certainly
intellectual work, carried out by a rational faculty on the basis of rich
experience and the most refined technique. The share of the intellect
is disclosed in the way the seemingly spontaneous motion is led toward
its predetermined goal in accordance with a well-conceived plan. The
fact that the composer never fails to provide the means for realizing
the plan testifies to his incomparable skill. And yet we feel that some-

thing else is involved here besides intellect and skill. These may suffice to account for the opening measures of the development, but the crucial event which clears the path for and touches off what comes directly after these measures, the seemingly accidental "error," cannot be attributed to intellect and skill. If the "wrong" note, b♯ instead of b, had been planned, i.e., introduced for a specific purpose, this purpose could have been only to lead the motion away from f♯ = $\hat{1}$. But this is the very thing that does *not* happen: the "error" is immediately corrected, and the motion swings back into the right path immediately after the momentary deviation. Only now might it dawn upon an intellect (not everyone's intellect!) that the repetition of the accidental "error" and the correction of it must lead to an overall shift to the next lower degree of the scale—a shift which actually takes place. Thus the event was not planned; rather, it was the event that suggested the basic element of the plan. An accident which, in retrospect, turns out to be pregnant with consequences, and to serve a plan that did not even exist when it occurred: this is indeed like a work of Providence, the result of "higher" inspiration. Here, if anywhere, "inspiration" is the right word, for in this instance the inspiration is not confined to itself, but affects everything that follows. The entire vast construction, latent in the "given," becomes actualized by this one flash of inspiration. We have mentioned previously that according to Schenker the plan of a musical work is an "ideal" factor operating from the background: here we see the plan actually operating in the foreground.

Our tacit assumption that the case discussed above is not exceptional can be fully justified only by a comprehensive study of classical development sections. The following analysis of the development section in the last movement of the same symphony will at least serve as a partial justification.

First of all, the theme. Here is the score (melody, bass, with the indication of one chord):

The crucial "event" here occurs in the second measure, directly after it begins, when the G minor triad, the harmonic base of the highest tone  reached in a steep ascent, is suddenly removed and a sound is inserted which transforms b♭ from $\hat{3}$ (g being $= \hat{1}$) into $\hat{6}$ (d being $=$ $\hat{1}$):  (the root of this sound is a, which at first is not actually played). The directly following blasts of the winds, , with the leading-tone step c♯-d, contribute their share to asserting the claim of d. All this can be schematically represented as

As a result of the violent shift of the center, the whole movement, in so far as it is dominated by the theme, takes on its distinctive character of a hectic pressing forward. In the second half of the theme (which sounds like a faithful copy of the first) Mozart achieves the opposite result, namely, the return to the center g by means of barely perceptible refinements. There is no need here to go into detail; the following schema should be sufficient:

(This time the terminal blasts of the winds serve to confirm the actual center, as is apparent from the difference between the basses in

the two cases: in the first [♪♫], in the second [♪♫].) Accordingly, the shifts of the center throughout the theme may be illustrated by the following outline:

$$g = \hat{1} \cdots I \quad\quad IV \; V \quad I$$
$$d = \hat{1} \cdots IV \; V \; I$$

Here we see the shift from g to d via the intermediary stage a, from d back to g after touching c. In terms of harmonic degrees, we have: first half, IV³-V-I, goal d; second half, IV-V-I, goal g.

Now, the development. The exposition has been concluded in B♭ major, according to the rule. What next? The main theme! Mozart rushes into it, with apparent recklessness, and immediately bogs down, stumbles, stutters:

What has happened? Is this an improvisation that has miscarried? Disjointed shreds of music, debris of the theme: what is the meaning of this?

After the close of the exposition in B♭ major, the development has begun with the theme in the same key. But the crucial event in the second measure requires the minor third, and so the motion rising in the first measure via the major third, d, ends on the minor third, d♭, at the beginning of the second measure: [♪♫]. But what is going on? The theme has begun incorrectly, not as elsewhere with the tone $\hat{5}$ and the fourth $\hat{5}$-$\hat{8}$, [♪], but with the tone $\hat{1}$ and the step $\hat{1}$-$\hat{3}$, [♪]. As a result the strong beat falls on the

---

3. The G minor chord I of the beginning re-interpreted as IV.

tone d, and the abrupt d♭ at the beginning of the next measure sounds all the more out of place—and this is fully intended, for all instruments play the theme in unison and no chordal prop is available. This is why the d♭, like the corresponding b♭ in the original theme, is heard as $\hat{6}$, not $\hat{3}$. (The chord to be added mentally, corresponding to the a chord in the second measure in the first statement of the theme, is here the c chord, [♪], the dominant chord of f = $\hat{1}$.)

The "incorrect" beginning of the theme has still another, very different consequence. Because the theme opens with [♪] instead of [♪], i.e., drops one note, the measure is short of this note: without it the highest point would be reached prematurely, [♪]. Therefore a note must be inserted somewhere. Here it is: [♪]. A new element, as though innocuous, seemingly emerging by accident, but once again the accident is pregnant with consequences: it has come to stay, and very soon its presence makes itself felt. Because the broken triad [♪] is expected, the ear cannot miss the inserted semitone step [♪]: it sounds like a special preparation for the directly following third, [♪]. Combined with the next semitone step downward, [♪], it forms a separate new little phrase, [♪], which immediately impresses itself upon the ear. The diagram opposite shows what happens next, and how to interpret the enigmatic opening measures of the development.

The thematic pattern requires the thematic continuation, which can be represented schematically as [♪]: the rising semitone step concludes the phrase as it did before: [♪]. But we have just heard the same step in the opposite function as starting a

new phrase. Because the same step now performs two functions, the row or chain formation shown in the first line of the diagram becomes possible. Although this makes little sense musically, it opens a path leading to music, namely, via condensation. Line 2 of the diagram shows how the two semitone steps are contracted into one step which performs both functions: end and beginning of each phrase overlap. This is, however, impossible metrically, for the semitone step at the end of the phrase falls on the "four-one" beats, whereas it falls on the "three-four" beats at the beginning of the phrase. Mozart cuts the knot by an abbreviation of genius. He simply eliminates the resolution tones $\hat{5}$ and $\hat{8}$ from the entire sequence of $\hat{6}$-$\hat{5}$ and $\hat{7}$-$\hat{8}$ steps (anyway, they are taken for granted after $\hat{6}$ and $\hat{7}$), retaining only the tension tones. Line 3 of the diagram shows what is left—the tones of the enigmatic opening measures of the development, which are thus "explained." Since the abbreviation has freed the tones from the metric scheme, any rhythmic arrangement has become possible.

The deeper meaning of the operation is expressed in line 4 of the diagram. The Roman numerals in the first line indicate the underlying chordal sequence: IV-V-I, the same as in the first half of the theme. In lines 2 and 3 we see how I is each time reinterpreted retroactively as IV:

$$\frac{I}{IV}\text{-V-}\frac{I}{IV}\text{-V-}\frac{I}{IV}\text{- and so on.}$$

Instead of a succession of separate links, we have a tightly constructed chain. How this affects the shifts of the center is shown in line 4. Whereas the ascending fifth in the first half of the theme, , was balanced by the descending fifth in the second half, , there is no such balancing here: what we have is an unbroken succession of ascending fifths, like a repeated breathing in with no breathing out. Moreover, since the first-degree sounds must remain silent because of the abridgment, only the tension tones pointing to them, the dominants (V), are audibly represented in the sounds.

"Incorrect" beginning of theme, with $\hat{1}$ instead of $\hat{5}$, as though by accident; casual insertion of a semitone step as a metric filler which at once gives rise to a new figure, the latter clearing the way for a chain formation, which in turn gives rise to the long, unbroken succession of fifths; the rising step of a fifth contained in the first half of the theme asserting itself by a chain formation of rising fifths, eventually becoming the law governing all that occurs subsequently in the development: just as in the first movement of the symphony, a seemingly accidental melodic twist proves pregnant with consequences and leads to realization of a plan which did not exist when the "accident" occurred. In both cases a kind of predestination, beyond all knowledge or skill, seems to be at work. Here, too, a seemingly accidental blunder, a rashly inserted semitone step, must be attributed to a flash of inspiration, if one insists on using this term.

The first half of the theme with its ascending fifth was contained in the abrupt succession of the opening measures; the opposite idea of the descending fifth asserts itself in the second half. The link between the two is supplied by the conventional transitional phrase we have encountered at the beginning of the development in the first movement, , $\hat{6}$-$\hat{5}$-$\hat{4}$-$\hat{3}$. But here—another bit of "predestination"—convention is immediately put in the service of the overall plan: when the theme starts again, this time in a form similar to its

second half, [♪♪♪], the transitional phrase suggests

the possibility of concluding not with the hard [♪♪], $\hat{6}$-$\hat{5}$-$\hat{7}$-$\hat{8}$,

but the soft [♪♪], $\hat{6}$-$\hat{5}$-$\hat{4}$-$\hat{3}$. The latter is practically obligatory,

for its "open" end clears the way for a new chain formation, one
of descending fifths, in keeping with the second half of the theme.
A short, hesitant alternation of ascending and descending fifths is
followed by a succession of descending ones only. The following
diagram shows how this is done (the new chain-forming phrase stands,

in each case, for the entire thematic phrase, e.g., [♪♪]

stands for [♪♪]):

Here the ascending fifths of the opening measures are balanced by
descending ones: the symmetrical pattern of the theme—ascending fifths
in the first half, descending in the second—has become the structural
principle of an entire section. This has not been done deliberately, as
though the composer had wished to fit the melody into a preconceived
plan, but has grown out of the unique thematic pattern itself, the whole
process touched off by a single, seemingly insignificant change in the
melody, suggested by the situation at the moment it was made.

All this, however, is merely the beginning. After a short intermezzo
in fugal style, the tendency to a chain formation reasserts itself with
increased violence, and now things are really carried to the extreme,
as can be seen from the next diagram:

We need no longer go into detail; only the overall picture is shown. The theme is repeated in every link of the chain (in the diagram it is indicated only in the first two links). Fifth follows upon fifth until the initial c has been transformed into c♯—its own negation, as it were. But shortly before the last step, the vehement motion is checked, dammed up with g♯ as V of c♯: a subordinate stage becomes the main stage, and when, after a longish wavering between g♯ and c♯, we reach the definitive cadence V-I, we hear this descending fifth—rather than the ascending one, f♯-c♯—as what is actually intended here. Thereby the reversal is introduced: the descending fifth comes into its own; the symmetrical balancing begins. What we have is a really precipitous fall:

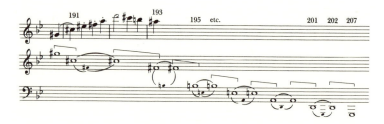

And now, in outline, a diagram of the whole, theme and development:

The diagram speaks for itself; no further comment is needed. We shall add only one observation and risk one modest speculation. The observation concerns the events at the peak of the three pyramids. In the theme itself, the two halves—the ascending and descending fifths—are sharply separated by a rest, a void. In the two larger pyramids the gaps are bridged, and in both cases bridged in the same way, by a standing still, a back-and-forth of two chords at the distance of a fifth, a kind of irresolute wavering between the two directions of the fifth. In the first large pyramid, the peak and standing still are reached with the A sound, directly followed by a wavering between A and D; in the second, with the G♯ sound, and the wavering (here twice as long) between G♯ and C♯. During the standing still, the decision is made to change direction, then the motion goes downward as irresistibly as it went upward before. Our speculation—it refers to the musical meaning of the development as a whole—is best expressed in a sketch:

: the first pyramid begins with b♭, the

second with c, and the end is d-g. The overall scheme would then be, simply enough, b♭-c-d-g, ⟨music⟩. The path from b♭ to c involves a long detour, but is still comparatively normal, as is apparent from the preceding diagram; but between c and the terminal d-g it is much more complicated: c becomes, so to speak, alienated from itself, is transformed into c♯, and the path which leads to the final g begins with an "alienated" g, namely, g♯. As a result, we have two intertwined paths: one from the initial b♭ over c (beginning of the second pyramid) via the strongly accentuated c♯ to d and g; the other from b♭ via the highest notes of both pyramids, a and g♯, to g—like this: ⟨music⟩.

XVI. The Single Creative Source

Now, what conclusions can be drawn from the foregoing considerations? The widely held notion of two distinct creative sources of music—inspiration responsible for the themes, and technical knowledge responsible for their elaboration—has proved untenable. This was demonstrated even in cases which, at first glance, seem to justify the notion. There can be no doubt that it is in development sections, where a given theme is elaborated according to rules, that a composer must rely primarily on his knowledge and technical experience. The breadth and boldness of the plans underlying the developments in the two movements of Mozart's G-minor Symphony we have analyzed, the sure mastery with which the material is used to further realization of the plan, are evidence of Mozart's incomparable compositional knowledge. But we have also seen that something else is involved. The crucial "events" that set things going and lead to all that follows are *not* a matter of knowledge or technique, are not dictated by a preconceived plan. In so far as one can speak of a plan, these "events" are accidental; they determine the plan rather than are determined by it. They originate in the themes—and this is what makes such developments so fascinating, so exciting; this is why we are spellbound, as if listening to a great storyteller. They sound like the actions and passions of a living thing, like episodes from the life history of a theme. Thus, it is not in those features of a development which it shares with other developments, but in those which distinguish it from others and make it as unique as a living being, that we grasp its innermost core. Consequently, it *cannot* be the product of knowledge or expertise. Knowledge and skill come with experience: thanks to them, old achievements can serve as the basis for new ones, provided that the old and the new are comparable, that is, have some features in common. Skill is gained and enhanced through application to essentially similar tasks. And because no situation is entirely new in every respect—even the unique individual breathes the same air as everyone else—no composer can dispense with knowledge and technical skill. However, they are insufficient to account for the unique, the *sui generis*, the incomparable—for something that has never been done before. Had he no more than this to rely on, a composer would be no better off than without them. To create something new, more is required.

A different source? Does $\begin{array}{c}\text{♪♪♪}\end{array}$ at the start of the development in our second example derive from the same source as $\begin{array}{c}\text{♪♪♪}\end{array}$ at the beginning of the movement? And if it does, is the source correctly designated by the term "inspiration"? We are using this term to denote something created out of nothing, something that fills a void not hitherto recognized. And nothing could be farther from a void to be filled than the start of this development: it is crammed with thematic patterns. Mozart does not set these patterns aside to accommodate some sudden inspiration—quite the contrary.

$\begin{array}{c}\text{♪♪♪}\end{array}$ is not conjured up out of nothing: the passage grows out of the richness and density of the musical materials on which the composer's mind is exclusively concentrated. It is not an idea occurring to the composer apropos of nothing or on occasion of something else, as in the case of Bach's bass line; it is an idea emerging out of something. The correct term when dealing with an idea that grows out of something is "discovery," not "inspiration"—discovery in the sense of a "finding" made in the course of examining given materials. Of course, findings or discoveries might be called "inspired":

not only are they unpredictable; they also produce unpredictable consequences. But in this usage "inspired" means something else. No
"higher" power is involved, not even Mozart's genius, but rather the
theme itself. The composer has merely helped the theme along, supplying a dynamic field within which the musical event can take place.
In such cases the composer may be likened to an architect who, instead
of arranging building blocks according to his own blueprint, urges them
to act and interact on their own—to arrange themselves according to
their own best interests—and who, observing their actions and interactions, makes their plan his own. This sounds like magic, and the
fact of the matter is that it is a greater miracle than the creation of
the theme itself, because it is creation not in the void but amid plenty,
and not in freedom but in confinement. The spiritual act involved here
cannot be called "rational" in the usual sense, yet it certainly cannot
be relegated to the domain of the irrational. The only justification for
evoking irrational sources, surely, is with reference to events so unpredictable or so utterly unprecedented that any attempt to interpret
them in terms of cause and effect must seem absurd. Here, we are
dealing with events whose distinctive characteristic is precisely this,
that they follow at once logically *and* unpredictably from what has gone
before: together with what precedes and follows them they form a tightly
knit whole. That there is a high degree of "rationality," indeed, even
"logic," in this kind of musical development cannot be denied. Moreover, as we have seen, the attempt to understand it is by no means
hopeless.

Viewed in this light, the distinction between rational and irrational—at any rate, the manner in which this distinction is used—scarcely
seems to apply. If specific events, correctly observed, cannot be subsumed into the one or the other of these two mutually exclusive
concepts, then something must be wrong with our definitions of them.
Could it be that we find it hard to understand what goes on in a musical
work because our concept of the rational is too narrow? And that we

are obliged for this reason to call "irrational" everything that does not fit this narrow concept? However that may be, when we are dealing with a Mozartian development, we cannot help feeling that our concept of the rational is inadequate to account for the facts of the case—not because the facts themselves elude rational explanation, but because our definition of the rational is not inclusive enough. What goes on in this development is rational even in the most customary sense, but is not fully accounted for thereby. As between the "events" themselves and our concept of the rational, who is to decide where to draw the line? Consider ♪♪♪♪♪. Who can break this down in illustration of the notion of two creative sources, especially two opposed sources? This phrase is whole and indivisible, could only have been created in a single spiritual act. To recognize that its creative source is rational up to a point—and no one doubts it—is to recognize that all of it must be rational. Only our narrow concept of rationality demands the dichotomy of two creative sources, one sharply distinguished from the other. We should stop forcing the facts to fit the concept, so that essential features of music are relegated to the domain of the irrational: that is, rendered unintelligible by definition. Rather, we should let the facts guide us toward a broader concept of the rational—a concept that more truthfully reflects the real power of thought, the true scope of the intelligible. At this point, however, a still broader question opens up. On what grounds are we justified in ascribing irrationality to music in the first place? May not the appeal to "higher" powers, to "inspiration," simply reflect the narrowness of our concept of the rational? For the time being we must leave this question unanswered and deal with another fundamental question: whether the spiritual act that produces musical events of the kind referred to above can be called an act of thought. What has been said so far is indeed insufficient to show that this designation and all it implies is the only proper one.

THE MUSICIAN'S HAND

Like any other artist, the composer handles a given raw material, confers on it a specific form, thus producing something that has never existed before, a new bit of reality: the work. In this sense, the sculptor, the potter, and the rug weaver may be called the archetypal artists: this not only because all the stages of artistic activity are strikingly illustrated in the way they transform their raw materials into finished works, but also because their activity involves primarily the hand, the organ in which the specifically human character of their activity is expressed more clearly than anywhere else.

Viewed in this light, the act that produces a work of art seems to be the direct opposite of an act of thought. Thinking operates with concepts; it draws boundary lines, makes distinctions, and creates relationships: it does not create new reality. It changes the world, to be sure, but never directly, always through the intermediary of an activity which involves the human body or a tool that improves its efficiency. Also language, this most direct creation of thinking, would not be a reality without the contribution of the body, which turns it into spoken words or signs. The artist's hand, however, is not guided by thought as defined above. To be sure, his hand is not blind, does not grope in the dark, but what guides it is representations or images, not concepts or judgments. This is at least what we feel compelled to believe. The hand's activity may depend on thought in the form of learning or experience: its decisive impulses do not originate in thought.

This being the case, can anything be gained from comparing the painter or sculptor with the composer? After all, the musician's raw material cannot be shaped by the hand. Or can it? Can one speak of a "musician's hand"?

In order to prepare the ground for the following discussion, we shall quote a few sentences from Heidegger's previously mentioned work

Albrecht Altdorfer: *The Battle of Alexander*. 1529. 62″ x 47″

Was heisst Denken? "There is something quite special about the hand," he writes. "It is generally believed that the hand is part of the human body. Yet the human hand can never be adequately defined as a bodily prehensile organ. . . . There is an unbridgeable gulf between the hand and all other prehensile organs. Only a speaking, i.e., thinking, being can have hands and produce handmade works. . . . Handwork is richer than is usually believed. Every motion of the hand in every one of its works is carried out in the medium of thought; every one of its gestures presupposes thought. All handwork is grounded in thought. For this reason thinking is the simplest and hence the most difficult handwork."

To begin with, the function of the visual artist's hand must be examined more closely. Is it really true that the activity of his hand is guided by the imagination, that it makes visible to the physical eye what has first been seen by the mind's eye? The potter's hands may be guided by his idea of the vessel's form when he is turning it, though this seems less certain when we recall that a vessel must be taken in one's hands in order to understand its form. Is it conceivable that the complicated design of a large rug is fully present in the rug maker's mind before the design has become actually visible through the activity of his hands? Did Altdorfer have a mental image of the lances in *The Battle of Alexander* before he actually put them on canvas? (See plate on facing page.)

As far as the last question is concerned, it can be answered only in the negative. Altdorfer may have conceived the plan for his enormous painting—enormous in content, not in dimensions—before he had begun to paint it: at the top the celestial drama, sun against moon, and the battles between storm-blown masses of clouds; in the middle area, the earth, mountains, seas, and human dwellings; at the bottom, the clash of hostile armies. And here are the lances, thousands of them, in every conceivable position—horizontal, vertical, diagonal, parallel, crossed, bristling like the quills of porcupine—an indescribable ordered confusion of lines and grids, in which the figures in the painting are caught just as are the viewers. No seeing eye will escape their truly magical power. Are we to suppose that the painter's inner eye saw this network with its thousand details before he put it on canvas? Let no one say that details do not matter. It is precisely those details that add up to create the whole, the overall design, the order—and without order there is no magic. That a mental image guided the hand here is just as unthinkable as that the hand worked blindly.

The questions concerning the priority of the inner over the outer image and the part played by handwork in the visual arts have been dealt with at length by Etienne Gilson in his great book *Painting and Reality*. After observing that paintings are man-made material objects and that "it is in the nature of things that the maker of a solid physical body has to use his hands to make it," Gilson says that the painter's hand (he refers most often to painting but what he says is true of all visual arts) is certainly not a mere tool subservient to a superior faculty, such as the mind or the imagination, is not merely an executive organ, but rather one educated to co-operate closely with the intellect. A painting is not conceived within the mind and then transferred onto canvas by the artist's hand: his hand is involved in the conception of the work. Indeed, the painter can often entrust his hand with doing all the work, let himself be guided by the hand. The painter does not think *with* his hands, but he thinks *in* his hands; his own hand is for him full of surprises: it solves his problems. "One of the main reasons painters find it so hard to make themselves understood when they speak of their art is that their hearers listen with their minds only, not with their hands." When Matisse was asked how he could distinguish between the good and less good among his many works, his answer was, "One feels it in his hands." A philosopher would have answered with considerations about beauty, order, and other aesthetic categories.

At this point one might ask, Where is the eye in all this? Gilson does not forget or deny that the eye is involved in the act of painting.

He refers to the continuous exchange between the painter's hand and eye. However, the eye functions predominantly as a receiving organ. Even though the eye is the source of all pleasure we take in the visible, especially in the visual work of art, the active, creative organ is the hand. In the continuous exchange between the two, the hand acts the part of the giver at least as often as the eye; it is the hand which, according to Gilson, gives definite form to the indistinct, incomplete pictures of the imagination and makes them visible to the eye. The first creative impulse, he says, does not originate in the eye, in something seen that might be reproduced on canvas: "Unless he feels in his fingers the curious itching that must have put a piece of charcoal into the hands of the men who painted the bison of the Altamira cave, nobody will ever acquire this art, much less use it. . . . A man has no creative perceptions . . . unless at the very moment he perceives certain external spectacles he feels in his hand an obscure urge to translate them into colors and shapes." It is not the eye, it is the hand that discovers the picture, the one to be realized. The term "motive" expresses this fact: what the painter sees becomes a potential picture by setting his hands in motion.

Gilson is especially illuminating on the creative function of the hand where he points out that paintings are creations *ex nihilo*, that the artist always starts from a void. "When the born painter finds himself confronted with an empty surface, he experiences an obscure desire to cover it with forms." It is a void, a visible nothingness, not a richly varied spectacle, that triggers the hand's first action, the first line drawn by the artist: the hand responds to the call of the void, while the eye merely looks on. To be sure, if the artist had not preserved in his memory all the things he had seen, the hand would not know what to do. What he has seen is, so to speak, in the back of his mind, but he has no specific spectacle before him that he wants to reproduce. What he has before him is a void that demands to be filled, covered with forms.

It may be possible to go beyond Gilson's reflections, which refer only to Western art. Certain Far Eastern drawings suggest that the hand responsible for them did much more than meet the demand of the void to be covered with forms. Here the hand seems actually to have created the void in the first place, and if one can speak of any demand made by the void, this demand was certainly not to be covered but to be made visible as a void. Where there was nothing to be seen before, now one sees the nothing, the void around things delimited by the lines, the void as their supporting ground, the things as creatures of the void. Anyone who has seen how a hand trained in the Far Eastern tradition draws the first line on an empty sheet, how the expressive gesture of the hand, starting anywhere, continues to draw, producing a network of lines out of which emerge, as though accidentally, shapes of objects—mountains, trees, human figures—cannot escape the impression of a dialogue between hand and void. The work originates in this dialogue, this encounter, this interplay, not in the intention to put on paper a picture seen by the mind's eye. Otherwise, the picture would have pre-existed in the imagination; the time needed by the hand to transfer it onto paper would not enter into the making of the work, would remain external to it. Here, however, we can see a work coming into being, and this process of coming into being, the time taken by the hand's motion, has been incorporated in the work itself, has become an essential element of the whole.

Here the spark of analogy leaps over to the composer's art. Let us go back to an earlier example, where we visualized Bach at the keyboard. His left hand strikes the deep note ♪; his right hand takes over, replies with ♪ —or ♪ and ♪ . A line of sound, traced by a hand in the silence, forms beginning to be outlined . . . Gilson, too, compares the process of creating a painting to that of creating a piece of music: just as visible form presupposes a void, he says, so audible form presupposes silence. Gilson refers primarily to the silence which is imposed before the beginning of a musical performance, from which the first tone emerges and in which the last tone dies away. But there is much more to it. The composer, too, must have created a silence around himself before beginning his first line of sound. This silence is not necessarily external: Mozart could compose in the midst of noise because he built around himself a wall of inner stillness. Also, it is certainly true of music, as it is of painting, that its task is not to cover the void or to do away with it. It may be said that one of music's functions is to lay bare the positive meaning of silence, to transform a silence when we hear nothing into an *audible* nothing. Unlike painting, music cannot make tangible the void around the forms; in musical space there is no "around" in this sense: each tone occupies all the available space when it sounds. But we experience the void in between, in the rest which, after all, is something very different from mere absence of tones and is an element of music as real as the tones themselves. "The tones stop, but the music goes on," as a wise child once said. And when can the power of silence be felt more compellingly than when the last tone of a melody has died away? (It may be noted here that many persons use music to mask a silence which they cannot bear because they feel only its negative aspect, the void. They could be cured of this error, this sickness, precisely by listening to music.)

Can the audible line be the work of the hand, like the visible one? After all, Bach's hands at the keyboard have merely struck keys, not produced sounds. The painter's hand produces the visible line directly—the trace of his hand's motion is recorded in the line—but the musician's hand merely operates an instrument, which produces the sounds. Whereas the painter's brush directly incorporates the hand's motion in the line, the musician's tone and hand are kept apart by an elaborate mechanical apparatus. And have we not stated explicitly that it is not at all necessary to suppose that Bach conceived his melody while actually sitting at the keyboard, that he could just as well have conceived it away from any keyboard? Where would the hand come in then? But must Bach's hands actually rest on a keyboard to create such a melody? Do the hands have less to do with it when it is created in the composer's mind?

The score

shows clearly where the fingers rest on the keys, where the motion passes from one hand to the other. Something like this could have been created only by hands moving on a keyboard—whether actually or mentally is beside the point. What Gilson says of the painter is also true of the musician: his hands solve his problems; the hands repeatedly have surprises in store for him. This is why Novalis could say, "In the painter, the hand becomes the locus of an instinct, and the same is true of the musician." And this is why it is misleading to praise a composer in such a case on the ground that he knew how to write "for his instrument," as though the instrument confronting him and his hands were merely a thing to be mastered or operated effectively, when in truth the instrument is an extension of his hands. It would be more exact to say the opposite, that his instrument writes for him; indeed, one often wonders whether his hand has discovered a melodic turn on his instrument or whether his instrument has played it into his hand. In a Chopin, a Domenico Scarlatti—masters of the highest rank who composed almost exclusively for the keyboard—hand and instrument are as inseparable as hand and brush in a painter. A Chopin melody seems to be traced by the playing hand, as a visible line is traced by the painting hand. A composer must not sit at the keyboard to do this: he always has the keyboard in the spirit of his hands.

What about instruments such as the flute which require less manual work than the keyboard? Does a melodic line drawn into the silence by means of a keyboard lose this character when played on a flute?

The hands that hold the flute, opening or closing the keys or holes, are not of the kind that can be described as being "the locus of an instinct." If any actual or mental activity produced the melody in this case, it would be breathing. And what about song, the mother of all melody, all music? What have the hands to do here? Nowhere are they needed less than for singing. Finally, the idea that orchestral music is in any sense the work of the hand seems completely absurd: here the hand would have to play all the instruments of the orchestra simultaneously.

In one respect, however, all music, whether made to be sung or played on the keyboard, flute, or any instrument whatever, is handwork: it must be recorded in writing if it is to exist objectively as a work. Just as the painter's hand records the pictorial work on canvas, so the musician's hand—the writing, not the playing hand—records the musical work on paper. Now it becomes clear how painting differs from composing. Whatever one may think about how the hand is related to the artist's mind or imagination, it will not be contested that the hand is actually responsible for the last stage of the work; whether the step from the mental image to the picture on canvas be large or small, it is a step: mental image and finished painting are not the same. It is even possible to ask whether the step involves a gain or a loss. Nothing like this is true of the musician. His writing hand records only what is a finished musical pattern in his mind; his hand does the very thing that the painter's hand never does: it merely copies. The music in the mind is the whole music and the hand contributes nothing; there is no difference between the imagined and the realized musical pattern. In a well-known letter to his sister, Mozart wrote: "I am sending you a new piece, a prelude and fugue for the clavier. Don't be surprised that the fugue comes first. I had it in my head and while I was setting it down on paper I composed the prelude."[1] We see clearly here that

---

1. Dated April 20, 1782, this letter refers to K. 383a [394].

the writing hand has nothing to do with the task of composing. Can you imagine a painter who, while painting one canvas, is painting another in his mind?

To the assertion that the writing hand has nothing to do with the task of composing, one case would seem to offer a spectacular and, at first glance, conclusive exception: Beethoven. He *did* compose while writing, *did* write while composing. In his case, the two activities—his sketchbooks bear witness to this—are more closely interwoven than in the case of any other composer. Later we shall discuss his way of composing in greater detail; here we are concerned only with the "writing hand." When Beethoven loses his way after writing the felicitous beginning of a melody, in looking for the proper continuation, he invariably starts again from scratch, and writes—*writes*—it, often in great hurry yet never omitting a single note, obviously in the hope (there is no other explanation) that the momentum of his hand will carry him beyond the critical point and put him on the right track. Is this momentum really that of his writing hand? Yes and no. Yes, for if his writing hand had nothing to do with it, he would not need to write at all; no, because the motion of the tones is certainly not—and cannot be—that of the writing hand, if only because each proceeds at a different pace: where the motion of the music is rapid, the hand lags considerably behind; where it is slow, the hand runs considerably ahead. Consequently, if the hand is involved, it is not the physical but the thinking hand, which is, of course, not at all the same thing as the mental image of the physical hand.

That the idea of the musician's "thinking hand" is not a fiction will become clear when we compare his activity with the painter's.

The visual artist works in a visible medium. Because everything visible, everything perceived by the eye, is an object or the property of an object in the external world, production of a visible work requires an external, "outgoing" organ: the hand. In the audible world, too, there are many things that the ear perceives as coming from the outside, e.g., all noises and natural sounds. Musical sounds, however, the audible in its most refined form, are not objects or properties of objects in the external world. When I hear I hear "Bach," not "clavier." Although the sound comes to me from outside, it has been inside before being outside: the thing—instrument or human body—is merely a station through which it passes on its way from inside to outside and back inside. The tone I send out when I sing it is the same as the one I take back when I hear it. The ear that opens to hear it does not react to it in the same way as the eye reacts to color, for the ear lets the tone come back, return home to join other tones. Whoever works in tones does not need to go out to them; he always has them within himself (this is why man can emit sounds but cannot emit light, unlike some animals). This is also why no external, outgoing organ, no bodily hand, is needed to form tones; no corporeal organ could grasp the incorporeal substance of music. The organ here must be as incorporeal as the substance to which it gives form; if it is to grasp tones, it must go inward, not outward.

The painter or sculptor needs two organs, a perceiving one and a working one, the eye and the hand: the eye sees what the hand does. The musician can, as it were, dispense with the eye. His work is done inside, not outside himself. In his case, external perception, actual hearing, at best serves to confirm the correctness of what he has done inwardly or to verify it for the purpose of subsequent adjustments. Composing at the piano, letting oneself be guided by the outward sound, has always been regarded as a sign of amateurishness. The creative composer's ear is an organ of inner rather than outer perception, but not in the sense that it perceives what is inside one's body. More generally, it does not serve to apprehend something already present. The ear does not perceive in the same way as the inner eye perceives a dream image. The composer's ear is directed at a void: what it perceives it creates, summons into existence from the void. It is eye and hand in one, but more hand than eye, a hand that does not find the material to be formed outside itself. The formed material here rather seems to come directly from the forming hand itself; the boundary between forming hand and formed material becomes fluid. Before music becomes external sound or written score, an inner ear has apprehended it, an inner hand has formed it—and this is true of music for any instrument or voice, whether one or many. It is especially true where the composer is completely unconcerned with external sound, with realization by instruments, and thinks in terms of pure sound. Bach's *Art of the Fugue* is a frequently cited example but certainly not the only one. And the same is true not only of works entirely or partially finished in the composer's mind before they are set down in writing but also of improvised works, where the composer has not thought in advance, where he abandons himself to the moment. Here, too, the inner ear and inner hand must be one breath ahead of the outer ear and outer hand. We have mentioned works which seem to be produced by a physical hand in direct contact with an instrument. When Bach at the keyboard begins ♮, he may do this by his fingers alone, which know how to find their way; next they look for , but no longer involves the physical hand alone. To be sure, the notes seem to meet the hand halfway, as though of their own volition, yet we feel the presence of something else which guides the hand from within. The sounds have become an expressive gesture. This gesture cannot be ascribed to the physical hand; should we ascribe it to the composer or to the tones? Here all such distinctions are pointless: the tones themselves have become hand, since they speak in gestures.

Some writers have toyed with the idea of a handless Raphael. Such speculations are not as absurd as might seem at first glance. Take the painter's hand away: certainly, what is left is not nothing. The will to form, to produce the work, is still present, although it cannot be materialized, since the organ that gives form to the material is lacking. But when the material is incorporeal, when the artist finds it within himself, the will to form can be realized. The handless painter is a musician.

We have begun by inquiring into the intellect's share in the creation of musical works; then we started on a new tack, viewing the work of art as a material object formed by the artist's hand; now we have come to recognize the musician's hand as a purely intellectual organ, and its formative activity as purely intellectual in character. So, after all, is his work the product of an act of thought? Our question about the share of thought in the musician's activity has gradually led us to the conclusion that his doing is indistinguishable from his thinking. This, of course, applies only to his musical activity proper: a musician may wonder whether he should compose a cantata or a string quartet, whether a phrase should be given to the strings or the winds, or—to cite the most famous example of a thinking process of this type—whether there is room for human voices in a symphony. In all of these cases his thinking deals only with preliminaries, not with the work itself. Beethoven may ponder whether and how song is to be introduced in the last movement of his Ninth Symphony, but he cannot just *think* about what melody is to be sung: in the very act of conceiving the melody he creates it. Here the organ of perception is indistinguishable from the organ of thought: thinking and creating have become one and the same thing.

MUSIC AND MATHEMATICS

The foregoing reflections throw a new light on the relationship between music and mathematics.

We take it for granted that tones are correlated with numbers, and that relations between tones correspond to numerical ratios. We learn at school that every pitch corresponds to a certain frequency of vibrations, and that the intervals of the diatonic system, which is the basis of our music, are expressed in terms of the simplest ratios. The interval of the octave corresponds to the ratio $1:2$, that of the fifth to $2:3$, the fourth to $3:4$ (hence that of the difference between fifth and fourth, one whole tone, to $8:9$, that is, the difference between $2:3$ or $8:12$ and $3:4$ or $9:12$), that of the major third to $4:5$ (hence the difference between the fourth and the major third, one semitone, to $15:16$), and that of the minor third to $5:6$. The series $1:2:3:4:5:6$ is sufficient to provide the basis for the whole system. Because this fact fits easily into our world view and into our belief, inspired by mathematical natural science, that all phenomena can be correlated with numbers, we take it merely as a confirmation of this belief and see nothing remarkable in it.

If, however, we look at this matter with unprejudiced eyes, a different picture is disclosed. The diatonic system is not a natural product. Apollo did not give it to the Greeks, the God of the Bible did not reveal it to the Hebrews, nor has any ancient sage constructed it according to a rigorous mathematical order and decreed that people be guided by it in their singing and playing. The system was developed gradually. At first people just sang and built instruments on which they could play their tunes. Eventually they began to reflect on their peculiar activity, and noticed that the same intervals kept recurring in their melodies. Only then did they discover the order governing them. "First come the melodies, then comes the scale." It was discovered (perhaps by an instrument maker) that in order to produce the tones occurring in the melodies a vibrating string or column of air must be divided into halves, thirds, quarters, and so on. All this suggests that the correlation between music and mathematics is anything but natural or self-evident. After all, inventors of melodies did not deliberately choose tones in such a way that their intervals could be expressed in terms of simple ratios! When making music nothing is farther from our minds than mathematics, measurements, or numbers. Mathematics operates secretly, as it were, behind the musicians' backs.

For a real understanding of what goes on in music, there is little to expect from considerations which start with the individual tone or interval and branch out into mathematics. I add nothing to my understanding of the auditory experience of $\hat{1}$-$\hat{5}$ when I learn that the ratio of frequencies corresponding to this interval is $2:3$. This fact has no bearing on the tonal pattern without which there is no music; it has nothing to do with the reality of music. What we are concerned with is not the correlation between music and numbers, but the less obvious similarities between the musician and the mathematician in respect of the nature of their activities. Nothing can be farther from the working musician's mind than counting, nothing farther from the working mathematician's mind than singing, and yet there is something common to both. In mathematics, just as in music (and nowhere else), doing is inseparable from thinking; more than that, in both doing is identical with thinking. What is true of tones is also true of numbers: to think them is to create them. Theologians say that God's thoughts are His creations, that God's thought posits existence; what God thinks, exists. Where human creation is concerned, the musician and the mathematician come closest to the divine model: however far removed from God they may be otherwise, here is the place where they meet.

It might be contended that what we have asserted about mathematical concepts is true of other scientific concepts, or even of all concepts. Concepts such as those of entelechy, dynamic field, mutation, surplus value, thing-in-itself owe their existence to acts of thought, exist only in so far as they are thought. Similarly, the concepts of cause, possibility, and freedom are what they are only because they are thought. Indeed, "animal," "plant," "mountain," "man"—all these owe their existence to acts of thought, and the same is true of terms such as "between," "however," "no." But each of these creations of thought refers to something "given" to thought, which thought defines, delimits, or, if you will, intellectualizes. In each of these cases thought is directed toward something it seeks to understand. Concepts do not produce what they define: the concept "thought" does not produce thinking; concepts do not posit existence. In the last analysis, thinking usually implies a reference to something that is not merely a thought, to something that exists independently of thought. The same is true of the word, which is the outward aspect of thought. The word, too, owes its peculiar mode of existence to thought and refers to something other than itself, something given; even the concept "word" is different from the many particular words subsumed into it. Not so numbers and, more generally, mathematical concepts: the mode of existence which they owe to thinking is of a different kind. 3, $\sqrt{2}$, π, ε, $\sqrt{-1}$, point, straight line, right angle, circle—none of these refers to something given, something that is not created by thought. Here nothing is given in advance, nothing pre-exists—or if it does, it is in the sense of "comes before": 2 comes before 3, 1 before 2, nothing before 1, the straight line before the circle, the point before the line, nothing before the point. What comes before is here invariably of the same kind as what comes after. The concepts are related, they form a chain, but every link in it is again a mathematical concept. The chain is anchored in another mathematical concept, not in something that exists outside thought. The ancient maxim that life can be created only by life itself may someday lose its validity (as is suggested by recent developments in biology), but there can be no doubt that numbers and geometric figures are always produced by other numbers and figures. In the words "three trees" (referring, say, to a maple, an elm, and a palm), the term "trees" denotes a set of qualities which three given trees have in common. These qualities do not originate in thinking: we perceive them; they are given. But "three" does *not* denote anything like that, e.g., something our three trees, a triangle, and a clock striking three have in common. That such a something is present I know only because I know the meaning of "three": the common element does not suggest the concept; the concept suggests the common element. Similarly, "circle" is not primarily what all given circles have in common: until the concept of "circle" was formed, there had been no given circles. Of course, once they have been defined, numbers and geometric figures can refer to the given, but their referents owe their existence to the concepts, not vice versa. All this is not intended as a contribution to the perennial debates concerning being and thought, but only to stress the distinctive character of mathematical concepts, which a mathematician, Andreas Speiser, formulated in the statement, "The concept of number has the power to posit existence."

But surely there is a paradox here. Are we not granting—to just that kind of thought (or concept) that allegedly has no roots in existence—the very power we have explicitly denied all thought or concepts? Actually, there is in ordinary life a very good example of the sort of thought that remains self-contained, even in operation: what is involved in playing games. Games like chess and Go are purely intellectual constructions that correspond to nothing outside themselves. Mathematics, in this connection, can be thought of as merely the most sublime of all games, in which the intellect plays with its own potentialities—and indeed mathematics has often been so described. At the same time, however, it must be admitted that playing with numbers or with geometrical figures is a very different game from the others. The difference is illustrated in the well-known saying of a mathematician, "God made the integers; all else is the work of man." It never occurs to chess players to think of the chessmen as divinely created. We only invoke the hand of God in connections where insight into reality is involved, whereas the distinctive appeal of games is that they enable us to escape from ordinary space-time limitations into a realm of comparative freedom, subject only to rules of our own devising. The rules and concepts of mathematics, for all that they may be without objective correlatives, nonetheless do refer to something real: to play the game of mathematics is to answer questions posed by the real world. We may well be unaware of this when working out a problem in mathematics, but the rules we follow and the kind of thinking mathematical operations require are ultimately bound up with the laws of nature. To be sure, mathematical concepts stand outside the world of sense perception, yet they are close enough to it to be affected by it and respond to it—just as a string tightly drawn emits a sound when anything causes it to vibrate. The order of numbers and figures is in tune with the order of nature. What distinguishes mathematical concepts from others is just this consonance between thought and existence, and this is why they can serve as symbols. Other concepts rise to the level of allegories, at best.

For the same reason, we speak of a mathematician's accomplishments as "works"; though fabricated of purely intellectual stuff, they posit existence. Winning a chess game or even a tournament, though undoubtedly a feat, is not a work in the sense that the *Conic Sections* of Apollonius is. And here we see something else that music— and only music—has in common with mathematics: not only do they both create works; they also create the materials out of which their works are made. Like numbers, musical sounds owe their existence entirely to the human intellect. It is not true that nature supplies the musician with his materials, though unreflective thinkers have often alleged it. "Pure sound," Paul Valéry writes, referring to musical sound, "is a kind of creation. Nature knows only noises." No one denies that the noises of nature have their own beauty, purity, and individuality; indeed, sound in nature is probably more richly elaborated than color is. However, it is as remote from music as the constellation Cassiopeia is from the number five. It is the sounds of nature that seem closest to music, that best illustrate the difference: the song of birds. Only people who know nothing about music suppose birdsong to mark an early stage in musical development or can think of music as "imitating" birdsong. Géza Révész observes that birds always sing in the same key. They cannot transpose, because to do this it is necessary to have an audible grasp of the relations between tones, their dynamic qualities. These are only possible within a tonal *system*, that is, a construct of the mind. The sounds birds produce form no system. When a bird breaks off its usual song, perhaps just before the last note, it is *we* who sense some "unresolved tension." When a melody breaks off before the last tone, then it is the tone itself that demands continuation and resolution. The tension is that of the tone, not ours. Nor must we have heard this particular piece of music before to have this sensation. To be music, sounds have to be organized into a system. The affinity between tones and numbers, due to their being purely intellectual creations, is best demonstrated by the fact that neither numbers nor tones exist independently of constructing them and putting them together in a system. No single number and no single tone is what it is without the others. This strange mode of existence—as relation, ratio, logos—is an essential characteristic of music as of mathematics. Like the mathematician, the musician deals in relation, ratio, logos. How, then, could the musician's activity be anything but logical and rational, how could it be something other than an intellectual activity, for all that he does not think conceptually?

At the start of these reflections, we assumed, in accordance with the generally accepted view, that all thinking is conceptual, and that since the musician has essentially nothing to do with concepts, his activity could not properly be called "thinking." But after listening carefully to music and observing what transpires, it now seems that the accepted view should be turned upside down: what the musician does cannot possibly be called anything but "thinking." Obviously, conceptual thinking is not the only kind.

In the next chapter we shall attempt, by observing the process of musical creation, to form a more definite idea of the nature of this "other" thinking and of the laws that govern it.

XVII. Musical Thought

CHOPIN'S PROBLEM

WE HAVE IT on George Sand's authority that, when they were staying on Mallorca, Chopin once spent a whole day working over a passage from one of his Preludes, trying to get it right. Yet all his strenuous efforts were in vain. He did not succeed in improving the passage, and had to leave it as it was.

What exactly is involved in such an attempt? What is the meaning of "right" or "wrong" in this case, and what tells the composer that something needs to be "improved"? His feeling? But this vague term "feeling" merely expresses our perplexity: we use it only because we have no better word for it, because we do not really know what it is. "Feeling" here certainly is not used in the sense of feeling love or hate or any other familiar "emotion," or of anything like feeling dizzy, but rather something akin to feeling pain—not just in the sense of hurting but also because it tells us what is hurting. Here the sensation has an objective counterpart: something is actually perceived by an organ of inner sense. Did Chopin hear the deficiency? Did his hand reach out to set it right? We recall the painter's observation that he could feel the difference between good and bad in his hands. But how is it possible to hear or feel something that is not there?

Here we have an opportunity to observe the composer at work; it is a particular instance of a common human situation: there is a problem to be solved requiring intellectual effort.

Actually, two related yet distinct problems are involved here. One concerns the composer: to find the right phrase. The other concerns the listener: to find out what is wrong (George Sand does not mention it). We shall consider the listener's problem first.

To begin with, let us formulate it in terms of logical thinking. Suppose a mathematical treatise contains one false step and I am given the problem of finding it. Now, this may be hard for me to do, but it is surely not impossible; in principle, indeed, I must be able to find the error, and if I should fail to find it nonetheless, the failure could be ascribed only to my personal intellectual inadequacy. In logical argument, each step is correct so long as it follows from the steps preceding it according to rigorously defined rules. The statement to which it leads is not necessarily true: it can be false, for instance, when the preceding steps involve false statements. But each logically correct step following from a true statement necessarily leads to a true statement. This is what distinguishes logical necessity from physical compulsion or moral obligation: not the step itself, but only its validity is at stake. In logic, the symbol used to denote this kind of necessity—necessity in the reasoning rather than in the argument's conclusion—is $\subset$, the symbol of implication. The very shape of this sign suggests what it stands for: to imply is to enfold, to envelop, to contain. Each step correctly deduced in the course of an argument is already implicit in the preceding step, wholly contained in it. It needs only to be taken; it does not, nor is it supposed to, add anything new to the preceding step—for if it did, it would *not* be logically correct. Each successive step merely makes explicit what was only implicit in the preceding, makes us see or recognize something that was always there but had until now been missed. One is reminded of puzzle pictures, in which you try to find something that is not immediately apparent; it is not a matter of adding anything to the picture, merely one of discerning what is hidden away in it already. Similarly, to insure correctness in logical reasoning, we have to ascertain that every conclusion is implicit in what has gone before; that is, it must be enveloped or "contained" in what is given, though this may not be immediately apparent. As we have noted, it is not always easy to solve such a problem, but we may be confident that a solution exists.

Analogous problems in music are literally insoluble.

In what sense can we speak of "right" or "wrong" in a musical context? Well, some things are obviously wrong: false notes, mistakes made by performers, arbitrary deviations from the text, misprints, slips of the pen in original manuscripts or copies. Concerning the latter, however, we are already on delicate ground. When can we be sure that a slip of the pen is just that? Richard Wagner attributed the dissonant first note of the horn at the end of the development section in the first movement of the *Eroica* to a slip of Beethoven's pen and "corrected" it. An early editor of *The Well-Tempered Clavier* assumed that an unconventional harmonic progression in Prelude no. 1 was due to an oversight on Bach's part, and added a whole measure of his own invention to correct it; this "corrected" text appears in many subsequent editions. In such comparatively obvious instances the matter can eventually be settled. Not so in other, less obvious instances. Did Beethoven forget to supply accidentals in a certain passage of the *Hammerklavier* Sonata (first movement, measures 237 and 239)? Is the first note of the cello in measure 24 of the first movement of the C♯-minor Quartet a d or a d♯? These questions remain open, although interpretation of the passages involved largely depends on how they are answered. Unlike logic, music seems to lack a reliable criterion for settling such matters.

We speak, not without reason, of "musical logic" or "musical syntax," i.e., a framework that should provide a clear-cut criterion. These terms designate a set of rules resulting from the dynamic relationships of tones, the qualities of tension and resolution of sounds, the relationship of consonance and dissonance, from basic rhythmic patterns and the elementary desire for symmetry, and lastly from the particularities of a given style. Such rules, however, are of no help in solving the kinds of problem we are concerned with here. Take a score composed in a familiar style, cover up a few bars, and ask a number of students of composition to supply the missing music. This is simply a matter of studying the preceding passages and continuing them in the style indicated. Any student of composition ought to be able to come up with a "correct," or at least not obviously "false," solution. Quite a number of different solutions to the problem will be put forward, all of them "correct," yet it is very unlikely that any of them will be identical with the original. Even when only a very few notes have to be supplied—something as musically obvious as supplying the missing word in the sentence "It must . . . rained yesterday"—even then, when it would seem that no one could possibly come up with something new, just then we may be in for a big surprise.

Here is a concrete example. Suppose that only the main section of the last chorus in Bach's *St. Matthew Passion* had come down to us, only the first forty-eight measures, and that the concluding measure of the last phrase, too, is missing—both where it is played by the instruments and where it is repeated by the chorus. Now, it would seem that the melody admits of only one possible conclusion: not only does it proceed 5̂-4̂-3̂-2̂, , on the way to its final resolution 1̂, ; the parallel passage at the end of the first phrase, , confirms that the missing conclusion can be only . Actually, sopranos, violins, and oboes all proceed that way—but not the flutes! The latter depart from the melody to produce just about the last sound we should expect: coming as though from nowhere, the sharply dissonant note breaks into the concluding and resolving C minor chord with shattering effect. For the duration of one long pulse beat the entire musical structure hangs in midair—and only after this is the note resolved into the final consonance [♪]. So there was another way of concluding the passage, although it would never have occurred to us had not Bach found it first and taught us to hear the preceding passage as requiring it. It is easy, after the fact, to say that the conclusion could not possibly be other than it is, and even possible to "justify" the unexpected melodic turn by pointing to an earlier one, for what is [♪] but a disguised repetition of [♪]? However, the parallel is so thoroughly hidden, so anything but obvious that—as the present writer knows from his own experience—one can have been familiar with the *St. Matthew Passion* for fifty years without having noticed it. Moreover, Bach's solution to his problem seems to have been dictated more by mechanical than musical considerations.

In his day the lowest note on the transverse flute was [♪]: it could not produce the [♪] of Oboe I! In compositional situations like this, which occur often enough, the unplayable note is usually transposed to a higher octave: here, in other words, the flutes would have to play [♪]. If Bach wanted to avoid this, however, another solution was available to him: to have the flutes play [♪] like Oboe II. Only one of these two solutions would have been considered today if the measure in question had actually been lost. However, to a composer like Bach a mechanical obstacle like this served as springboard to his genius. Could his flute, like ours, have played the note [♪], Bach might have simply concluded with [♪]—in which case [♪] would never have been created and the world would have been deprived of a deeply moving experience. (Strangely enough, were a computer asked to compose the last measure of the flute part, it would, among other solutions, propose "the quarter note b followed by the half note c." But hardly anyone would single this out as the correct solution.)

All of which shows how misleading it is to speak of "logic" with reference to music's peculiar coherence. For the decisive characteristic of logical coherence, implication—that is, the fact that every step is implicit in the preceding and hence can be deduced from it—is missing. In music no step necessarily follows from the preceding in the sense of being deducible through keen listening. This is true not only of "hearing" in the usual acoustical sense but also of interpretative, comprehending "listening." Every step in music can accomplish what no step in logic is allowed to do: it *can* go beyond the given and say something that does *not* follow from it by any known rule. Even when the use of the sign of implication, $\subset$, seems to be justified, when the new step actually is determined by the preceding and needs only to be taken—even then, as we have seen, the field remains wide open, and the situation is better expressed by $\subset$ than by $\subset$. Of course, this is not to say that music is just a succession of surprises. This would be unbearable; and, indeed, as everyone knows, what takes place in music is largely determined by convention. Time and again, what happens is exactly what is to be expected according to the currently recognized rules—in other words, it is *not* something new. But the conventional proceeds in an atmosphere of freedom, as it were: not because it must, but because the composer wants it to be so. In principle, every step in music might have been taken otherwise than it was, and so, from this point of view, even a conventional step is "new." This renders pointless any attempt to find, in a given piece of music, the passage that seemed wrong to the composer. If we cannot decide between what is and what is not right on the basis of what has gone before (as we do in logic), how are we to decide at all? If I cannot say of any step that it has to be just that and nothing else, then I cannot (within reasonable limits) call any step "wrong" or say that it cannot be right. How idle, then, to search through Chopin's Preludes for the passage he worked on so long without being able to improve it. The problem is insoluble not only in practice but also in theory; it is meaningless.

In the light of these assertions, however, the very notion of musical coherence has become questionable. If no step in music follows from the preceding, if a step may be "wrong" even when it follows and "right" even when it does not follow from the preceding, what is left of musical coherence apart from the psychological fact that a number of subjective impressions are linked in an individual mind, a fact whose objective validity can be denied? To this question only one answer is possible: if this were the case, Chopin's attempt to improve a passage would have been foolish. But a Chopin is no fool. His problem is *not* meaningless. His behavior expresses the reality of musical coherence no less clearly than the behavior of a magnetic needle expresses the reality of the magnetic field. If our notion of coherence proves inapplicable here, it is incumbent upon us to formulate it in such a way as to render the experiences and phenomena of music not meaningless but intelligible.

In his dialogue *Eupalinos or the Architect*, Paul Valéry has his architect say, "What is important for me above all else is to obtain from *that which is going to be*, that it should with all the vigor of its newness satisfy the reasonable requirements of *that which has been*." What Eupalinos says of architecture, the spatial art par excellence, is also true of music, the temporal art par excellence. The essential characteristic of musical coherence, which distinguishes it from both logical coherence and random successions, cannot be expressed more clearly and aptly. If we omit the words "with all the vigor of newness," Valéry's statement defines the law governing logical coherence; if we keep these words omitting the rest, it defines random succession. What is in question here, however, is neither of these alternatives, but a type of coherence that is not logical yet not irrational either. It is rather one that has a logic of its own, in which rationality is compatible with newness. "That which has been," i.e., what is given, makes a reasonable demand, i.e., a demand contained and recognizable in the given, capable of being satisfied, and addressed to "that which is going to be." The latter, in order to satisfy the demand, must supply more than what can be recognized or heard in the given or inferred from it, must display "all the vigor of newness." Whereas in logic only consistency matters, and any step can be only right or wrong, in music where the new is woven into the given context, such hard and fast decisions are impossible. The difference between right and wrong remains, but admits of degrees, as we have seen in our Bach and Chopin examples. The two elements of consistency and newness can never be kept apart, even in a concrete individual case. Nor are they a composite—consistency plus a bit of newness or newness plus a bit of consistency. The twofold requirement is satisfied by *one* step; a single act produces both consistency and newness. Every step reveals two aspects: once it has been taken, it is consistent, for otherwise it would not meet a reasonable requirement; before being taken, it is unpredictable, for otherwise it would not have the full vigor of newness. The listener to the finished work, who knows only the steps that have been taken, enjoys the consistency of the new; the composer inside his composition, who has to take all the steps, feels that he cannot predict what will be consistent. What each successive step must be in order to meet the twofold requirement, this the composer too cannot know until he has actually taken it. Until then, this is a secret which the tones betray to no one except the one to whom they owe their existence, and even to him they do not really reveal it; they merely point the way. They prod him to guess, they facilitate, even urge, but they do not compel. Chopin's vain attempt to improve a passage pinpoints the process at the critical stage. The attempt made necessary by the requirement of consistency failed to meet the requirement of newness. Nothing more fully characterizes musical coherence and the act that produces it than Chopin's failure to solve his problem.

We are all familiar with the situation in which we find ourselves when confronted with a task that requires intellectual effort. Solving a mathematical or technical problem, constructing a model for the purpose of gaining better understanding of a specific phenomenon, defining a term, choosing the best means to a specific end, understanding the way a man acts, interpreting a historical event, finding suitable words to express a thought or feeling—all problems of this type, however different otherwise, have in common that in each one thinking is directed toward something given. What is to be found is already present in the given; only something that is hidden can be discovered, as when a ray of light illumines a dark spot or when our thinking fits an element of the given in a new order. The composer's situation differs from all situations of this type, which are aptly characterized by a statement Albert Einstein once made in conversation, "I know exactly where I want to get, only I don't know how to get there." Those who interpret music as essentially a language of feeling believe the composer's situation is comparable to that of a person trying to find words to express a feeling for which no word exists. That is not so. When Chopin tries to solve his problem, his thinking is only seemingly directed toward the "given" he has before him: the passage he wants to improve. Actually he has nothing before him; his thinking is not directed toward, or focused on, the given; it starts from the given, but is directed toward something beyond the given, toward a void. The given is behind rather than before him; he seeks not within it but together with it—together with the given he seeks something which is not in the given. Nor can he expect to discover something in the void. Here only one thing matters: to find something that does not exist, i.e., to invent it. Nor can he avail himself of a criterion for appraising his invention, such as is available in other cases. Even the word to be found can be tested against the inner experience it is supposed to express, in order to ascertain whether or not it serves its purpose. A composer has no such criteria, nothing which could help him in his predicament, no objects, rules, concepts, or feelings; he has only the tones themselves. Their momentum no doubt can carry him up to a certain point, but then they fail him, abandon him, cast him into the void, where he must gain a foothold without their help. And only an elusive inner sense tells him—and him alone—whether he has found the solution he has sought. Even in the awareness of his failure he is alone: anyone else can say what he has *not* found; the composer cannot. For he could say it only in the tones he has been unable to invent.

And there is something else: the mathematician's failure is temporary; the musician's is final. What one mathematician fails to find, others after him may be able to find, and even were it never to be found, it is "there" in a sense, though unseen; to search for it is not absurd. What Chopin failed to find does not exist and will never be found; to search for it makes no sense. The great mathematician Fermat wrote on the margin of a book that the equation $a^n + b^n = c^n$ is not solvable in integers for any n greater than 2, and added that the proof he had found was too long to write in the narrow margin.[1] This statement was discovered after Fermat's death, and for the last three hundred years mathematicians have vainly tried to find the proof of his theorem, whose truth no one doubts. The proof exists: it is implicit in the "given," although we do not have it. The proof would exist even if his note had not been discovered, even if he himself had not found it. But what Chopin failed to find—or if he found it failed to write down—exists in no form whatever, not even hidden in the notes, where others might resume his search for it. In his *Traité de la lumière*, Huygens wrote, "I cannot bring my wave theory of light to accord with certain optical phenomena, but I stick to my theory in the conviction that other, better minds will succeed in solving this problem." The problem was solved by other minds, not necessarily greater than his. Could better minds than Chopin's solve his problem? The solution cannot be looked for in the tones; it can be looked for only with them, from inside their

---

1. For example, whatever the sum of $11^3 + 17^3$ may be, it cannot be the third power of an integer. (But $3^2 + 4^2 = 5^2$.)

living motion, and no one can get in there except the man who was inside their living motion to start with because he helped it come into being.

Earlier we asserted that music has this in common with mathematics: that in either one thinking is indistinguishable from doing, and that thought has the power to posit the existence of both numbers and tones. Now we have found that in this respect there is an essential difference between numbers and tones. If it is true that what mathematicians think existed before it is actually thought and would exist even if it were not thought, then it seems that musical thought is far superior to mathematical thought where positing existence is concerned. But this only seems so. The proof of Fermat's theorem may exist although no one thinks it, but it is part of the theory of numbers, which is a creation of thought. It certainly makes sense to say that all of arithmetic is implicit, i.e., exists, in the idea of number—indeed, in the idea of the first number (especially if we regard two as the first number as the Greeks did), whereas not the slightest bit of music, let alone all of music, is implicit in the idea of the tone or any specific tone. In music only that exists which is actually created: this expresses not music's greater power to posit existence, but its close affinity with time. In this respect, number is the direct opposite of tone. To be sure, time is needed to think a mathematical thought, like any other, but in mathematics, time is merely a psychological backdrop, a "mere formality"; time flows by, so to speak, outside mathematical thought, which is just as extraneous to time as the text of a book is to the light I need to read it. What the mathematician thinks is what it is, even if there were no such thing as time; one might almost say that only time prevents mathematics from unfolding in all its dignity and splendor. (Curiously enough, Kant, who first denounced the dangers of psychologism, lapsed into its worst errors precisely when he confused number with counting, and asserted that arithmetic was grounded in time just as geometry is grounded in space. No musician could ever have been so misled.) In logical explanatory thinking, time is merely a psychological condition. In his *Regulae ad directionem ingenii*, Descartes describes the process of deductive reasoning as a chain of propositions, observing that "we must pass so quickly from the first to the last that practically no step is left to memory, the whole being viewed all at the same time" (Rule XI). In other words, if time were eliminated the process would not be affected in any way. If it were eliminated from musical thinking, nothing would be left of the latter. How could one think a melody if not as a specific succession of tones in time? Do we think more effectively when we imagine a slow melody moving fast? No, here time is not a mere formality, flows not outside thought, but within it; time is not merely a general condition of thought, but is consubstantial with the tones themselves, with the particular melody they form. Here one thinks not in time but with time; indeed, one thinks time itself in the form of tones, the only form in which time can be thought. This is why only the composer can think to the end a melody he has begun. The time he thinks is his own time, and though it is possible in some cases to continue another man's work, it is impossible to continue his "time."

Our discussion of Chopin's case has taught us a thing or two about musical thought. We may learn more from the case of a composer who, unlike Chopin, succeeded in improving one of his melodies.

SCHUBERT'S SECOND THOUGHTS

In the introductory note to this section we referred to Schubert's song "Wasserflut" and his alteration of its original ending. We shall now examine more closely what we have called the paradigm of the creative act.

"Wasserflut" is one of the simplest songs of the *Winterreise* cycle. The original poem consists of four four-line stanzas. Schubert's setting extends over the first two stanzas and is repeated for the second two stanzas. Here is the voice part (prelude, interludes, and accompaniment are omitted):

What we see is two graceful melodic curves, one for each stanza, each of them subdivided in mid-stanza.

The character of the melody is at first determined by the ♪♪♪ ♩. rhythm, announced in the short piano prelude: advancing at the beginning of the measure, halting at the middle. If the triplets fell on an upbeat and the longer note began a new measure, thus: ♪♪♪ | ♩. , the effect would be that of a natural progression toward a goal (as in measures 7–8,). But what we have here is the opposite. The halt on a weak beat after the advance on a strong beat contradicts the natural metric scheme, seems forced, like a motion carried out against resistance. What the rhythm hints at is strikingly expressed in the melody itself: first, by the resolute ascent to the highest tone (which is also the root, in the key of

E minor) reached on a weak beat [♪♪♪♩] (compare

with the natural [♪♪♪♩]), then by the sharp descent

[♪♪♪♩ ♪♪♪♩] carried out as though in response

to the warning "Thus far and no farther!"—as though the note [♩]

were a kind of ceiling not to be pierced, so that what goes on must

remain under it. Contributing to the same effect are perhaps the two

octaves [♪♪♪♩] and [♩♪♪] in measures 5 and 6,

which play off the root note and the fifth against each other. The upshot

of all this is something like an enforced rigidity and tenseness, as if

something were being held back that is seething under the surface. This

would account for a tendency to outbursts, the first of which occurs

toward the end of the first melodic curve, in measures 11 and 12. Here,

at the point where the first stanza of the poem ends, a normal eight-

measure period might be completed with an ascent followed by

a descent, in this fashion: [♪♪♪♩ ♪♪♪♩♩].

Instead, we have an ascent running through the entire span marked

off by those two octaves, [♩] and [♩], namely,

[♪♪♪♩ ♪♪♪♩]. Even so, the period could be concluded

with the note [♩] reached at the beginning of measure 12, were

it not for the chord [chord] which, breaking in at this point,

changes for the moment the dynamic value $\hat{8}$ of [♩] into $\hat{5}$, thus

preventing the conclusion and forcing the extension of the period by

two measures and the repetition of the last line of the stanza. More-

over, it pushes the melody beyond its apparent goal, [♩], to

[♩]. So this was what the preceding long ascent meant: a

straining to pierce the ceiling! Only now can the motion be reversed, the ascent balanced by a descent, and the ending sought and found (measures 13 and 14).

The second arc begins with a gently descending motion, [musical notation] , not with a steep ascent like the first. After the piano interlude has effected a shift to the key of G major, everything seems relaxed; the soft, flowing motion down and up the octaves, [musical notation] , has replaced the sharp up-and-down motion interrupted by a halt. Only the unmotivated, unnaturally high leap in measure 25, [musical notation] , reminds us that there is some unfinished business. Nevertheless, in measure 26 the eight-bar period ends normally, but, unfortunately, at the wrong place—g, not e, as $\hat{1}$. So this, after all, is not the ending? For a moment everything is in suspense, then the real ending comes abruptly, when least expected. The "error" is corrected; everything is set right; with one powerful blow the ceiling is pierced. After [musical notation] no return is possible: now the melody can end only with the e in the higher octave—an ending that is not a resolution. The effect of this ending is so overwhelming that everything preceding it is now felt as an inexorable progression toward this predetermined goal, as though the entire melody existed only for the sake of this very ending.

As mentioned earlier, this melody at first had a different ending. What cannot be other than it is, was nonetheless other. The final gesture which sums up everything that preceded it, which seems as inevitable as a logical inference, might have been an entirely different gesture, the one that served as the original ending, which did not pierce the ceiling. The traces of erasure in the manuscript leave no doubt: Schubert himself, when he first jotted down this melody, was completely unaware of the ending which to us seems to be the only possible one; what he had written was

The original ending cannot be interpreted as a slip of the pen. In no sense can it be described as "wrong." Had Schubert died directly after writing it down instead of a year later, no one could have pointed his finger at the last two measures, saying, "Wrong! This won't do! Something else is needed here!" What could be wrong here? The basic idea is the same as that of the ending familiar to us: the abrupt correction of the "error" in the two preceding measures. The misleading phrase ♦♦♦♦ which might have suggested a conclusion on g is convincingly disavowed by being repeated, but this time at the right place: ♦♦♦♦. And the beginning of the measure which leads to this concluding phrase, ♦♦♦♦—does it not echo the beginning of the melody? Beginning and end summed up in a single gesture: is a more effective ending conceivable? No, all of us would have accepted the song as it was originally, without the slightest objection, and would have loved and admired it as a masterpiece of Schubert's best period.

And yet, although his days were numbered, Schubert felt compelled to go back to the finished, perfect melody. Something troubled his creative conscience, kept reminding him that he had not done full justice to his own creation. In the course of his reflections on the melody it suddenly dawned on him what the trouble was: not until now had he really *understood* his melody, and seen that it could fully realize its potentialities only if given another ending. Unlike Chopin, he was able to create the new ending the moment he perceived that it was required by the melody. It would be a mistake to minimize his accomplishment on the grounds that any good composer could think of a dozen different endings, or that Schubert, having for some reason been dissatisfied with the first ending, replaced it with one he preferred—in short, that all this is purely a matter of taste. Such arguments may often be to the point, but not here. They cannot be refuted when, as in the case of Chopin, we know only that the composer tried to change something, not what the improved version might have been. But in Schubert's case we know both the old and the new ending, and it can be shown that he did not merely replace one with another equally good, but a good one with a better. Such a change cannot be accounted for by the composer's taste, but only by the specific nature of the melody itself. To use once again a disreputable pair of terms, Schubert was guided not by subjective but by objective considerations, not by his taste but by his thinking.

What Schubert failed to see at first, what must have dawned on him after he thought about it, was what goal this melody tries to achieve with the octave . Not that this was a rational idea—it was only an impulse to think another musical thought. After all (Schubert may have reflected), the whole story of the melody revolves around these two tones: where is the melody (and where am I) at home—at the lower e, at the higher, at both, or in an alternation of the two? Both appear in the short piano prelude; how significant they are one realizes only later:

Here the higher e is no more than a mirror image of the lower, is only hinted at; the motion rooted in the lower e immediately reasserts itself. But when the voice begins with , we have something different. Although the higher e falls on a weak beat, it does fall *on* a beat, on "two," not as just before, on the last time unit of a beat. Moreover, it has come to stay for a beat and a half instead of being dropped at once: the tone has now asserted its independence. It has a life of its own, although it is still too weak to sustain the melody, which soon falls back to the lower octave. Two measures later the same thing is repeated, but then something decisive takes place. As though the higher e were now trying to draw the melody to itself, to capture it, and as though the melody were willing to submit, we now have a long ascent passing through all the intermediate tones of the octave 𝄞; the melody reaches 𝄞 on the strong beat, and continues beyond it: 𝄞. For a moment it escapes from the pull of the lower octave. Then the latter gets hold of it again and, yielding, the melody descends slowly, reluctantly, to the last note of the phrase, 𝄞. By this time, however, the higher e has grown gradually stronger than the lower; at the end of the first partial curve the outcome hangs in the balance. It remains for the second partial curve to take the last step, to meet the demand of what has preceded, to settle the issue. Schubert's first ending fails to do this:

simply ignores the conflict and goes back to the situation that obtained at the beginning as though nothing had happened. But 𝄞 brings the final decision, finishes what has been begun by reaching the melody's goal, 𝄞 toward which it had tended from its initial note on, 𝄞. But to be really definitive 𝄞 must be reached from a higher note. What the piercing of the ceiling, the breaking of the mirror, 𝄞, has foreshadowed does come to pass in the last phrase, 𝄞. (Consequently, what characterizes 𝄞 is not that, sung to the word "grief," it expresses this feeling, but that the turn which expresses grief fulfills the decisive function of preparing for the closing phrase of the melody.) Represented schematically, this is the story of the melody, the gradual overcoming of the lower e by the higher:

. An arm is raised, drops impotently, is raised more vigorously, stays up, and what remains in the end is the picture of a raised arm. Behind it, the

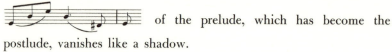

of the prelude, which has become the postlude, vanishes like a shadow.

Let no one object that our account of how Schubert discovered the new ending to his melody is due to hindsight, that it is an explanation after the fact. This is certainly true, but it is not an objection. An explanation before the fact would list the reasons for something happening as it did. But where nothing "must" happen as it does, where everything might have happened differently, such an explanation would be pointless. To explain an event before it has occurred is possible only if the situation in which it occurs can actually occur again or be artificially repeated, as in a scientific experiment. Only recurrence of the event proves whether the explanation is correct, that is, whether the event must really occur in the given situation. Where the event is unique, where recurrence is impossible in principle, such an explanation obviously serves no purpose. The situation in which Schubert found his new ending could not occur before he had found it, nor can it recur in the future. It could not occur before because the melody itself did not exist, and when it existed with the first ending, it was not the same melody; the situation cannot recur in the future because the new ending retroactively changed the situation in which it was found. After all, the new ending could not have existed hidden somewhere in the tones before it was found. The melody as we know it today did not exist before the new ending was found, and if Schubert had not found it, it would not exist, any more than the melodies he would have composed had he lived longer. It was the new ending that retroactively produced the melody; the demand that the new ending satisfies, the new meaning of the melody, the melody itself—all these were created retroactively. How could an explanation before the event account for such a process? In order to explain and understand such a case, one must look not for causes but for meaning; the question confronting us here is not "Why?" but "What is the meaning of . . .?" What is the meaning of the change from the old to the new version? What is the meaning of the new ending? What meaning does it create? Where our purpose is to interpret meaning, explanation after the fact is not pointless; indeed, in no other way can we do justice to an act of creative thought.

That Schubert's "improvement" is an act of creative thought will be readily granted; but why do we call it a paradigm of the creative act? After all, to say that there is such a thing as creative thought, a kind of thinking that does not fit our notions of the logical and the rational, is not to say that there are no creative acts of a different type. The examples so far discussed, which illustrate the musician's creative thinking and its share in musical masterpieces, have all been of one type; in all of them the process of creation was what theologians used to call *creatio in re*, not *creatio ante rem*. In these examples the creative process never began in a void, not even the comparative void of still unformed material; it always involved working over something given, elaboration of something already formed, development of higher from lower forms—creation in the sense of transformation. But what about the other kind of creation, *creatio ante rem*, which, even though it does not create out of nothing, yet does create original forms out of unformed material, forms which are later elaborated? What about the theme, the "flash of inspiration"? After all, when we deal with the creative process in music, it is the inspired theme that first comes to mind. It is the theme that is primarily responsible for the current view that the main source of music is inspiration, something different from and higher than thought, rather than a kind of nonlogical thought. If we are to maintain that the musician's creative act is always and essentially an act of thought, we must show that the theme, too, the originally "given," owes its existence to thought, not to a sudden flash of inspiration.

We are now confronted with the crucial question of how the inspired theme comes into being. The question seems to be self-contradictory: if the theme is due to inspiration, it does not "come into being," it is there. It is always a beginning, and the question of what comes before the beginning is meaningless. And yet, as we shall see, this question, however paradoxical it may sound, is not self-contradictory or meaningless. The flash of inspiration, like everything else, has antecedents—not just psychological (these do not concern us here) but also morphological. The flash of inspiration, too, is a creature of time, not of the moment.

BEETHOVEN'S SKETCHBOOKS

"Nothing ever equals the perfection of what we see in our mind at the moment of conception!!" These words are from a letter addressed to his publisher by Adalbert Stifter—a candid witness if ever there was one. And yet the exclamation involves an illusion typical of all creative artists. There may be such a thing as "the moment of conception," but at this moment the artist has nothing before him in his mind. If he had something before him, his task would consist merely of copying what he sees. Chopin would have been spared his exhausting, fruitless efforts; Schubert would never have recorded the first ending of his "Wasserflut." The artist may have something in the back of his mind or deeply buried in it; he has nothing "before" him. He is pushed, driven, pressed on, not pulled, not guided by a beacon. What he has before him is only something he wants to get over with, to go beyond, without knowing whither. What he has before him is only a void. Here every step confronts him with an open horizon. The other shore he wants to reach is invisible; it does not exist. He will conjure it up only by progressing step by step into the void. Conception is not birth; the artist who conceives a work cannot know what it will be like after his conception has become a reality. His work may fall short of his conception, because between conception and delivery there is a period of gestation, and the latter, like all living processes, involves the possibility of failure, of unfulfillment, as well as that of fulfillment. Only the creator himself knows or suspects where he has failed. We others benefit in either case.

Beethoven's Sketchbooks, to which we now turn, constitute a deeply moving, poignant record of the stages through which a work goes before it comes into the world, a record of the composer's struggles, defeats, and victories. Five thousand pages have come down to us—the only known musical document of its kind. How a musical work comes into being is recorded here in visible, tangible form. It is as though Nature's process of hidden creation—which we know only by its finished products—had here become transparent and revealed her inner workings: we can literally see the process of creation.

The importance of this document was first recognized by the musicologist Gustav Nottebohm. His little volume bearing the modest title *Beethoveniana* appeared more than a century ago. A second, larger volume, *Zweite Beethoveniana,* was published after his death. What these books revealed was so surprising, so exciting, that their inadequacies were at first unnoticed. They contained only short selections from the original manuscripts, which might be likened to tiny fragments cut out at random from an immense canvas. Moreover, the selection— as was to be expected—was determined by the scholar's personal interests. Nottebohm also published separately abridged selections from two of the Sketchbooks. That was all—until, a century later, the Beethovenhaus at Bonn began publication of a complete edition. The first volume appeared in 1952; it contains all the sketches for the *Missa Solemnis,* without omission of a single note or sign, reproduced in ordinary type, not in facsimile (this would have served no purpose because Beethoven's handwriting is illegible to the uninitiated). Only those who have seen the original manuscripts can have an idea of how much labor was involved in deciphering and transcribing the text. Some pages look as though a man beside himself with excitement were expressing his inner storms with a blunt pen. Had it not been for the staves one would scarcely realize that this is music. The observer marvels that this is how an organized structure of the highest order could be produced. Other pages seem at first glance to consist of blanks, so faint are the notes jotted down at wide intervals by the lightest of hands. Such differences, of course, cannot appear in the printed version; nevertheless, we have now a faithful reproduction of the document, the visible record of a continuous creative process.

The immense quantity of these sketches—and what has come down to us is only a fraction of what Beethoven wrote—can be accounted for only if we assume that to him composing was inseparable from writing. It is known that on his long walks he always carried music paper with him in the form of small notebooks, whose condition shows that they were used out of doors. Formerly it was thought that he wrote only because he distrusted his memory, because his stream of ideas was so abundant that he feared some might escape, but closer examination of the sketches shows this hypothesis to be unfounded. Other composers record ideas, a finished tonal pattern that may still be deficient in some parts, or outline a finished piece omitting details. By contrast, Beethoven in his sketches never records a finished melody; the latter appears only in the manuscript of the work (where, however, it often undergoes further alterations). The sketches contain only what precedes the definitive version; what they record is how it comes into being. We see—literally see—how the patterns develop from embryonic beginnings, the stages through which they pass as they come gradually closer to the end result (which we know, but which Beethoven did not know). This is not the "ideal" reconstruction of the creative process to which we referred in our discussion of Schenker's theory—the self-unfolding of a "background" through its successive "middleground" transformations to the "foreground"; as we have stated explicitly, no musical work is actually produced in this way. In the sketches, we have before us the process of real growth in real time. A particularly fine example follows.

The marvelous melody that serves as theme for variations in the slow movement of the Quartet op. 127 must seem to every listener a model of a heaven-sent flash of inspiration. As the melody emerging from the introductory measures gradually assumes form, begins to breathe, to trace its pure line in the tonal space, surely every listener feels that here is perfection. He feels himself in the lap of the gods as he savors every moment, exalted, carried along on the wave of music, deeply satisfied by its logic and exquisite proportions. In what other way could such a work have come into the world than as the whole it is, at one stroke, as a gift from on high? Well, the sketches tell a different story. The visible record of the days, perhaps weeks, of incessant labor to which this melody owes its existence fills more than twenty large music sheets. This famous melody was pieced together bit by bit; continually, new possibilities were tested and discarded. At some points the composer lost his way completely and had to start afresh, or hesitated endlessly between paths that led him nowhere. Such is the real face of heaven-sent inspiration.

Here is the finished melody, without the opening and closing phrases, changes of register, accompaniment, and countervoices:

The key is A^b major, the time signature $\frac{12}{8}$ in a rocking ♩ ♪ rhythm; a sixteen-measure period, divided in the middle by a cadence to the dominant E^b; each half is articulated by weaker caesuras into two four-measure phrases: twice two four-measure phrases, the second repeating the first with slight alterations, the fourth being an exact repetition of the third.

Here are the first four measures:

A broad upbeat, $\hat{5}$-$\hat{6}$-$\hat{7}$-$\hat{8}$, leads to the root tone; this is followed by a gradual ascent to the sixth and two descents, the first beginning with f, $\hat{6}$, and the second with e♭, $\hat{5}$. Next comes a leap of an octave ♩♩, followed by a gradual descent. Schematically represented, the motion is ▬▬▬. The phrase ends on the unresolved note b♭, $\hat{2}$, in the middle of the fourth measure. The second phrase seeks the resolution: the three opening measures repeat those of the first phrase, but the end of the seventh measure (not counting the upbeat) deviates sharply from the previous course with ♩♩♩. In this way a resolution is found, but only a provisional one, for the last tone is not the root a♭ but e♭, $\hat{5}$. The center has been shifted from $\hat{1}$ to $\hat{5}$. The original center will have to be restored in the second half of the melody. It begins with the still unresolved tone b♭, $\hat{2}$ (the last tone of the first four-measure phrase), reached via the upbeat, ♩♩♩, and leads it to the sought-for resolution $\hat{1}$, but—a surprising idea—it is the a♭ of the higher octave! This is, as it were, a gentle reminder that the melody owes something more to the leap ♩♩ than was accorded it there. And so it is only for a brief span that the motion after the [♪] which begins measure 9 descends to the lower a♭; then it changes direction, begins to ascend slowly, measure by measure, reaching [♪], $\hat{3}$, which begins measure 10, and [♪], $\hat{4}$, which begins measure 11. From this point on, however, the way having been cleared, the motion proceeds irresistibly toward the higher a♭ and even beyond, so that it can be reached via the step [♪], $\hat{2}$-$\hat{1}$. Now only does the motion descend rapidly and gently [♪] until it reaches the actually intended resolution note [♪], with which it comes to a rest. The phrase is then repeated, as though to confirm and savor the happily found resolution. (The impression that by measure 11 the way has been cleared is probably accounted for by the fact that from here on the desired goal can be attained merely by following the same path as in measure 1. The sketches confirm this.)

Let us now see how all this came about. On page 35 of one of the Sketchbooks, among other things, we suddenly find this: [♪]. A nothing, out of nowhere; a gradually ascending scale, followed by a descent, a rocking rhythm. Who could have suspected its potentialities? Of course, we who know what Beethoven made of it easily recognize the seed of the future pattern. The first measure discloses its future profile; the second is still amorphous. Only the first and the three last notes, the very notes which will reappear in the definitive pattern, are clearly legible; the others are barely decipherable.

This nothing seems to contain a powerful form-giving element. It settles down and begins at once to grow, to unfold. Still on the same page we find this:

The form has begun to breathe: it has found its own breathing span of four measures. The second measure is no longer amorphous; it has entered a higher stage (even the syncopation 𝄞 in the definitive pattern is already present). However, we can barely sense the future pattern in measures 3 and 4. But 𝄞 at the end, similar to 𝄞 in the finished melody, shows that the developmental forces are at work.

There follow various experiments with details, but then, two sheets later, comes a surprise. It looks like this:

The phrase suddenly shows another face. It is in a different key, C major instead of A♭ major. In Beethoven such a change indicates a step toward greater simplicity and lightness. The rhythmic alternation of longer and shorter notes and of states of gentle tension and resolution has given way to a uniform, relaxed sequence of eighths. To us, who know what Beethoven at the time did not yet know, namely, what this growing process was heading for, this change may appear as a deviation from the direct path. But the paths of organic growth whose goal is latent are not the paths of the planning intellect which sets itself its goal in advance. The less ponderous C major, the more relaxed sequence of eighths: who can tell—perhaps the task required at this point that some ballast be thrown overboard. What seems to us a deviation from the direct path may turn out to have been a shortcut in terms of organic growth.

Clearly, this change marks decisive gains. The will to shift the center to the dominant—here from c to g—has asserted itself in the simplest and most striking manner: the motion of measure 1 is repeated in measure 3, only now f♯ has replaced f; that is, the C major order has

given way to the G major order. At the same time, measure 2, leading
to the new beginning of measure 3, finds, as though accidentally, its
definitive form. But the greatest surprise comes in measure 4. It is jotted
down in two versions: one of the upper register is tried and obviously
rejected—it never recurs; the other is retained. But in this latter version
measures 3–4 are nothing but the final phrase of the definitive melody,
merely transposed by a semitone downward and in $\frac{4}{4}$ time. Beginning
and end of the melody have been found, but nothing else so far. The
whole of the developing pattern is now outlined as concisely as possible.

To achieve this advance, however, important elements had to be
sacrificed: the four-measure scheme, the organic breathing span. What
we have here is four measures, not a four-measure phrase. We have
two two-measure phrases, clearly distinguished from each other because
the second phrase makes a fresh start; it does not continue the first,
but is rather symmetrical to it, an independent unit. Moreover, measure
4 has a real ending, whereas the previous four-measure attempt ended
with the unresolved tone $\hat{7}$, thus indicating that the first stop was to
be reached only at the end of the second four-measure phrase. It is
impossible to know it at this point, but later it will become apparent
that in the first two attempts the lines of the future battle are clearly
drawn. Four-measure phrases, shift of the center: these two demands
inherent in the developing pattern are here expressed as two mutually
exclusive alternatives which lead to two radically different, mutually
exclusive solutions. The four-measure phrase excludes the shift of the
center: the shift of the center splits the four-measure phrase in two.
The composer is now confronted with the task of reconciling the
seemingly irreconcilable, of satisfying both demands.

It must not be forgotten, however, that such insights are due to
hindsight. At this point Beethoven did not know, could not possibly
have known, what goal he wanted to attain—had he known, he would
have had the whole melody; he even thought here that he should further
lessen the weight and the tension. And so he replaces the eighths with

sixteenths: [musical notation] ; the melody be-

comes playful. A later experiment in the same spirit results in a

somewhat blurred outline: [musical notation]. And whereas

Beethoven added the word "V.cello" in the last eighth-note sketch—
that is, planned it for string quartet—Schindler (Beethoven's assist-
ant and testamentary executor) wrote on the margin of the sixteenth-
note sketches that they were intended to be used in a piano sonata
for four hands. Apparently Beethoven at this point toyed with the
idea of an entirely different work, but he soon abandoned it. For a
while he pursued experiments in counterpoint with the sixteenth-note
material, but the next sketch marks a return to the original idea:

adagio

The eighths are back; the explicit indication "adagio" emphasizes
the rejection of playfulness. But this is much more than a return to
the earlier idea. It also marks an essential advance. For the first time
the whole structure, consisting of sixteen measures (as indicated by the
repeat signs in the middle), comes into view; the definitive result is
outlined; and we learn that it will be formed by the repetition of two
four-measure phrases. Furthermore, its beginning and end, the two first
and two last measures, have been given their definitive form (apart from
a slight change at the end). The rest of the melody, however, is still
half-formed. The first half resembles the first sketch in C major: for
the time being progress has bogged down. Repetition of the phrase
turns the previous gains into weaknesses: the two-measure phrase
combined with the cadence on the dominant (which is now repeated)
sounds short-winded; the brief oscillation of the center between $\hat{1}$ and
$\hat{5}$ lacks internal justification. By contrast, the process of growth has
been carried much farther in the new second half of the sketch. In
respect of their motion, the slow stepwise ascent from measure to

measure, the two first measures after the repeat are now very similar to the corresponding measures in the definitive pattern, above all in that they are designed to lead in an ample ascent toward the "climax" of the two last measures. Consequently, what we have here, in contrast to what we have in the first half, is a genuine four-measure phrase. And the "climax," the concluding phrase with which the sketch arrives at the final pattern, is nothing other than the repetition of measures 3–4 of the first half, except for starting from f instead of c, thus reading c instead of g. Previously misplaced, here it is absolutely right; it fits perfectly. The paths of growth are peculiar: was it really necessary that the phrase should first appear at the wrong place and then by repetition be put in the right place? It is also worth noting that at this point Beethoven already recognized that after the half close on the dominant the second half of the melody must begin directly, without transition, in the key of the root. However, the second half begins with $\hat{1}$—this is its weakness—not with the tension tone $\hat{2}$, as in the definitive pattern. As a result, the beginning of the second half sounds like an entirely new beginning; the whole breaks into two separate parts. And there is another weakness: the concluding phrase has been anticipated in the last measure of the first half (even twice). Consequently, its marvelously liberating effect in the definitive version is missing here. The tension that informs the arc of the final melody is not yet in sight.

In the following sketches, Beethoven addresses himself to the point where the process of growth had lagged behind most. Since the two-measure scheme of the first half is wrong, he tries to find another continuation of the opening two measures. He concentrates on measures 3–4, as can be seen in the beginning of the next longer sketch:

. This is a true four-measure

phrase, similar to the one in the last sketch in $A^{\flat}$ major, but closer to the definitive version because this time it ends "correctly" on $\hat{2}$. What is decisive, however, is the change in measure 3:

. Although this is not the definitive solution, that is present here in a peculiarly hidden way, as will be seen presently. The sketch is very elaborate: it aims at an entirely new content for all of the sixteen measures, but trails off without result. What is remarkable is that toward the middle the melody suddenly, for no reason, shifts to A^b major. The original key has not been forgotten; the impulse to return to it continues to be active underground. Very soon it will assert itself openly.

One of the sketches on the next sheet shows Beethoven experimenting for the last time with sixteenths; what follows, however, is surprising: .[2] This is a return, slightly veiled (the profile is unclear; the meter is different), to the original key and rhythm. But what is decisive is that the third measure opens with a leap of an octave, where the sketch breaks off. We can almost feel the composer's hand stopping instantly with the realization that he had hit on the right step. (He realized this only *after* writing.) Then, sure of himself, he proceeded to jot down the next sketch, where the upbeat makes its first appearance:

This is the definitive pattern of the first four-measure phrase: leap of an octave, followed by a gradual descent. The same sketch also shows how measure 3 of the definitive version was prefigured in the preceding sketch: . Both the leap and descent are here, but in reverse order! As one problem is solved, another arises: the four-measure phrase cannot be stretched to eight measures by being repeated, for it does not shift the center to $\hat{5}$. Yet the shift must be effected by the eighth measure.

---

2. The first half of the second measure is illegible.

In consequence, a new content effecting the shift must be found for measures 5–8. The sketch shows the first of several attempts, none of them satisfying. The time is not yet ripe for further growth.

And so Beethoven attacks another problem: once again he concentrates on the structure as a whole, all of the sixteen measures. To begin with, he tries to improve the middle section of the melody where, in the earlier complete sketch in C major, it split into two separate parts because the second half started with $\hat{1}$, which produced the effect of an entirely new beginning. He jotted down the following very rapidly, as though to record at once a possibility that had just occurred to him:

At first glance this looks like a step backward. The previously attained final pattern (of course, Beethoven did not know it was final) of the first four-measure phrase is sacrificed; the earlier two two-measure phrases are back again. But this is of no matter here; what Beethoven is now concerned with is to reach the middle with the shifted center, if possible in one sweep that would carry him onto the right continuation and proper linking of the two halves of the melody. For the time being, nothing better is available to him for filling the whole stretch from beginning to middle than the two two-measure phrases with repetition. But the attempt proves fruitful. What appears now at the breach in the middle is nothing other than the upbeat of the beginning, repeated here, but now it leads toward $\hat{2}$ instead of $\hat{1}$. In other words, instead of the previous ♪♩ ♪♩ we now have ♪♩ ♪♩ in the middle, a link as simple as it is solid, which ties the two halves into a single whole.

On the next page we find a sketch of all sixteen measures. The upbeat is not jotted down, but a prelude is indicated (the first two measures are to be read in the bass clef), and the change of register is effected. The melody is divided between violin and cello:

Beethoven wrote this down twice, the second time with the indication of a higher countervoice, which subtly differentiates between the first occurrence of the concluding phrase and its repetition. (The note ♭𝅘𝅥 of the countervoice, last note in the third measure from the end, makes the opening note 𝅘𝅥 of the next measure sound like $\hat{1}$ for a moment, so that here the concluding phrase begins with d♭ = $\hat{1}$ and ends with a♭ = $\hat{1}$. Thus here—but not four measures earlier, where it first occurred—it has exactly the same shape in which it first appeared, though in the "wrong place," in the first sketch in C major!) Except for measures 3–4 and their repetition in measures 7–8, everything appears here as in the definitive version—but we know what problem is hidden behind these two "unfinished" measures. To master this last task a great deal remains to be done.

For some time the development is not carried further. On the next two pages we find suggestions of variations. Beethoven even toys for a last time with C major and eighth notes. He experiments with possible preludes and postludes; he attends to the countervoices. Then, slowly, the last stage of growth begins, and at the same time all sorts of other ideas occur to him. With the next sketch he tries to discard the two-measure periods in the first half; the sketch begins with the correct first four-measure phrase, but fails to find the continuation, which is supposed to lead to the dominant four measures later. He writes, crosses out, writes again and crosses out again; the notes have no direction. The result of the fruitless effort is a new attempt, the last, with the two-measure form, almost identical with the one last cited, only enriched by a postlude. Then he goes back to the four-measure phrase of the beginning, thus:

A new content for measures 5-8 *and* a repeat sign? That makes sixteen measures. Where is the second half? Does Beethoven intend to extend the melody to thirty-two measures? Once again, it seems, all the laboriously achieved gains are being put in jeopardy. Actually, however, we are now quite close to the end. This is only a last try before the decisive step—a try in the opposite direction. What we find on the next page is already the last sketch:

At first we hardly notice that the decisive step has been taken, for here Beethoven acknowledges that the first four-measure phrase must be repeated. Just like the second half of the melody, so the first half requires repetition of a four-measure phrase. This is acknowledged without reservations; the phrase is repeated literally. As a result of this repetition, the shift of the center and the conclusion on the dominant in measure 8 are eliminated, but only the superficial observer will conclude that this is another attempt to achieve the impossible. Actually,

---

3. Uncertain.
4. The second half of the measure in numerous different shapes.

all that is needed now to arrive at the definitive version is a tiny change, one so slight that it is hardly worth while recording in a further sketch. This change appears only in the finished melody, in the manuscript: in measures 3-4 has become in measures 7-8. That is all that is needed to attain the goal immanent in the growing process, i.e., to realize the two mutually exclusive tendencies—that to a four-measure articulation and that to a shift of the center in the middle—within one coherent pattern.

Let it be said once more: our presentation of the sequence of musical sketches as a meaningful process, an unfolding, a growing whose predetermined goal is reached, however peculiar the approaches may be, with a kind of somnambulistic sureness—such a presentation has been possible only because we know the outcome. To those who do not know the end, who cannot see what comes after each successive stage, long stretches of the process may seem like a planless wavering between equally unpromising possibilities. A creative artist's torments are due to the fact that he is in that same situation: he does not know the goal of the process; indeed, before reaching this goal he does not know whether it exists. It takes a great deal of strength, courage, and faith to persevere in such a situation. Not until the very last step can the artist say, This is it, this is what I have been seeking without knowing what it was, without even knowing that I was seeking it. Only after he has the finished melody before him can Beethoven understand what the whole long process was about, what kind of problem he has had to solve (provided that he is interested, which is doubtful). We are reminded of Valéry's saying that a felicitous line in a poem is the solution of a problem which arises only after it has been solved. Paul Klee, too, said, "An artist knows a great deal, but only in retrospect."

The sketches cited above are again reproduced, in sequence, in the table (facing): a purely audible development can also be made visible—can present a meaningful picture to the eye—and thus we are able

1

2

3

4

5

6

7

8

9

10

11

12

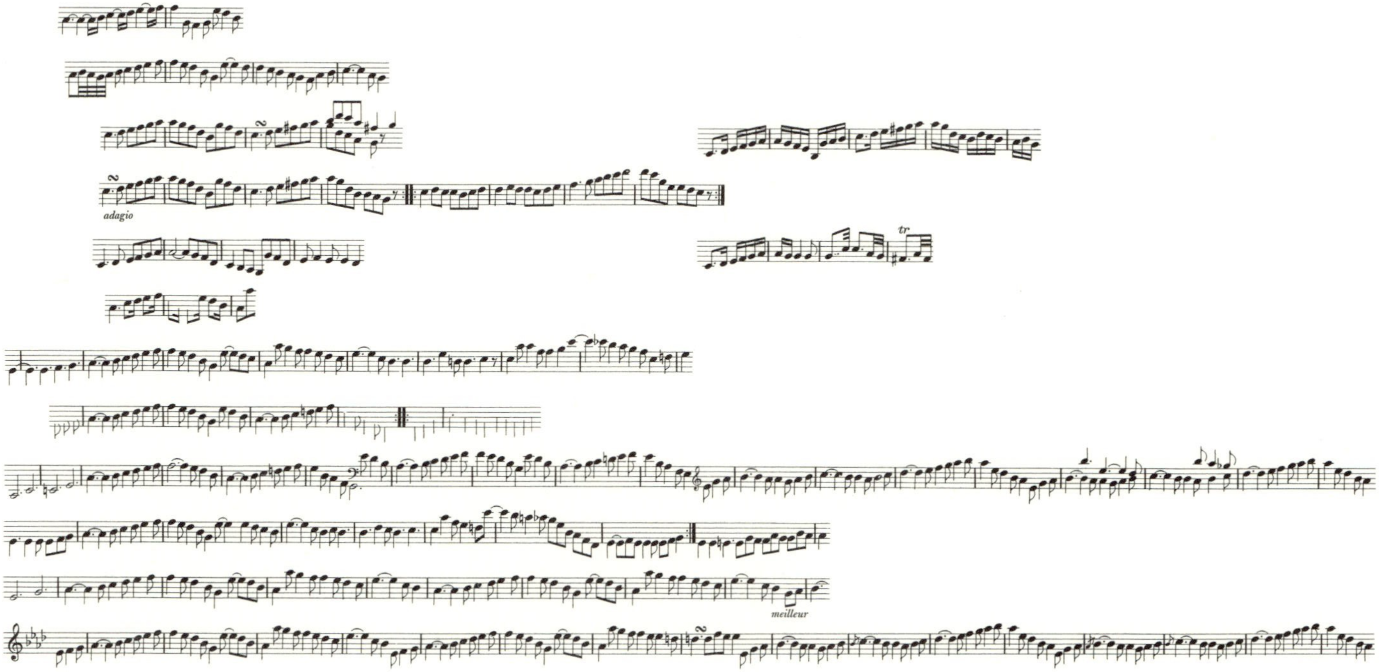

to see what "inspiration" looks like once the veil of mystery has been lifted. What has happened to the much vaunted sudden illumination, the voice that seems to come from on high and to which the entranced creator listens intently? Who could be more uncertain than Beethoven is here about his own creation, about what his own inner voice tells him? The flash of inspiration, the moment of grace, is seen to extend in time, to take more and more time. Instead of the sudden "Here it is!" we see a long process, a slow gestation. And the time we are referring to is not the time an artist needs to impose his will on refractory material, nor is this a process like that, say, of building a house, stone being added to stone until the form conceived by the architect has become reality. It is the time of growth, comparable to organic growth, a process that takes place independently of the artist's will or imagination: he cannot actuate it; he can at best only regulate its course. From its beginning as a seed to the final emergence of the finished pattern, this process is anything but a straight development. It is marked by false starts, detours, second thoughts; yet it is not blind, is not a groping in the dark, even though at some points that is what it seems to be. Rather it might be said to follow an invisible scent: it is a *tâtonnement dirigé* ("a purposive groping"), as Teilhard de Chardin characterizes the development of living things. It is as though the composer had nothing to do with it, as though the tones did it all by themselves. We see no Prometheus here, no Titan actuated by pride: what we see is a man struggling against obstacles, doing his utmost to help the tones striving to be born, acting as a midwife, an anti-Prometheus, intent only on discovering the hidden will of the tones. It is a deeply moving experience to see how Beethoven—for instance, when he tries to find the correct continuation for measure 4—begins his search not with measure 5 but with measure 1. As mentioned before, he repeatedly starts afresh, writes all the opening four measures note by note, often in feverish haste, as though he knows that he can find what he is looking for only in the tones themselves, that he must let himself be carried by their motion, move with them time and again until their momentum takes him over the hurdle and puts him on the right track. For he does not know how the melody will continue, and only the tones can tell him. And they do, time and again. It is they that tell him, not a voice from on high. This is inspiration, if you will, but its source is neither a higher power nor the artist himself: it comes from the tones.

It might be contended that, unlike biological growth, the process just described begins at a point that can be exactly located. When the phrase ♪♪♪♪ emerges for the first time, something actually comes out of nowhere, is suddenly "there," the creation of a moment, not the result of a process—in other words, a sudden illumination, a genuine flash of inspiration. The creation of a moment, yes; but of a moment of grace, an "inspired" moment? Is it really necessary to use such lofty words to account for the existence of ♪♪♪♪? After all, to think is always to think of or about "something." A musician will naturally think of tones, unless something else forces itself on his awareness. When a musician's consciousness is left to itself, as it were, it will be a consciousness of tones, in the form of more or less loosely assembled groups. ♪♪♪♪ : an ascending scale, a rocking rhythm—this is simply what psychologists call a primary content of consciousness. Its presence requires no special explanation. Since composers are conscious beings, such primary contents of consciousness must exist, too. In other words, the existence of ♪♪♪♪ is not a morphological but only a psychological problem.

That the process described here is typical of Beethoven's creative method is convincingly established by his Sketchbooks. As mentioned before, his method represents an exceptional case, in that his composing is inseparable from writing. But this does not necessarily imply that what can be learned from this special case has no general validity. Something has come to light here which may very well be present (though it is usually hidden) in the work of other composers. And so we assert emphatically that it is the process of musical creation per se which is revealed in Beethoven's Sketchbooks, that musical creation is always a process of spontaneous growth, and that every genuine tonal pattern is something grown. In most cases, however, the stages of this process succeed one another so rapidly that the composer cannot record them—he is probably even unaware of them—or (this is what must actually be assumed) the process takes place in the unconscious, and only its result, the finished pattern, crosses the threshold of consciousness. What composers experience as a flash of inspiration would then merely be the moment in which they become conscious of the finished, gradually developed pattern—that moment when Beethoven stops writing in his Sketchbook and proceeds to write the autograph. Such an assertion cannot be confirmed or refuted by observation; it cannot even be called a hypothesis; moreover, we must grant that it is less plausible than the objections that will be raised against it, by artists who have experienced flashes of inspiration and by others. Only this may perhaps be said in its favor. No one will deny that the melodies produced by Mozart, Beethoven, and Schubert belong to the same type, for all the individual and generational differences they disclose. Now, Beethoven's creative method is the very opposite of Mozart's and Schubert's; they composed effortlessly and rapidly, as though drawing upon an inexhaustible supply of finished patterns. Is it not true in a general way that affinity of type points to affinity of source? Is it conceivable that melodies so closely related are produced in radically different ways—that some presuppose a long process of growth while others are, so to speak, conjured up by a magic wand, a "Let there be . . . "? However, the less one tries to prove here, the better: after all, our assertion is admittedly an act of faith, a postulate of the kind even the most exact sciences

cannot dispense with, whose validity is measured only by its contribution to our knowledge and understanding.

"Perfection is not supposed to be something grown." Under this
heading Nietzsche writes in *Human, All Too Human:* "In the presence
of perfection, we seldom ask how it came about. We are content to
enjoy it as a gift, as though it were conjured up by magic. This is
probably because we are still influenced by a primitive, mythological
attitude. . . . The artist knows that his work is more highly praised
if it gives the impression of having been produced by the miracle of
a sudden illumination, and so he encourages the belief that in the
creation of a work of art the only active force is blind inspiration. . . .
His purpose is to deceive the viewer or listener, to make him readily
accept the idea that perfection implies no work. . . . It is the art
historian's duty . . . to dispel this illusion and to expose the fallacies
and bad habits which lead the intellect into the net spread by the artist."

The romantic notion of the artist, which Nietzsche denounces here,
has long since become a thing of the past. Yet even today, after it has
been "deromanticized," we are justly reluctant to deny that there is
something miraculous in the work of art and that a voice from on high
has a share in its production. At the same time we cling to the notion
that "miracle" is the opposite of process, and believe that a higher
power can act only by magic—as though gradual growth were beneath
its dignity. Perfection is not supposed to be something grown. This
view is still as commonly held as it was in Nietzsche's day. Have the
nineteenth-century scientists and their camp followers rendered us
incapable of experiencing the wonder and awe of the miracle of growth?
Do we still listen to their facile explanations and share their adulation
of the intellect? Do we never listen to the swelling chorus of more
recent voices? However that may be, there is certainly no better way
to regain a capacity for wonder and awe than to study Beethoven's
Sketchbooks.

XVIII. Cognitive Thinking and Creative Thinking

THAT MUSICAL patterns are created through a process of growth was the overwhelming impression conveyed by the series of examples discussed above. Many another example could be cited from Beethoven's Sketchbooks. In every case, the earliest conception is amorphous, yet contains elements capable of development, and the forces that activate and direct this development toward the finished form seem to be inherent in the tones themselves. Assuming, as we have to, that the same is true of other composers' work, the whole domain of music appears rather close to that of nature, where forms similarly germinate, grow, and mature. The one difference is that plants and animals, upon reaching maturity, generate others of their kind and die, whereas works of art reproduce themselves by coming alive again each time we experience them.

Contemplating this aspect of music we almost forget that, unlike plants or flowers or fruit, its patterns are man-made. And if they appear to be organically grown, they are at the same time the results of human activity. The miracle of the organic growth of Beethoven's melody is one aspect, but there is also the miracle of thought: Beethoven the man stooped over his labors, seeking and finding, solving problems and creating new ones, every single step consciously taken, produced by thought. If any doubts remained concerning what produces tonal patterns, here they are laid to rest: it is thought, a continually renewed intellectual endeavor. The activity of the mind when it concentrates on an issue that confronts it, like a problem, when it finds solutions that turn out to be partial and pose new problems, and when at last it reaches the goal that represents the solution to all problems—we cannot but call this thinking. Admittedly, this type of thinker does not quite fit the traditional image of a man who relies on the resources of his mind, where he seeks guidance to reach his decisions. The thinker as composer is rather lost in his mind, which does not vouchsafe him guidance; he looks for guidance in his subject matter, the tones, and it is out of the tones that inspiration comes to him. Now we may apply the term without having to trouble man's genius or God or the Muses. Nor is there a contradiction between the composer's activity as a midwife helping a melody to be born and the character of the work as a man-made creation. For the tones are not something radically different from man, wholly outside him. The tones themselves are created by man, and the spirit of the tones is the spirit of man. When the composer seeks guidance from the tones, he seeks guidance in his own thinking: he thinks not only in tones but out of the tones. A tonal pattern, a work of music—they stand before us wholly the product of human thought.

How do thought and inspiration collaborate in the process of composing? By now, surely, this age-old question has become all but meaningless. Any and every element of the musical work—whether theme or elaboration—has its origin in a single source, a source for which there are no better words than thought, thinking, sustained intellectual reflection, but in a sense different from that they have in logic.

The process we have studied is undeniably a concrete instance of nonlogical thinking. There was a time when its reality was denied, when all known forms of nonlogical thinking—organic or intuitive, image or object thinking—were held to be primitive, prelogical stages of logical thinking. Such a view can no longer be justified: a document such as

Beethoven's Sketchbooks is sufficient to show this. An inhabitant of the desert might believe that life is impossible outside the atmosphere, but he would be compelled to admit his error if he were shown a fish. That there is such a thing as nonlogical thinking, and that it is not merely a stage preliminary to logical thinking but equal to it in status and performance, is no longer a matter for debate. The only thing that still remains in question is the nature of this other kind of thinking and its mode of operation.

As is well known, logical thinking deals with concepts and propositions, the latter defining concepts and linking them according to rigorous rules. As for its mode of operation, the model example is supplied by Euclid's *Elements*. Its supreme law is implication: no proposition is valid unless it follows necessarily from the initial axioms and definitions. All logical thinking does is to make explicit what is implicit in the axioms and definitions, to lay bare, to uncover what is hidden—often hidden so deeply that only the most strenuous intellectual efforts can bring it to light. The proof of the Pythagorean theorem that "in right-angled triangles the square on the side subtending the right angle is equal to the squares on the sides containing the right angle" is wholly contained in the definitions of point, straight line, right angle, triangle, square, and so on. Though hardly anyone could find the proof without assistance, it *must* be implicit in those definitions, for otherwise it would not be valid. Its validity is proved precisely by showing that it is implicit in them. (Incidentally, this is why the *Elements* can be read backward, starting from the end, as was done by the young Pascal.) However unexpected the things that come to light in this way, they can never be "new." The whole force of a logical argument consists precisely in this, that it never says anything really new, that it only makes us see what we have not seen before. What is really new lies beyond the reach of logical laws. This is why in the domain of logic no problem is in principle insoluble, nothing is in principle unknowable. Here, what is unknown today may become known tomorrow; what one man has failed to discover, another may be able to discover: for whatever can be discovered is already there, as it must be if it is to be discovered without violating the laws of logic. (Incidentally, it is interesting to note that the one personal trait in Euclid's system—the idea which might not just have occurred to anybody—is a nonlogical step: the idea that one proposition of a system must be "new," i.e., not contained in previous propositions and therefore not deducible from them. Modern logic, however, has demonstrated that Euclid's idea to posit the parallel postulate as undemonstrable was nevertheless a logical one: it has been logically demonstrated that every complete logical system must include at least one logically undemonstrable postulate.)

Musical thinking deals with motions and links them into patterns. Why music has always been experienced and recognized as motion has been shown in detail elsewhere.[1] Music *is* motion, pure motion, freed from all ties with material objects, and for this very reason a kind of motion that can be realized in thought. That musical patterns are patterns of motion is confirmed by the way they are produced. We have seen that Beethoven invariably rewrote his melodies from the beginning whenever he was at a loss how to continue. What he did would have been a completely senseless waste of time had not his purpose been to move with the tones, to discover new motion by moving with the old. What he seeks by writing ♪♪♪♪♪♪ and finds when writing ♪♪♪♪♪♪ is tonal gestures, tonal motions. Each motion communicates its impulse to the next; the latter realizes and balances it, but invariably overshoots its goal, so that again a new motion must be sought, must be invented. The new motion is new in the full sense of the word: here thinking does not proceed under the laws of logic as a searching and finding of something already there; it is inventing something that is not there, not yet there, not implicit in the given, but demanded by it. Logical thinking is deductive, brings something

---

1. Cf. *Sound and Symbol: Music and the External World*, pp. 73–148.

to light; its goal is to discover the hidden; it is like developing an exposed photographic plate. Musical thinking articulates, gives form to an amorphous impulse; its goal is to fulfill; it is like the development of a living being, self-development. The former is a making visible, the latter a becoming real. For this reason, what is true in logic, namely, that every step can in principle be taken by anyone at any time, is not true of music. Logical thinking is an impersonal function: it can in principle be performed, though with varying efficiency, by any individual; the thinker here is the pure logical subject. Where music is concerned, the thinker is a living individual, for he shares a living motion which involves man as a whole.

We see now: the distinctive feature of musical thinking is the same as that of musical hearing. Just as the "I" of objective hearing, the hearing of noises, is different from the "I" of musical hearing, the hearing of tones, cognitive thinking is different from creative thinking. The "I" of cognitive thinking is determined by the opposition between subject and object; whatever it thinks must become its object, must be something it is not. It cannot think itself without becoming an object, alienated from itself. Thinker and thought are separated by an un-bridgeable gulf. The "I" of creative thinking does not think anything outside itself; it is itself motion and it thinks motion; it can think itself without becoming alien to itself; it encounters, as it were, from the outside what it thinks inside. Instead of the separation of thinker and thought, we have here a togetherness of both.

Now, when the function and the bearer of the function cannot be differentiated; when the human being does not have a function, but is a function, wholly function that projects now one, now another aspect; when the function is not directed toward a separate or separable object among many; when, grammatically speaking, subject, predicate, and object are in constant mutually influential motion: then the split into the three grammatical parts of speech becomes misleading. The same togetherness, closeness, interaction which characterized the relation between the singer and his song at the primal stage characterize that between Beethoven and his melodic patterns. The thinking subject is also the hearing subject; he lets himself be guided by his creation. The latter is invariably both grown *and* invented, never one *or* the other. Our customary distinction between subject and object simply does not apply where musical experience is concerned. This experience is not mystical. Although it is similar in structure to the musical experience, in the latter the subject is not completely submerged by the thought; the two aspects of the process involved remain distinct. But here the distinction has an entirely different sense from our customary distinction between "subject" and "object."

There is, then, such a thing as logical thinking, thinking in concepts, and there is such a thing as musical thinking, thinking in motions. Conceptual thinking leads to judgments, musical thinking to tonal patterns. Every concept is a concept "of" something, a reflection of reality. Motion is real in itself. Conceptual thinking is cognitive, its purpose to add to our store of knowledge. Musical thinking is productive, its purpose to add to our store of reality. Conceptual thinking owes its internal order to the laws of logic which govern it: it is natural to assume that musical, productive thinking owes its internal order to laws of its own. What the laws of logic are is known: it should be possible to gain insight into the nature of those other laws from what we have learned about musical thinking.

XIX. The Musical Law

FIRST OF ALL, let us try to define the sense in which we employ the term "law."

As commonly used, it denotes a general statement that covers a vast number of individual instances. Laws of nature are statements about natural processes; they refer to certain observed uniformities and can be reduced to the formula "It has always been so and will always be so." The laws of thought or logic are reducible to the formula "It is so." Moral laws express an "ought to be." What is common to all these laws is their universality. Each individual instance subsumed into the universal law may differ from all the others, but from the point of view of the law, the differences are inessential, mere matters of chance or circumstance. A false inference does not invalidate the laws of logic, but rather confirms them by its consequences. The wind that blows leaves upward is no "exception" to the law of gravitation. To kill in self-defense is contrary to the moral law, even should the action go unpunished. Any phenomenon that meets the general requirement of a law may be said to be "governed" by that law: its universality is not affected by the particularity of the individual instance. The law's formulation (and the law is not laid down or discovered until it has been formulated) is on another level than the phenomenon it governs. A commandment, "Thou shalt" or "Thou shalt not," is not the same thing as a deed, nor is a mathematical equation a natural process. A rule in logic is not a judgment: neither true nor false in itself, the rule's purpose is to determine when a judgment is true or false.

That laws or rules of this type operated in Beethoven's composing will not be contested by anyone who has followed our analysis of the sketches discussed above. Such laws or rules derive their validity from the specific tonal and metric system on which a composer relies. That Beethoven used ordinary music paper and the customary notation shows that he accepted the conditions of the diatonic system and the metrics of the major-minor epoch. The entire series of sketches is governed by the laws of this system, e.g., in the way the tonal center is shifted to the dominant and in the fact that the four-measure phrases are being balanced against each other. Like the laws of nature, the rules of logic, and moral laws, those of the diatonic system have a certain universality: they are in force wherever music expresses itself in the language of the major-minor tonality and its metrics. Their validity, however, is of a different kind—different from the "It will always be so" of the laws of nature (which leaves no choice as to what is going to happen), from the "ought to be" of moral law (which implies the possibility of obeying or disobeying the law), and different, too, not least of all, from the categorical "It has to be so" of the laws of logic, so very certain concerning what is true and what is false. The laws in question here might rather be formulated as: "If this . . . then that," so as to express not so much a combination of freedom and conformity to law as a certain variability or flexibility in the law itself. In this respect these laws resemble linguistic conventions the aim of which is exact correlation between form and content, the "how" and the "what." I am free to say what I want to say, and I may say it in any way I choose (though the "how" will always affect the "what"), but if I want my statement to be understood, I must express myself in a form conventionally prescribed for my kind of statement. (For example, if I intend to ask a question, my words must not be cast in one of the forms conventionally used for answering questions, or I am very likely to be misunderstood.) It is not impossible to make statements departing from conventional usage, nor are such statements necessarily false; they are simply meaningless. (This is why one can also speak of laws of meaning.) Of course, I may want to say something for which no conventional expression exists and so find it necessary to coin a new word, thereby departing from current usage. When I do this, however, I am not breaking any rule, merely altering it. (The term "style" has deliberately been avoided in this paragraph: it is too vague; one manages better without it.)

In any case, it is certain that Beethoven's musical sketches do not owe their fascination to the application of these laws, i.e., the conventions of key, time signature, metric scheme, rhythm, shift of the dominant in midpassage, and so on—all the features Beethoven's music shares with many other composers', as musical theory teaches. What did fascinate us, and was worth inquiring into, was rather how Beethoven took an amorphous initial group of tones and transformed it into a unique musical structure. We may be confident that he was thoroughly familiar with the laws or rules of the tonal and metric system he inherited, that he had assimilated all the lessons of musical theory, but this knowledge was of no help to him when, for instance, he worked on the third measure of the melody. It could not help him, because no general rule can possibly be formulated for the necessity of jumping an octave at this particular point in the melody. The only problem to which this is the solution was the particular problem that confronted Beethoven at this particular point in this particular composition. And we may say the same at every stage in his search for the melody. Had there been general rules governing its growth, each successive step could have been deduced from the preceding, and Beethoven would have known exactly what notes he had to write down at any given point. But, as we have seen, this is precisely what he did not know (or, should we say, did not yet know): the law governing his melody. He could not possibly know it because this law did not exist (or, should we say, did not yet exist). That the way he worked was law-governed throughout, that it was a process of growth unmistakable as such for its internal consistency, developing out of a logic of its own, no one can deny. But then the law governing it must have lain hidden within the compositional process itself. Beethoven had to find it for himself: it did not pre-exist; it was demanded from him. One might almost speak here of a process in search of the law that governs it. We only recognize it as law after the fact, once the compositional process has ended and the musical work has been created. The law in question here is no more or less than the terminated work in all its uniqueness and particularity. "Thou shalt search and find thy law"—this might be how to put in words the law that governs the process of musical composition. This implies, however, that the process is law-governed only in so far as it actually finds its law. If the manuscript of the Quartet op. 127 had not come down to us, if we had only the preliminary sketches, we would have no idea of what Beethoven was actually getting at. Instead of a process of well-ordered growth, we would have only a number of seemingly haphazard attempts leading nowhere. It would occur to no one to speak of a law-governed process.

What all this amounts to is that in the domain of musical forms there are as many laws as there are individual musical patterns, and that each law is valid only for a given instance. Ought we, then, in this connection, speak of "individual" law? The term is not unheard of in other connections, but what sense would it make here? How are we to interpret it? A law that is applied only once, the validity of which vanishes as soon as it has been recognized and realized—surely, this is the very opposite of law. A situation in which there are as many laws as individual instances, each law holding sway over only one instance—what is this but anarchy? It might be argued that the law governing a musical structure is universal in the sense that every step in the process of composing is a particular instance subsumed into it. But even granting this, how can we speak of law when it is hidden, when it cannot be detached from the process it is supposed to govern, when it cannot be formulated independently of the process it governs, the formulation of which, rather, is simultaneous with the loss of its effectiveness and validity? Can there be such laws? There *must* be laws of this type: otherwise art would be a domain not of order but of anarchy. And art is a domain of order—not only and not essentially because it is also governed by general laws relating to materials, formal organization, historical epochs, generations, styles, but in a much deeper sense. The affinity between a landscape by a Sung painter and one by Dürer is an affinity closer than that between a painting by Dürer and a painting by one of his pupils. To account for such facts, we obviously must revise our habitual notions of law and conformity to law.

In his *Critique of Judgment*, Kant recognizes that art has no room for universally binding laws, and that at the same time works of art undeniably display an order that cannot be purely subjective, a mere matter of personal taste. He attempted to master the difficulty involved here by putting forward a notion of "conformity to law" in a situation "where no law applies." Because his own experience of art was limited, he left it at that, contenting himself with a negative formulation. Our concern, however, is to gain positive insight into the nature of what we have called "the hidden law," hidden by definition, as it were, for it ceases to operate as soon as discovered and has no application or validity beyond the single instance it governs. It does not operate via causation (like the laws of nature), via motivation (like moral laws), or via formal rules (like the laws of logic). To assume that it operates via purposes—the final pattern as the secret purpose guiding the creative process—would even be wider of the mark. If, with Kant, we define purpose as "the concept of an object, so far as it contains the ground of the object's actual existence," we certainly cannot speak here of a "guiding purpose." Our analysis of an example from the Sketchbooks shows unmistakably that in creating his melody Beethoven was never actuated by a "guiding purpose." No such concept existed in his mind, for had it already existed, there would have been no need to search further. To say that it existed elsewhere—in God, in the thing-in-itself, in the realm of the Platonic ideas, or in any other inaccessible place— might be acceptable to those who believe that "perfection is not supposed to be something grown," but contributes nothing to our understanding. If Beethoven's melody had come to him all at once, it would make sense to say that it pre-existed in some higher realm and was revealed to its "creator" in an inspired moment. But then there would be no growing, no problem of growing, and no hidden law. We see now that the latter does not operate through purposes any more than through causes, motives, formal rules, or any kind of compulsion. At best we can speak only of the composer's "obscure impulse" to search for it. Even the term "operates" is misleading here, for the final pattern is certainly not the result of the law's "operation." Rather, it is the law's self-realization, the form it assumes on emerging from its hiding place, when it finally manifests itself.

As mentioned before, this kind of "emergence" does not resemble the lifting of a veil, as when something hitherto invisible suddenly becomes visible. What happens, rather, is that something crosses the threshold of existence: something that never existed, save potentially, now is made actual. We are reminded of the Aristotelian distinction between existence δυνάμεια (as force, as tendency) and existence ἐνέργεια (as actuality). Because the hidden law is not given beforehand but is to be found, and because it does not reveal itself until it has been found, the kind of process it governs combines conformity to law with newness, internal consistency with unpredictability. Under universal laws such a combination would be self-contradictory, for in processes governed by such laws every step is predetermined, prefigured, predictable, and hence not really "new." Aesthetics has expended a great deal of labor fruitlessly trying to eliminate the seeming contradiction, the pseudoproblem of how conformity to law can be reconciled with freedom in artistic creation, as though the freedom involved were a thing apart from conformity to law! So long as aesthetics, taking its cue from other disciplines, aims at discovering universal laws, it cannot get rid of this contradiction, and so is diverted from its real task. For unlike natural science, whose universal laws add to our knowledge and understanding, aesthetics must seek the key to understanding not in universal laws, but in what is unique and unrepeatable, the single one of its kind.

In this light, still another notion current in aesthetics appears untenable, the notion (which is more or less taken for granted) that creating works of art and experiencing them are two different processes, the former directed to the finished work, the latter starting from it. The process of creation is most often studied from the psychological point of view, whereas the problem of aesthetics is located in the recipient's experience of the finished work. The fact that in the primal stages of music—in folk music, for example—it is impossible to draw a line dividing creators from listeners or interpreters, or to speak of musical "works," should be sufficient to show, at least as far as music is concerned, how superficial are all such distinctions. At the other pole, where composer and listener are as far apart as possible, our example from Beethoven's Sketchbooks proves beyond all doubt that the creative process in music is first and foremost *musical*, that the main problem involved—the problem of how a musical structure comes into being—is not psychological but morphological. Here, production of the pattern and the pattern itself involve the same type of problem, but more than that, both are governed by the same law. Even before we discussed the genesis of a tonal pattern, we saw that the latter is essentially a union of conformity to law with newness, internal consistency with unpredictability. The same law governs the process when the composer works over patterns already existing, when Mozart elaborates thematic material, when Chopin tries to improve a passage in a prelude, and when Schubert alters the ending of one of his melodies. In all such instances we have observed how unpredictable steps can be "right," how in each case a hidden law governs the process of musical composition. As the composer penetrates ever more deeply into the pattern he has himself created, he senses which of its inherent potentialities have not yet been fully realized. And his search *within* the pattern is essentially no different from his search *for* the pattern: they are governed by the same law. Indeed, there is no better way to describe what we actually hear in a Beethoven melody (or any good melody) than a process of organic growth, of gradual self-realization, each successive step new and unforeseeable, yet, once taken, somehow satisfying an urgent requirement hitherto unrecognized. We have the same experience every time we hear such a passage of music, and no matter how often we hear it. Even when we know exactly what every next step is going to be, we still experience it as unpredictable and are delighted all over again. No clear line can be drawn between the finished pattern and the gradually emerging pattern. The process of organic growth does not end in the finished pattern, it continues in it. So it is not quite correct to say that the hidden law ceases to operate once it has been embodied in the pattern: it has merely moved from the realm of Becoming to that of relative Being, from the realm of the unrepeatable to that of the repeatable. Repetition of the unrepeatable (totally incomprehensible by the terms of any universal law) is in music an everyday occurrence: every time we experience the pattern, the hidden law is revealed afresh.

Will anyone raise the objection that all this has nothing to do with any law of musical thinking, only with the law governing tonal patterns and musical compositions? Such an objection would be unfounded, for these are not two different kinds of law. Just as the laws of logical thinking are the same as those that govern the thought it produces—a work of mathematics, say—so it is with musical thinking and its productions. And now this has to be said: even though music is the creation of musical thinking, and of that alone, music is not somehow cut off from the rest of the world. Other things besides music are musical:

the law that governs musical thinking has applications beyond music, where other than musical processes are involved. It is not just a poetic metaphor to speak of the world's "musicality."

Of course, actually to chart the furthest extensions of musical thought would be a task no less arduous than that of doing the same for logical thought. It goes without saying that we cannot attempt to do so, at the close of reflections already too lengthy. We may still call attention, however, to a few essential points.

If we were to look for the crucial characteristic distinguishing musical thinking from logical thinking, it would most probably lie in their radically dissimilar attitudes to time. Generally speaking, the laws of music hold sway wherever time operates as an active force. In logic, time does not exist; in music time is essential. In all processes governed by laws of a "logical"—a universal—type, time is a mere formality; in all processes governed by musical laws, time is their very flesh and blood.

Time enters into all types of process, no matter under what laws, but processes governed by universal laws (which imply a "logical" character) are unaffected by the flux of time. They of course occur in time, but time as such adds nothing to them, serves merely as a conveyor belt carrying parts in our direction. There is no differentiation between past, present, and future: all merge in a gray indifference. The past can always be rediscovered, and the future is already present in all essential respects. All that is missing is the "mere formality" of tangible emergence in the here and now. This formality, too, will be taken care of when the predetermined span of time has elapsed. Were it otherwise, predictability could never have been made the touchstone of universal law. In so far as the process runs its course in conformity to law, time has no part in it. Temporality is not inherent in it, but an extraneous element added by the observer or thinker who perforce is born and must die. The nonhuman processes studied by the natural sciences especially exemplify this peculiar timelessness.

No observer can fail to notice that musical processes require time in a very different sense, that time is their very content, the air they breathe, so to speak, at each and every step. What takes place in music is a union of tone and time, meter and time. Tone is more than an audible event that occurs in time: it is audible time. Meter is a "now" signaling a "whence" and a "whither," a "no more" and a "not yet" in one.[1] Time is so active a force in music that we should not be surprised that all other processes in which time is an essential factor are governed by laws similar to those governing musical processes. Readers familiar with the debate concerning the problem of time which has been going on in philosophical thought for more than half a century must have noticed that many of our formulations and interpretations have echoed that debate. The seeming paradoxes of time—an existent made up entirely of nonexistence—dissolve when we are confronted with a law that produces a concrete reality out of "no more" and "not yet." For music is the concrete manifestation of an order that, far from excluding the new, requires and embodies it. Novelty does not destroy consistency in music, but creates it: here, unpredictability is the very touchstone of law, not any lapse from it. In making evident that time is something more than a "mere formality," more than the factor t in physics, music provides us with a model of a law-governed process whose essential features are not subject to any universal law, yet in which the unique, the particular instance, is not a matter of chance but necessity—the model of genuine Becoming as a mode of Being in its own right, rather than subordinate to Being. Processes governed by musical law and accessible to musical thought may be assumed to involve genuine Becoming wherever interpretation in terms of universal laws runs into difficulties. Earlier we saw that the concept of the organic provides a link between the domains of music and biology. Thus, in accounting for the genesis of a musical pattern we were obliged to use

---

1. Cf. *Sound and Symbol: Music and the External World*, where all of this is discussed in detail (pp. 151–264).

the term "growth," and in music, as in biology, we speak of seeds, growth, development, of how embryonic forms are "transformed" into mature forms. It might be contended that the similarities between music and biology are superficial and probably deceptive. After all, biological growth is cyclical—it starts with a seed and produces seed, and so starts all over again—whereas artistic growth ends at a definite point. How, then, can we extend to biology the operation of a law characterized by its application solely to single specific instances? Whatever law may govern the development of the cherry pit into the cherry tree or the egg into the chicken, it has to be valid for all cherry pits, all eggs—it has to be of universal application to all given instances. Biology is perfectly entitled to study organic growth in this way, and to be supremely uninterested in the form of individual cherry trees or the features of individual chickens: in the realm of organic nature individual characteristics are inessential and are looked upon as accidental, not worth the trouble of accounting for. Not so in the realm of art. Even though we know little today about the laws of biological growth, they are not "hidden" in the same sense as musical law: they can be discovered, and once they have been discovered, they will not cease to govern growth. Their effectiveness does not depend on their being hidden.

It is, however, possible to view these things from a different angle. Whether universal laws will ever account for organic growth as completely as they account for the growth of crystals is a wide-open question. Even biologists whom no one suspects of neovitalist tendencies acknowledge that "the problems of organic growth extend far beyond physics and chemistry"—in other words, they lie beyond the range of universal law. It is only in so far as the process of organic growth is *repeated* in every individual growing thing that universal laws apply and the process can be predicted. However, apart from individual characteristics (which are a matter of chance as far as their growth is concerned), organisms are at the same time *essentially* unique, as representative of their species. If their individual growth is viewed as an instance of the unique pattern of growth characteristic of each species, then the "musical" aspect of the process becomes apparent at once: it is unique, law-governed, complete only once a final pattern has been arrived at, and not "repeatable," strictly speaking. Like patterns of music (which can be replayed any number of times), those of living things are reproduced not produced, re-created not created. It is just as impossible to infer the form of the mature organism from a germ cell of an unknown species as to infer the final pattern of a melody from its "seed," whereas the course of biological growth in an individual of a known species is as predictable as the course of a familiar melody. As we have seen, predictability in the latter case (reproduction, not production, of a tonal pattern) is not incompatible with the continued effectiveness of the "hidden law" and the unpredictability of the processes it governs: predictability and unpredictability apply to different aspects of the process. In other words, one and the same process may be governed by both types of law. We might carry our comparison one step further. Suppose that phonographs grew like plants and emitted patterns of sound the way flowers give off scent: then "physicists and chemists" might be eager to investigate how musical phenomena are governed by universal laws, but it would not take them one inch closer to the heart and core of the musical process, namely, the tonal pattern. When we search for universal laws of organic growth—however important, significant, and difficult itself—are we not like those physicists and chemists studying the mechanical reproduction of unique tonal patterns?

However, when we deal with the human individual's development and self-realization, there is no question that we stay within the bounds of musical law. Here, too, the law is not given beforehand but forever to be found, and not a single step is predictable, for the law governing it must first be found. Nor does any step follow necessarily from what has gone before; although the end result is internally consistent and meaningful, every single step is taken in perfect liberty. The meaning of a human individual's life can be grasped only in retrospect: we act as we do because we are what we are; we become what we are because we act the way we do. The process is a gradual one of progression from amorphous beginnings toward ever more sharply defined forms and is complete only when the last step has been taken. A man's death, then, might be compared to the birth of a melody—to the moment when it has ceased to "grow" and enters actual existence. What we asserted at the beginning of this book can now be confirmed in a deeper sense. Musicality is not an individual gift, but one of man's basic attributes; man's very nature predisposes him to music. In music, man does not give expression to something (his feelings, for example), nor does he build autonomous formal structures: he *invents himself*. In music, the law by which he knows himself to be alive is realized in its purest form.

There are other processes within human history and experience that are similarly characterized by uniqueness. Think of those great collective individuals: peoples, nations, states, supranational communities, even mankind as a whole, the historical individual par excellence. Disputes over the "laws" of history are all vitiated because the only interpretation admitted of "law" is the universalizing one of logic and the mathematical sciences. Yet historical processes are obviously governed, at least in part, by another type of law entirely. History is essentially unpredictable and unrepeatable, although some situations may repeat themselves in the sense of reproduction. The meaning of an event is disclosed only after the fact. All peoples are in search of their own hidden law, their history this very search. The pattern is fully revealed only at the end. All these features are characteristic of musical processes, and so the meaning of history is more readily grasped by "musical" than by "logical" thinking. The notion of universal laws governing all historical events must surely come down to no more than a wish fulfillment inspired by the natural sciences. There are good reasons to believe that there are as many historical laws as there are historical collectivities. If so, the only true historical law would be one that could be shown to govern all mankind. But the search for such a law is not the business of historians; mankind as a whole is searching for it, is on its way toward realizing it. Today daring thinkers, trained in the rigorous school of natural science, are applying the concept of history to the universe as a whole—the universe on its way from subatomic initial states toward a final state when it will be consummated and its hidden law will be revealed; the universe as a whole in search of its hidden law: a truly musical conception. Finding support in this quarter for the idea of the musicality of the world should help to rid it of the taint of being fantastic. Moreover, it was a student of mythology, not a musician, who wrote, "Music rests upon an inherent quality of existence, musicality." Music could not move us so deeply if we did not sense in it the operation of a law that embraces both us and the world and an intimation of the heartbeat that animates the whole of the universe.

Here we may pause and reflect.

The world, man's world, shows us two faces: the face of logic and the face of music. We cannot do without either of them. Both laws were created by man before he encountered them in the world, and of both he discovered afterward that they are also the order of the world. Wonder at the inconceivable logical order of the world was the beginning of philosophy; Kant's tremendous intellectual achievement has made the inconceivable conceivable in principle without taking away from the wonder or curtailing reflection. The analogous wonder and reflection about the musicality of the world have not yet appeared, though both aspects, as yet undifferentiated, may have been present in the teachings of Pythagoras. No intellectual effort on the Kantian scale, however, is required to apprehend the world's musicality: in music, after all, man is not radically separated from the world as a subject from an object, but each is turned toward the other as in the togetherness of an encounter. The truth of music, like that of mathe-matics, consists in this, that it serves us as a key to understanding the world we live in.

Logic and music do not divide the world into two separate Cartesian compartments. The world is one, governed by given laws and on the way to laws yet to be found. Man, who alternates between conceptual and musical thinking, is also one. In the last analysis, logic and music need each other, for neither is quite complete without the other. As previously mentioned, logic reaches its culmination in the proof that every complete logical system must include at least one logically un-demonstrable proposition, i.e., one that is "new," that cannot be logically deduced. That is, logic must borrow from music. That works of logic, like works of music, presuppose a process of growth is attested in Pascual Jordan's book *Verdrängung und Komplementarität*. "A prominent living mathematician [John von Neumann]," Jordan writes, "once described to me the process of mathematical discovery. First a specific conjecture is formulated, then the proof of it is sought. Bit by bit, disconnected fragments of an eventual proof are dredged up. It is like linking an island with the mainland, but not in the usual manner of working from the mainland out. Rather, it is as though the bank of earth grew of itself from the bottom of the sea upward, and very unevenly, parts of the eventual causeway emerging here and there above the water long before the rest." The process so described is obviously akin to that which we traced in our example from Beethoven's Sketchbooks.

That more than musical thinking is involved in music should be clear from the existence of music theory, an indispensable part of every composer's education. We might compare it with the role of physics and chemistry in organic life. Schenker was right to call attention to an essential aspect of music which involves conceptual rather than musical thinking. That the gradual unfolding of the fundamental struc-ture in the background must be understood as a purely "ideal" reconstruction, not to be confused with the actual process of growth in real time, was mentioned earlier. It is true that Schenker's diagrams must be interpreted in dynamic terms, yet it is clear that his "foreground" pattern is contained in the background in a way that comes close to implication—not at all in the way Beethoven's finished melody is contained in the seed of his first sketch. This is, indeed, why Schenker could expound his theory *modo geometrico*, deductively, beginning with hypothetical primal forms in the background, inferring middleground patterns from them, gradually making them more explicit. The analytical method of conceptual logic, however, takes us no further than the middleground structures: the leap to the foreground is beyond the powers of logic.

PUBLISHER'S NOTE

The original manuscript continued here for some pages, as the draft of a summing up of the volume. The author's present conclusion—the final three paragraphs—is a summary of the third part, "Musical Thought," rather than of the entire book. Death prevented him from reformulating his final pages in such a way that they would serve as an appropriate end to this volume.

LIST OF WORKS
CITED

LIST OF WORKS CITED

BEETHOVEN, LUDWIG VAN. *Skizzen und Entwürfe*. Edited by Joseph Schmidt-Görg. (Beethovenhaus Gesamtausgabe.) Bonn, 1952– (in progress).

BÖRNSTEIN, WALTER. *Der Aufbau der Funktionen in der Hörsphäre*. (Abhandlungen aus der Neurologie, Psychiatrie, Psychologie, und ihren Grenzgebieten, ed. by K. Bonhoeffer, No. 53.) Berlin, 1930.

CASSIRER, ERNST. *An Essay on Man*. New Haven, 1944.

COMBARIEU, JULES. *La musique et la magie*. (*Etudes de philologie musicale*, III.) Paris, 1909.

DESCARTES, RENÉ. *Regulae ad directionem ingenii*. Paris, 1930.

EHRENFELS, CHRISTIAN FREIHERR VON. "Über Gestaltqualitäten." *Vierteljahrsschrift für wissenschaftliche Philosophie* (Leipzig), XIV (1890).

EHRENSTEIN, WALTER. *Probleme der ganzheitspsychologischen Wahrnehmungslehre*. Leipzig, 1947.

GEBSER, JEAN. *Ursprung und Gegenwart*. Stuttgart, 1949–53. 2 vols.

GILSON, ETIENNE. *Painting and Reality*. (The A. W. Mellon Lectures in the Fine Arts, 1955. Bollingen Series.) New York, 1957.

GOETHE, JOHANN WOLFGANG VON. *Zur Farbenlehre*. In: *Naturwissenschaftliche Schriften*, 1. (Gedenkausgabe, Vol. XVI.) Zurich, 1949–54.

———. *Faust, II*. Passage translated by R. F. C. Hull in: *The Spirit in Man, Art, and Literature*. (Collected Works of C. G. Jung, Vol. 15.) New York and London, 1966. (p. 131.)

GURNEY, EDMUND. *The Power of Sound*. London, 1880.

HANSLICK, EDUARD. *The Beautiful in Music*. Translated by Gustav Cohen. London and New York, 1891.

HEGEL, GEORG WILHELM FRIEDRICH. *The Philosophy of Fine Art.* Translated by F. B. P. Osmaston. London, 1920.

HEIDEGGER, MARTIN. *An Introduction to Metaphysics.* Translated by Ralph Manheim. New Haven, 1959.

————. *Was heisst Denken?* Tübingen, 1954.

HELMHOLTZ, HERMANN LUDWIG FERDINAND VON. *On the Sensations of Tone as a Psychological Basis for the Theory of Music.* Translated by Alexander J. Ellis. London, 1875.

HINDEMITH, PAUL. *A Composer's World.* (The Charles Eliot Norton Lectures, 1949–50.) Cambridge, Mass., 1952.

HOPKINS, GERARD MANLEY. "Henry Purcell." In: *The Poems of Gerard Manley Hopkins.* Edited by W. H. Gardner and N. H. MacKenzie. London, 1967.

HUYGENS, CHRISTIAAN. *Traité de la lumière* . . . Leiden, 1690.

JAMES, WILLIAM. *Psychology: Briefer Course.* New York, 1920.

JESPERSEN, OTTO. *Language, Its Nature, Development, and Origin.* New York, 1921.

JORDAN, PASCUAL. *Verdrängung und Komplementarität.* Hamburg-Bergedorf, 1947.

KANT, IMMANUEL. *Kants Werke.* Edited by Ernst Cassirer. Berlin, 1912–22. 11 vols.

KOFFKA, KURT. *Principles of Gestalt Psychology.* New York, 1935.

LANGER, SUSANNE. *Feeling and Form.* New York, 1953.

————. *Philosophy in a New Key.* Cambridge, Mass., 1942.

Li Chi. See: *Li Gi; Das Buch der Sitte.* Translated into German by Richard Wilhelm. Jena, 1930.

MACH, ERNST. *Die Analyse der Empfindungen und das Verhältniss des Physischen zum Psychischen.* Jena, 1900.

NEWTON, SIR ISAAC. *Philosophiae Naturalis Principia Mathematica.* London, 1687.

NIETZSCHE, FRIEDRICH WILHELM. *The Birth of Tragedy.* Translated by Francis Golffing. New York, 1956.

————. *Human, All Too Human.* Translated by Helen Zimmern and Paul V. Cohn. (The Complete Works, Vols. VI–VII.) Edinburgh and London, 1909–23.

NOTTEBOHM, GUSTAV. *Beethoveniana*. Leipzig and Winterthur, 1872.

――――. *Zweite Beethoveniana*. Edited by Eusebius Mandyczewski. Leipzig, 1887.

OGDEN, C. K., and RICHARDS, I. A. *The Meaning of Meaning*. New York and London, 1923.

PAULI, WOLFGANG. "The Influence of Archetypal Ideas on the Scientific Theories of Kepler." In: C. G. Jung and Pauli. *The Interpretation of Nature and the Psyche*. New York (Bollingen Series LI) and London, 1955.

Penguin Book of Lieder. Translated and edited by S. S. Prawer. Harmondsworth and Baltimore, 1964.

RÉVÉSZ, GÉZA. *Introduction to the Psychology of Music*. Translated by G. I. C. de Courcy. London and New York, 1953.

RILKE, RAINER MARIA. *Briefe*. Wiesbaden, 1950.

――――. "Die Sonette an Orpheus." In: *Gesammelte Gedichte*. Frankfort on the Main, 1962.

SCHENKER, HEINRICH. *Der freie Satz*. Edited and annotated by Oswald Jonas, Vienna, 1956.

――――. *Harmony*. Translated by Elizabeth Mann Borgese and edited and annotated by Oswald Jonas. Chicago, 1954.

――――. *Das Meisterwerk in der Musik*. Munich, 1925–30. 3 vols.

――――. *Neue musikalische Theorien und Fantasien*. Vienna, 1906–35. 4 vols.

――――. *Der Tonwille*. Vienna, 1922–24. 9 vols. in 3.

SNELL, BRUNO. *Der Aufbau der Sprache*. Hamburg, 1952.

SPEISER, ANDREAS. *Die mathematische Denkweise*. Basel, 1945.

VALÉRY, PAUL. *The Art of Poetry*. Translated by Denise Folliot. (Collected Works, Vol. 7.) New York (Bollingen Series XLV) and London, 1958.

――――. *Dialogues*. Translated by William McCausland Stewart. (Collected Works, Vol. 4.) New York (Bollingen Series XLV) and London, 1956.

WITTGENSTEIN, LUDWIG. *Tractatus Logico-Philosophicus*. Translated by F. P. Ramsey and edited by C. K. Ogden. London, 1922.

INDEX

INDEX

A

"absolute music," 54
adjunct note, 246-48, 259
Aesculapius, 1
Aesop, 1
aesthetics, 343-44
all-together, *see* together
Altamira, cave of, 277
Altdorfer, Albrecht, *The Battle of Alexander* (Munich), 275 *and pl.*
Apollo, 1, 286
Apollonius, *Conic Sections,* 290
architecture, 298
Aristotle, 66, 219, 343
art music, 22, 162-63, 169-70, 172, 195
art song, 31, 38 *n*
audible world, 83-88
audience, *see* listener

B

Bach, Johann Sebastian, 15, 18, 70, 114, 163, 178, 231, 249-51, 279; *Art of the Fugue,* 284; Cantata No. 21, final chorus, quoted, 126; *Goldberg Variations,* 84, 251; Partita No. III in E major for Unaccompanied Violin, 87; *Passion According to St. John,* Chorale (Nos. 7 and 27), 250; *Passion According to St. Matthew,* Chorale (No. 55), 250; Chorale (Nos. 21,

23, 53, 63, 72), 250-51, 271; final chorus, analyzed, 295-97, 299; Sonata No. II in A minor for Unaccompanied Violin, second movement (Andante), quoted, 227; *The Well-Tempered Clavier,* Book I: Prelude in C major, analyzed, 127, 233, 294; Fugue in C major, quoted, 244-45; Prelude in D major, quoted, 245; Fugue in D minor, theme analyzed, 173-74; 178, 187-88; Prelude in E♭ minor, 113, 115; Fugue in E♭ minor, theme analyzed, 112-15; Fugue in E♭ major, theme quoted, 114; Prelude in G♯ minor, analyzed, 231-32; Book II: Prelude in C major, analyzed, 242-48; 278, 284; Fugue in C minor, theme quoted, 283; Prelude in F major, analyzed, 233-44; 278, 280
background, *see* foreground
Beethoven, Ludwig van, 18-19, 53-55, 129, 174, 177-78, 182, 188, 191, 252, 282, 337, 345; *Diabelli Variations,* 252; *Eroica* Symphony: opening theme analyzed, 124-26; slip in development, 294; *Fidelio,* 161 *n; Hammerklavier* Sonata, 294; *Missa Solemnis:* 19, 55; sketches for, 313-14; Ninth Symphony: 54,